HORSES, PEOPLE AND PARLIAMENT IN THE ENGLISH CIVIL WAR

T0304079

Horses, People and Parliament in the English Civil War

Extracting Resources and Constructing Allegiance

GAVIN ROBINSON

LONDON AND NEW YORK

First published 2012 by Ashgate Publishing

2 Park Square, Milton Park, Abingdon, Oxon OX14 4RN
711 Third Avenue, New York, NY 10017, USA

Routledge is an imprint of the Taylor & Francis Group, an informa business

First issued in paperback 2017

British Library Cataloguing in Publication Data
Robinson, Gavin.
  Horses, people and parliament in the English Civil War : extracting resources and
  constructing allegiance.
  1. Great Britain – History – Civil War, 1642–1649 – Logistics. 2. Great Britain – History
  – Civil War, 1642–1649 – Social aspects. 3. Civil-military relations – England – History –
  17th century. 4. War horses – England – History – 17th century.
  I. Title
  942'.062–dc23

Library of Congress Cataloging-in-Publication Data
Robinson, Gavin.
  Horses, people and Parliament in the English Civil War : extracting resources and
  constructing allegiance / Gavin Robinson.
      p. cm.
  Includes bibliographical references and index.
  ISBN 978–1–4094–2093–4 (hardcover : alk. paper)
  1. Great Britain – History – Civil War, 1642–1649. 2. Great Britain – Politics
  and government – 1642–1649. 3. War horses – Great Britain – History – 17th century.
  I. Title.

  DA415.R556 2012
  942.06'2–dc23   2011052193

ISBN 978-1-4094-2093-4 (hbk)
ISBN 978-1-138-10960-5 (pbk)

Contents

Contents

List of Tables and Figures

Figures

Tables

Abbreviations and Conventions

All dates are given in the Old Style Julian calendar, but the year is taken to start on 1 January. Abbreviations for manuscript sources are given at the head of the Bibliography.

A & O	C.H. Firth and R.S. Rait, *Acts and Ordinances of the Interregnum* (1911), (http://www.british-history. ac.uk/source.aspx?pubid=606)
AV	Authorized Version of the Bible
BL	British Library, London
CCAM M.	A.E. Green (ed.), *Calendar of the Proceedings of the Committee for Advance of Money, 1642–56* (London: HMSO, 1888)
CCC	M.A.E. Green (ed.), *Calendar of the Proceedings of the Committee for Compounding 1643–60* (London: HMSO, 1889)
CSPD	*Calendar of State Papers Domestic*
CJ	*Journal of the House of Commons* (http://www.british-history.ac.uk/catalogue.aspx?gid=43)
ERO	Essex Record Office, Chelmsford
HMC	Reports of the Historical Manuscripts Commission
JP	Justice of the Peace
LJ	*Journal of the House of Lords* (http://www.british-history.ac.uk/catalogue.aspx?gid=44)
MP	Member of Parliament.
OED	*Oxford English Dictionary* (http://www.oed.com/)
ODNB	*Oxford Dictionary of National Biography* (http://www.oxforddnb.com/)
PA	Parliamentary Archives, Westminster
TNA: PRO	The National Archives of the UK: Public Records Office, Kew, Surrey
TT	Thomason Tracts, British Library
VCH	*Victoria County History* (http://www.british-history. ac.uk/catalogue.aspx?type=1&gid=153)

Acknowledgements

This is not 'the book of the thesis', but my new arguments are partly based on material from my PhD research. This was generously funded by a three-year studentship from the Reading University Research Board. My parents have given me lots of support over the years, including paying for my MA. Without that step I could not have got any further. Frank Tallett was a very good PhD supervisor and has since helped with job applications and article submissions. Peter Edwards has been an unofficial mentor, guiding me through the maze of SP 28, sharing his notes, giving me opportunities to present papers and get published, and giving valuable comments on my work, including a large part of this book. Martyn Bennett has provided useful feedback during and since examining my PhD thesis and has also written job references. Tom Crawshaw has given me lots of important information and interesting conversations about the finances of Essex's army, and read part of my typescript. Nick Poyntz has inspired me with his knowledge and enthusiasm, and has looked over several parts of this book, saving me from some mistakes. John Tincey sent me his transcript of SP 28/131, part 5, and gave me the idea of using databases to analyse SP 28. The Life in the Suburbs project gave me a well-paid job when I really needed it, and working with Gill Newton and Phil Baker was a good experience. The Essex Record Office and the Parliamentary Archives both saved me from expensive research trips with their detailed online catalogues and efficient reprographic services. The UK National Archives continue to be way ahead of other repositories, allowing and encouraging readers to photograph documents and share them on Flickr, and providing spaces for user-created content. Embryonic parts of this book were presented in seminar papers at Bishop Grosseteste University College, Lincoln, and the FORWARD network at Nottingham Trent University. I have learnt a lot about Python programming and text mining from Bill Turkel. The Roy Rosenzweig Centre for History and New Media at George Mason University deserves everyone's thanks for developing Zotero, which is so much more than just a citation manager, and completely free. Research and writing would be much harder without it. Holly Matthies proofread the entire text, saving me from some embarrassing mistakes. Apart from final formatting in Microsoft Word, this book has been written using free software.

Introduction

This book is not about the causes of the English Civil War. Some of the biggest names in British history have tried and failed to explain why war broke out in England in 1642. As Malcolm Wanklyn and Frank Jones have stressed, this obsession with the question of how the First Civil War started has been accompanied by a lack of interest in how it ended.[1] The historiography has been dominated by what Wanklyn and Jones have defined as a determinist explanation of Parliament's victory. This traditional model has recently been summed up by Clive Holmes:

> In fact, parliament enjoyed a number of key advantages that rendered its ultimate victory almost certain ... The combination of elements that guaranteed Roundhead victory was complex. The parliamentarians' control of the navy and of London were vitally important, as was their greater success in negotiating effective alliances. Parliament ultimately proved more adept in mobilising resources for war, and in developing an effective command structure. Finally, the morale and commitment of a leaven among the parliamentarians was better able to sustain a prolonged conflict.[2]

This paradigm has been so dominant that even a book entitled *Naseby: The Decisive Campaign* could (perhaps had to) assert that 'From the beginning of the war Parliament had the advantage in resources through its control of the wealthiest areas of England ... Parliament's command of resources should have enabled it to win the war far sooner'.[3] To argue that the result of the war was 'almost certain' or 'guaranteed' is incredibly ambitious. We should be very suspicious of a causal explanation of complex and imperfectly documented historical events which confidently claims to be almost as reliable as Newtonian mechanics. One of the biggest problems for determinism is the battle of Edgehill. Holmes admitted that this 'ended in anti-climax. Neither side won an outright

---

[1]   Malcolm Wanklyn and Frank Jones, *A Military History of the English Civil War* (Harlow, 2005), pp. 11–12.

[2]   Clive Holmes, *Why Was Charles I Executed?* (London, 2006), p. 73. This was published after *A Military History*, but probably too soon for Holmes to be able to respond to Wanklyn and Jones before going to press.

[3]   Glenn Foard, *Naseby: The Decisive Campaign* (Barnsley, 2004), p. 329.

victory', but did not attempt to explain why the battle was so indecisive.[4] If determinism cannot offer any kind of explanation for this then we have to ask whether tactical contingencies had any influence, and what might have happened if the battle had gone differently. Holmes simply tried to close down discussion of 'what if' questions without properly explaining why they should be considered illegitimate.[5] Edgehill can only be dismissed by assuming the conclusion that battles are always irrelevant and refusing to consider other possibilities.

I have to admit that even I accepted and contributed to determinist historiography.[6] That changed after I read Wanklyn and Jones. Their work challenged the determinist consensus, arguing that the resources available to both sides varied but were usually adequate, and that battles, which could have gone either way, were crucial for deciding the outcome of the war.[7] Battles have been given even more attention in Wanklyn's subsequent work.[8] Wanklyn is right that resources did not make the outcome of the war inevitable and that we need to bring tactical and operational contingency back into the picture. His focus on battles and operational strategy was necessary in order to correct various misconceptions and redress the balance which had been skewed by determinism, but there is still more to be written about resources. Battles had to be fought by armies, which had to be recruited, paid and supplied. A sufficient and necessary explanation for the start or the end of the war would have to account for where these armies came from and why they were not bigger or smaller than they actually were. Resources must have played some role in this, but not in the way that determinist explanations assumed. Trying to add up the population and wealth of areas which were nominally under the control of one side or the other does not tell us whether either side had an advantage, because resources did not automatically flow from civilians to the military. Like battles, resources were contingent. Jan Glete has changed the terms of the debate by

---

[4]   Holmes, *Why*, 71.

[5]   Ibid., 73.

[6]   Gavin Robinson, 'Horse Supply in the English Civil War, 1642–1646' (PhD, Reading University, 2001), pp. 235–7. See also pp. 20–21 for an example of how male privilege made me entitled to comment on feminism despite not knowing anything about it. I hope the present book proves that I got better.

[7]   Wanklyn and Jones, *Military History*, 11–26, 277–81. Ian Roy and Malcolm Wanklyn both argued for contingency in their theses in the 1960s, but these arguments were not widely accepted. See Ann Hughes, 'The King, the Parliament and the Localities During the English Civil War', *Journal of British Studies*, 24/2 (1985): 240–41.

[8]   Malcolm Wanklyn, *Decisive Battles of the English Civil War* (Barnsley, 2006); Malcolm Wanklyn, 'Oliver Cromwell and the Performance of Parliament's Armies in the Newbury Campaign, 20 October–21 November 1644', *History*, 96/321 (2011): 3–25.

showing that 'explanations emphasising "lack of resources" as limits of medieval and early-modern warfare are political rather than economic'.[9]

In order to fight the Civil War, both sides had to construct administrative systems and make them work. This book will show just how difficult it was for Parliament to extract resources from civilians. Several different approaches were tried with varying degrees of success. This is not a narrative of progress from the wrong systems to the right one. What was appropriate depended on circumstances, which changed during the war. Chapter 1 will show that in 1642 Parliament depended on voluntary contributions, which were initially large and would have been perfectly adequate to fight a single campaign. It was possible for either side to win the war by Christmas 1642 because most of their resources were concentrated into their main field armies, but because battles were unpredictable neither was guaranteed to win. When the Edgehill campaign ended indecisively they had to adapt to a longer war. Military force was not an adequate method of extracting resources (Chapter 3). In 1643 defeat in battles, shortages of resources, and factional divisions brought Parliament dangerously close to losing the war (Chapters 3 and 4). From the middle of 1643 politicians and administrators started to construct more sustainable systems which could maintain armies through a long war (Chapters 4 and 5). Even with reliable tax revenues and a reformed army, victory was not inevitable. Administrators had to work as hard as generals and soldiers in order to make victory possible.[10] Without the resources to keep armies in the field, defeat would have been inevitable.

The contingency of battles, operations and resources cannot be separated, because they influenced each other. The availability of resources and the logistics of moving them placed constraints on where armies could go and how quickly they could march. Sometimes operations were hampered by shortages of draught horses.[11] Even without battles, attrition was constant: armies wasted manpower, horses, money and food just by existing. Resources were required in order for armies to fight battles, but battles could also influence the availability of resources. Defeat often caused serious losses of men, horses and equipment, and even victories might be costly. Generals could never be certain of the outcome of a battle. They had to risk losing everything in order to have a chance of winning. If an army was destroyed, extra resources would be needed to rebuild it, while existing armies would be under more pressure. This could have serious

---

[9] Jan Glete, 'Warfare, Entrepreneurship, and the Fiscal-Military State', in Frank Tallett and D.J.B. Trim (eds), *European Warfare 1350–1750* (Cambridge, 2010), p. 301.

[10] James Scott Wheeler, *The Making of a World Power: War and the Military Revolution in Seventeenth Century England* (Stroud, 1999), p. 84.

[11] Peter Edwards, *Dealing in Death: The Arms Trade and the British Civil Wars* (Stroud, 2000), p. 164; *CSPD 1644*, 476–7.

and unexpected consequences for civilians. After Waller's army was destroyed at the battle of Roundway Down in Wiltshire, the remnants of his cavalry tried to replace their losses by seizing many horses in Hertfordshire (Chapter 4). The actions of armies could affect resource gathering in even more indirect ways. In 1645 Sir Samuel Luke, parliamentary governor of Newport Pagnell in Buckinghamshire, wrote:

> the hearts of the people in these parts being so stricken by the loss of Leicester, together with the late alterations in Parliament affairs, that though I have summoned in this county and Beds. to my assistance, yet cannot get one man, and but very little provisions. Neither can I get but very few to come into the works without forcing them.[12]

The King's capture of Leicester had not directly affected the physical power of the Newport Pagnell garrison, but Luke claimed that the news of it had changed the way that civilians responded to his demands. A further complication was that both sides had multiple armies and commanders operating independently. This led to competition for resources between armies on the same side as well as with civilians and the enemy. Factions in Parliament and at Court backed rival commanders, bringing high politics into logistics and operations.[13] The problems of why the First Civil War started and why it ended as it did intersect at the question of how the armies were created and maintained. This question is important in its own right and deserves more attention. This book will show that things were more complex and more interesting than either traditional determinism or Wanklyn's operational history implied. Neither the start nor the end of the First Civil War was determined by economic forces, but there was far more to the story than battles and generals.

The Value of Horses

Early-modern armies depended very heavily on horses. Until the mid twentieth century, mounted troops were the only truly mobile ground forces available. While cavalry had lost their dominance on the battlefield since the high middle ages, they could not be dispensed with because victory in battles depended on combined arms.[14] Civil War armies spent relatively little time fighting battles, but cavalry were also vital for more routine operations. Without an adequate

---

[12]   Foard, *Naseby*, 156.

[13]   Holmes, *Why*, 81.

[14]   Clifford J. Rogers, 'Tactics and the Face of Battle', in Frank Tallett and D.J.B. Trim (eds), *European Warfare 1350–1750* (Cambridge, 2010), p. 203; Wanklyn, *Decisive Battles*, 202–3.

screen of cavalry, infantry on the march were very vulnerable to attack and could be slowed down by having to go into battle formation to protect themselves from enemy cavalry. There were more garrisons than field armies, but they also needed cavalry. The day-to-day role of a garrison was to control the surrounding area, which could not be done without a mobile force. Cavalry of garrisons such as Newport Pagnell were constantly active in scouting the surrounding area, raiding enemy territory and bringing in contributions. Scouting and raiding were also carried out by field army cavalry.

Both sides raised very large numbers of cavalry. The planned establishment of the New Model Army in 1645 included 6,000 cavalry and 1,000 dragoons.[15] This was the largest mounted force actually raised by Parliament, but the need for more cavalry had already been recognized earlier in the war. A new army planned in 1643, but never completed, was to have 6,500 cavalry (see Chapter 4). The Eastern Association field army actually had 4,000 cavalry in service in 1644.[16] Even at their weakest, parliamentary field armies usually had thousands of mounted soldiers. In July 1643 Essex's army was down to 2,500 cavalry, which was represented as a cause for concern.[17] A muster taken in 1644 showed that Essex's army had 2,300 cavalry of its own and a further 400 on loan from the London militia.[18] Loss of records makes it impossible to arrive at accurate numbers for the King's armies, but they must have been comparable to Parliament's, and were probably superior at certain times and places.

Horses were not exclusively for cavalry and dragoons. Infantry and artillery could not move or be supplied without horse-drawn transport. Artillery usually required fewer horses than the cavalry in this period, but absolute numbers of draught horses were still quite large. Essex's army and the New Model each had around 1,000 horses in their artillery trains.[19] Official records probably under-represent draught horses because they do not record the private victuallers who sold food directly to soldiers.[20]

---

[15] Ian Gentles, *The New Model Army in England, Ireland and Scotland, 1645–1653* (Oxford, 1992), p. 10.

[16] Clive Holmes, *The Eastern Association in the English Civil War* (Cambridge, 2007), p. 236.

[17] *LJ*, vol. 6, 160.

[18] Richard Symonds, *Diary of the Marches of the Royal Army*, C.E. Long and Ian Roy (eds) (Cambridge, 1997), p. 97.

[19] TNA: PRO, SP 28/146, fol. 183; TNA: PRO, SP 28/145, fols 60–64; *CJ*, vol. 4, 71; *A & O*, vol. 1, 653–5.

[20] Aryeh J.S. Nusbacher, 'Civil Supply in the Civil War: Supply of Victuals to the New Model Army on the Naseby Campaign 1–14 June 1645', *English Historical Review*, 115/460 (2000): 145, 148–9, 155.

Getting the thousands of horses needed to build a new army was only the start of the problem. A constant supply was needed to replace horses which died, went lame or became diseased, or which were captured by the enemy, stolen or otherwise lost. Battle casualties varied wildly. Sir Samuel Luke claimed that his troop in Essex's army had lost 30 horses at Edgehill and another 18 at first Newbury, but Richard Griffin's troop in the Earl of Manchester's cavalry regiment had only three horses killed when it fought under Cromwell at Marston Moor.[21] Griffin had left another six horses behind in various places because they were lame, and had five taken away by deserters, three of whom were alleged to have joined the King. From April to July 1644, Thomas Noakes, a captain in a parliamentary regiment in the midlands, lost 12 horses to deserters and only two in battles.[22] Richard Atkyns, who served in the King's forces, wrote that three side-changers, 'all very well horsed and armed', joined his troop at Oxford.[23] The New Model Army replaced more than 60 per cent of its cavalry horses in a year (see Chapter 5).

Some of the things needed by armies only had military uses or were used by civilians in relatively small quantities. Weapons, armour and ammunition were imported by both sides in the early years of the First Civil War because domestic supplies were inadequate.[24] In 1642 prices of most commodities were very high because demand was much greater than supply. By 1644 the English arms industry, particularly in London, had increased its output and prices had fallen drastically.[25] Horses were very different because they were owned and used by many civilians. Oxen were still used sometimes, but they were in decline during this period. Wagons, carts and pack horses were the only viable way of moving large quantities of goods over land. Horses also provided power for ploughs and other machinery such as mills. Breeding, training, buying and selling horses were major economic activities in their own right.[26] While many people had to travel on foot, riding a horse was not limited to the elite. Owning and riding expensive horses was a conspicuous display of wealth and status which was increasingly available to the upper middling sort as well as the elite in early-

---

[21]   TNA: PRO, SP 28/127, part 2, fol. 26r; TNA: PRO, SP 28/266, part 1, fol. 32.

[22]   TNA: PRO, SP 28/38, part 4, fol. 318.

[23]   Richard Atkyns, 'The Praying Captain: A Cavalier's Memoirs', Peter Young (ed.), *Journal of the Society for Army Historical Research*, 35/141 (1957): 6.

[24]   Edwards, *Dealing in Death*, 175.

[25]   Ben Coates, *The Impact of the English Civil War on the Economy of London, 1642–50* (Aldershot, 2004), p. 211; Edwards, *Dealing in Death*, 72.

[26]   Peter Edwards, *Horse and Man in Early Modern England* (London, 2007), pp. 44, 183–209; Peter Edwards, *The Horse Trade of Tudor and Stuart England* (Cambridge, 2004), pp. 10–18.

modern England.[27] Despite this potential devaluation, the elite were still able to set themselves apart using equestrian portraits, jousting, manège, hunting, racing, and importing and breeding eastern horses.[28]

The value of horses to civilians was both an advantage and a disadvantage for Civil War armies. England almost certainly had a very large equine population. English horse breeding had improved immensely throughout the sixteenth century, and by the early seventeenth century there was a strong export trade. During the civil wars horse were probably diverted to armies, but by 1657 the trade had recovered so much that export restrictions were lifted.[29] Unlike arms, there is little evidence that horses were imported to England in significant numbers in the 1640s.[30] Although prices rose because of wartime demand, and there were temporary shortages, there were usually enough horses available for both sides.[31] This did not mean that getting them was easy. Because horses were so valuable in so many ways, their owners were often reluctant to give them up or unable to do without them. Voluntary contributions of horses were adequate at first, but proved unsustainable (Chapter 1). Taking remounts by force was surprisingly ineffective (Chapter 3). Horse ownership was disputed and negotiated in courts, Parliament and print as well as directly between soldiers and civilians.

Humans, Animals and Property

The ownership of horses was contested during the Civil Wars, but all parties in every dispute shared a common assumption that horses were property. This was ideological consensus, but perhaps not quite in the way that revisionists employed the term. The assumption that animals could and should be owned or used by humans occurs in many texts which were written or read in the early-

---

[27] Edwards, *Horse and Man*, 2–3, 75; Gavin Robinson, 'The Military Value of Horses and the Social Value of the Horse in Early Modern England', in Peter Edwards, Karl Enenkel and Elspeth Graham (eds), *The Horse as Cultural Icon: The Real and the Symbolic Horse in the Early Modern World* (Leiden, 2011), pp. 351–76.

[28] Peter Edwards and Elspeth Graham, 'Introduction', in Peter Edwards, Karl Enenkel and Elspeth Graham (eds), *The Horse as Cultural Icon: The Real and the Symbolic Horse in the Early Modern World* (Leiden, 2011), pp. 6–7.

[29] Peter Edwards, 'The Supply of Horses to the Parliamentarian and Royalist Armies in the English Civil War', *Historical Research*, 68/159 (1995): 54–8.

[30] Robinson, 'Horse Supply in the English Civil War', 238–42; ERO D/Y 2/8, p. 63.

[31] Edwards, 'Supply of Horses', 52–4, 57, 66.

modern period and was rarely challenged. Perhaps the most widely available was Genesis:

> And God said, Let us make man in our image, after our likeness: and let them have dominion over the fish of the sea, and over the fowl of the air, and over the cattle, and over all the earth, and over every creeping thing that creepeth upon the earth. So God created man in his own image, in the image of God created he him; male and female created he them. And God blessed them, and God said unto them, Be fruitful, and multiply, and replenish the earth, and subdue it: and have dominion over the fish of the sea, and over the fowl of the air, and over every living thing that moveth upon the earth.[32]

Justifications for human domination of animals ranged from this simple assertion to the sophisticated Neoplatonist concepts of plenitude and the Great Chain of Being.[33] Thomas Cranmer's conservative and authoritarian homily of obedience, which was still being printed and read in the 1630s, insisted that 'Almighty God hath created, and appoynted all things, in heaven, earth, and waters, in a most excellent, and perfect order', presenting human social hierarchies and domination of birds, beasts and fish as the natural God-given order.[34] Although Fifth Monarchists looked forward to a time when man would stop 'devouring his fellow creatures' (an ambiguous phrase which could mean all species or only humans), radical groups in the revolutionary period tended to represent nature as a resource to be exploited by humans.[35] John Locke argued that in a state of nature all people had an equal right to use animals for their own preservation, necessarily denying animals the same right to 'subsist and enjoy the conveniences of life'.[36] Asking questions about animals makes it slightly easier to see property rights as arbitrary and historically specific rather than natural or inevitable. In the seventeenth century, English law defined different types of ownership for different types of animals. Absolute property only existed in domestic animals which served a useful purpose. Wild animals could not be owned to the same extent, but could become property if they were captured, tamed and marked. Pets which were kept only for pleasure were not formally classified by the law,

---

[32]   Genesis 1:26–8 (AV).

[33]   Keith Thomas, *Man and the Natural World: Changing Attitudes in England 1500–1800* (London, 1983), pp. 124–5.

[34]   Thomas Cranmer, *Certaine sermons or homilies appoynted to be read in churches. In the time of the late Queene Elizabeth of famous memory. And now thought fit to be reprinted by authority from the Kings most excellent Maiesty* (London, 1635), p. 69.

[35]   Brian Manning, *The Far Left in the English Revolution 1640 to 1660* (London, 1999), pp. 58, 118.

[36]   John Locke, *Two Treatises on Government*, (London, 1821), pp. 98–100, 190.

and some writers of legal treatises denied that they could be owned or stolen.[37] In practice, wild deer tended to be treated as the private property of the owners of the parks where they lived. In 1638 the Doncaster quarter sessions enforced Sir Francis Wortley's demand for £3, 6s, 8d compensation for each deer which had been poached from his park.[38]

People needed to assert and challenge property rights because they were competing for resources. Animals were part of this competition in three ways: they consumed resources because they needed feeding, accommodation, routine care, veterinary treatment, clothing and equipment; they were used as resources themselves because humans killed and consumed them for food or harvested food and raw materials from them; and they were a source of labour for extracting and transporting resources. Jason Hribal has argued that animals are part of the working class.[39] His old Marxist tendency to reduce everything to class has its limitations. Even in the most oppressive and exploitative capitalist societies it is not usual for the bourgeoisie to kill and eat workers. But Hribal's model is particularly apt for horses because there was, and still is, a very strong taboo against eating horse flesh in Britain.[40] Horses had many symbolic functions in the culture of early-modern England and were used for conspicuous display, but they were rarely displayed without at least some pretence of doing something. In contrast, monkeys and parrots were kept as pets purely for their symbolic and aesthetic value and did no physical work.[41] The practical roles, social value and cultural meanings of horses were all related to work. Hunting and racing were leisure activities for humans but hard work for horses. The situation of horses in England was similar in many ways to that of chattel slaves.[42] Both horses and slaves were treated as less than human but better than many other species. This is what Bruce Boehrer has defined as relative anthropocentrism: the belief that humans are superior to animals but that some people are more human than others.[43] Owning, exploiting and dominating animals helped to define the identity of humans as well as providing resources.

---

[37] Erica Fudge, *Perceiving Animals: Humans and Beasts in Early Modern English Culture* (Urbana, 2002), pp. 125–33.

[38] Andrew J. Hopper, 'The Wortley Park Poachers and the Outbreak of the English Civil War', *Northern History*, 44/2 (2007): 98.

[39] Jason Hribal, '"Animals Are Part of the Working Class": A Challenge to Labor History', *Labor History*, 44/4 (2003): 436, 453.

[40] Edwards, *Horse and Man*, 33.

[41] Fudge, *Perceiving Animals*, 133.

[42] Hribal, 'Animals', 436.

[43] Bruce Boehrer, *Shakespeare Among the Animals: Nature and Society in the Drama of Early Modern England* (New York, 2002), pp. 17–18.

Relative anthropocentrism was not only a justification for human exploitation of animals. It intersected with many other aspects of identity, particularly gender, race and social status. Boehrer showed that almost any out-group could be identified as less than human, and in early-modern England these groups included women, foreigners, catholics and poor people.[44] Low-status people were also treated like animals in practice when they were subjected to corporal punishments from which the elite were usually exempt.[45] The words 'man' and 'horse' both had double meanings: they could refer to a whole species, or only to males (and in the case of horses, specifically uncastrated males). The passage from Genesis quoted above used 'man' to include all humans, but this is only clear because it was explicitly qualified by 'male and female'. In many other cases 'man' and 'men' were ambiguous, often working as false universals which privileged men and excluded women.[46] It is not anachronistic to point this out, because the double meaning caused confusion in the seventeenth century. It was not at all clear whether the Protestation was to be taken by women, and practice differed from parish to parish.[47] In 1650 Henry Marten substituted 'men' for 'persons' in an act to require taking the engagement to the Commonwealth; a contemporary newsbook explicitly claimed that his intention was to protect women.[48] These words were still contentious in 1867, when John Stuart Mill proposed changing 'men' to 'persons' in a suffrage bill.[49] Ann Hughes has warned that 'it is still common for scholars to write of how human beings or "people" are understood within republican thought when men specifically are clearly intended'.[50] Even the word 'person' could be a false universal which privileged men, not least because women were often said to be less perfect, and therefore implicitly less human, than men.[51] While these false universals denied the agency and humanity of women, they still allowed limited opportunities. Some

---

[44]   Ibid., 18.

[45]   Thomas, *Man and the Natural World*, 45.

[46]   Hilda L. Smith, *All Men and Both Sexes: Gender, Politics, and the False Universal in England, 1640–1832* (University Park, PA, 2002), pp. 2–4, 14, 17, 21–4.

[47]   Edward Vallance, *Revolutionary England and the National Covenant: State Oaths, Protestantism and the Political Nation, 1553–1682* (Woodbridge, 2005), p. 110.

[48]   Ivor Waters, *Henry Marten and the Long Parliament* (Chepstow, 1976), p. 52; David Martin Jones, *Conscience and Allegiance in Seventeenth Century England: The Political Significance of Oaths and Engagements* (Rochester, NY, 1999), p. 279.

[49]   Jose Harris, 'Mill, John Stuart (1806–1873)', *ODNB*.

[50]   Ann Hughes, 'Men, the "Public" and the "Private" in the English Revolution', in Peter Lake and Steven Pincus (eds), *Politics of the Public Sphere* (Manchester, 2007), p. 197.

[51]   Anthony Fletcher, *Gender, Sex and Subordination in England 1500–1800* (New Haven, 1995), p. 72; Alexandra Shepard, *Meanings of Manhood in Early Modern England* (Oxford, 2006), p. 47; Fudge, *Perceiving Animals*, 134; Boehrer, *Shakespeare Among the Animals*, 18.

women could potentially take actions which were required of 'persons' or avoid obligations which were imposed on 'men'.

Early-modern England was a patriarchal society in which a male elite was privileged over women and many men. The revolutionary changes of the 1640s did not fundamentally transform this situation.[52] This is part of what Judith Bennett has defined as patriarchal equilibrium: the position of women might improve, but patriarchy always adjusts to ensure that they never quite achieve full equality or humanity.[53] But women's rights were at least contested more than animal rights. Women in Blackfriars disputed the views of their minister, William Gouge, on the subjugation of wives to husbands.[54] In the first half of the seventeenth century there was not yet any consensus among men that women were, or should be, legally barred from voting in parliamentary elections. Since voting rights were derived from property, widows who held land in their own right could have a valid claim, which some candidates tried to encourage in order to get more votes. In Suffolk, propertied widows tried to vote in the elections for the Long Parliament in 1640, and although Sir Simonds D'Ewes, the presiding sheriff, disallowed their votes in a very hostile and condescending manner, he had to admit that there was no legal justification for his actions.[55] William Prynne, whose misogyny went beyond what was normal at the time, opposed votes for women, servants and poor people, or the 'very scum of the people', as he called them.[56] While there was apparently ideological consensus about the subordination of animals to people, there was much less consensus over who should and should not be counted as 'the people'.[57]

The supposedly 'natural' order was actually very unstable. Cranmer desperately claimed that 'The water above is kept, and rayneth downe in due time, and season. The Sun, Moone, Starres, Rainebow, Thunder, Lightning, Clouds, and all Birds of the ayre doe keepe their order. The Earth, Trees, Seeds, Plants, Hearbes,

---

[52] Ann Hughes, *Gender and the English Revolution* (Abingdon, 2011), pp. 60, 90, 125, 148.

[53] Judith M. Bennett, *History Matters: Patriarchy and the Challenge of Feminism* (Manchester, 2006), pp. 54–81.

[54] Christopher Brooks, 'Professions, Ideology and the Middling Sort in the Late Sixteenth and Early Seventeenth Centuries', in Jonathan Barry and Christopher Brooks (eds), *The Middling Sort of People: Culture, Society and Politics in England, 1550–1800* (Basingstoke, 1994), p. 124; Hughes, *Gender*, 11–12.

[55] Derek Hirst, *The Representative of the People? Voters and Voting in England Under the Early Stuarts* (Cambridge, 1975), pp. 18–19. D'Ewes was returned as MP for Sudbury even though sheriffs were legally barred from election: Mary Frear Keeler, *The Long Parliament 1640–1641, a Biographical Study of its Members* (Philadelphia, 1954), p. 156.

[56] Christopher Brooks, 'Professions', 127; Frances E. Dolan, *Whores of Babylon Catholicism, Gender, and Seventeenth-Century Print Culture* (Notre Dame, 2005), pp. 96, 98, 119–20, 144.

[57] Christopher Brooks, 'Professions', 126–7; Hughes, *Gender*, 6, 109.

Corne, Grasse, and all manner of Beasts keepe themselves in order.'[58] It is hard to see rain, thunder and lightning as ordered. The theory, practice and equipment of horsemanship made it very clear that rather than keeping themselves in order, horses were difficult to control and had to be carefully trained to obey humans.[59] The very existence of the book of homilies shows that rulers did not trust nature very far and made efforts to train people in obedience. Gender stereotypes presented women as subordinate to men but 'always on the verge of escaping control'.[60] It was difficult to judge the effectiveness of obedience training or predict future actions. Whatever their motives and intentions might have been, people and animals continued to do things which they were not supposed to do.

Undoing Allegiance

The outbreak of civil war complicated the competition for resources and the construction of human identities. Rival claims for allegiance by King and Parliament created new aspects of identity. The study of allegiance has traditionally been founded on a binary opposition between royalist and parliamentarian. There are many theoretical reasons to be suspicious of this dichotomy, but it can also be opposed on empirical grounds because it is an abstraction which oversimplifies messy and complex reality. It is generally accepted that both court and Parliament were divided between different factions with conflicting aims. Jason Peacey has warned that 'it is not clear how sensible it is to talk about "royalists" and "parliamentarians", at least in terms of their attitudes to print and propaganda, since both were to some degree internally divided over their attitude towards print and the public'.[61] In practice, more historians have acted as if these groups are only subdivisions of royalist and parliamentarian which do not disturb the fundamental categories, despite the problem that many Scots and English Presbyterians went over to the King during the Second Civil War. A bigger problem is that many people cannot easily be fitted into either category. Making them fit has required more oppositions and categories, but these have still mostly been subordinated to the labels 'royalist' and 'parliamentarian'. On the questions

---

58   Cranmer, *Certaine sermons*, 69.

59   Edwards, *Horse and Man*, 28, 42–4, 52–4, 133–4; Pia Cuneo, 'Just a Bit of Control: The Historical Significance of Sixteenth- and Seventeenth-Century German Bit-Books', in Karen L. Raber and Treva J. Tucker (eds), *The Culture of the Horse* (Basingstoke, 2005), pp. 155–6, 158.

60   Hughes, *Gender*, 16.

61   Jason Peacey, *Politicians and Pamphleteers: Propaganda During the English Civil Wars and Interregnum* (Aldershot, 2004), p. 307.

of whether allegiance was internal or external, and fixed or changeable, historians have tended to privilege one without fully considering the other.

B.G. Blackwood, David Underdown and the early work of Mark Stoyle tended to privilege fixed and internal over changeable and external. Although Stoyle's *Loyalty and Locality* rejected Underdown's conclusions about why people chose sides, it unquestioningly accepted the same assumptions about what allegiance was and how it could be measured.[62] All three of these historians wrote as if allegiance was a fixed underlying state. They would not necessarily have described their work as essentialist, but their evidence depended very heavily on allegiance being essential. In identifying people as 'royalists', Blackwood, Underdown and Stoyle all used lists of suspected enemies of the state compiled during the rule of Cromwell's major-generals, 1655–56.[63] This assumed that nothing had changed in up to 14 years. Underdown acknowledged that the sources he used to quantify allegiance were 'totally silent on the extent to which outward allegiance reflects *real* preferences—on what proportion of apparent supporters of each side were *really* neutrals driven into their respective camps by compulsion or force of circumstance' (emphasis added), which implies an assumption that there was something underneath which was more real than external actions.[64] Similarly, Stoyle accepted that external factors such as military occupation could change people's outward conformance, but treated this as less real than what was supposed to be underneath: 'few towns and villages are known to have shifted their underlying allegiance in response to changing circumstances ... as soon as they got the chance, or as soon as the situation became too much to bear, most communities would revert to their true allegiance.'[65] This argument required that people had an essence which made them always royalist or parliamentarian regardless of what they were saying or doing. Blackwood's project depended so heavily on classing people as royalist or parliamentarian that he slipped between internal and external without explanation. After defining 'Royalist' and 'Parliamentarian' gentry as 'those who, at some time or other between 1642 and 1648, served either the King or Parliament in a military or civil capacity', the same essay goes on to suggest that 'King's

---

[62] Mark Stoyle, *Loyalty and Locality: Popular Allegiance in Devon During the English Civil War* (Exeter, 1994), pp. 155–6, 253.

[63] B.G. Blackwood, 'Parties and Issues in the Civil War in Lancashire and East Anglia', in R.C. Richardson (ed.), *The English Civil War: Local Aspects* (Stroud, 1997), pp. 271–2; David Underdown, *Revel, Riot, and Rebellion: Popular Politics and Culture in England 1603–1660* (Oxford, 1985), pp. 195–6, 199–206; Stoyle, *Loyalty and Locality*, 76–7.

[64] Underdown, *Revel, Riot, and Rebellion*, 183.

[65] Stoyle, *Loyalty and Locality*, 74.

Lynn seems a good example of a town that was Royalist in terms of military occupation but Parliamentarian in terms of opinion'.[66] There does not seem to be any logic to this jump from actions to opinions, other than the need to classify as many people as possible as royalists or parliamentarians. Similarly, Blackwood introduced an opposition between active and passive, but used it mainly to expand the numbers of people aligned with one side or the other.[67] For essentialist historiography, the existence of people who changed sides was an awkward fact which had to be explained away. Blackwood maintained the purity of his royalists and parliamentarians by putting side-changers into a separate category which was neither, and then dismissing this group as 'statistically insignificant'.[68] Stoyle claimed that turncoats were exceptional and provoked hostility, but by doing this he had to admit that they existed.[69]

John Morrill strongly opposed Blackwood's approach, which he described as putting people into boxes marked 'royalist' and 'parliamentarian'. Morrill made an important distinction between enthusiastic militants and people who went along with one side or the other reluctantly. He also pointed out that people who reluctantly supplied one side might be perceived and treated as enemies by the other side, and that circumstances changed so much during the 1640s that people could find themselves aligned with a different faction without changing their own opinions.[70] In Morrill's view, allegiance was contingent and was not binary, but he still privileged the internal over the external, objecting that the records used by Blackwood 'tell us a great deal about a man's activity, much less about his beliefs'.[71] Anthony Fletcher took a similar position, making claims about 'MPs who in their heart of hearts felt attachment to the king rather than parliament'.[72]

In 1998 S.L. Sadler defined the problems of allegiance more clearly than anyone had before. While she was influenced by Morrill's approach, she offered a more sophisticated model in which allegiance operated on several different levels. The first level was 'allegiance as it really was in Cambridgeshire; that is, the natural preferences of all local people'.[73] Sadler's thesis worked from the

---

[66]   Blackwood, 'Parties and Issues', 262, 270.

[67]   Ibid., 263.

[68]   Ibid., 263.

[69]   Stoyle, *Loyalty and Locality*, 112.

[70]   John Morrill, *Revolt in the Provinces: The People of England and the Tragedies of War, 1630–1648* (London, 1998), pp. 128, 187–9.

[71]   John Morrill, *The Nature of the English Revolution* (London, 1993), p. 204.

[72]   Anthony Fletcher, *The Outbreak of the English Civil War* (London, 1981), p. 403.

[73]   S.L. Sadler, 'Cambridgeshire Society During the First and Second Civil Wars c.1638–c.1649: Some Aspects of Patterns of Allegiance' (PhD, Anglia Polytechnic University, 1998), p. 16.

premises that there was an important distinction between internal and external allegiance, and that 'the study of an internal state of mind rather than its external expression, is a proper way into an understanding of the Civil Wars'.[74] Although Sadler acknowledged that it would be difficult or impossible to discover internal states, and that internal and external factors interacted, her language tended to privilege the internal as more real and authentic, mentioning 'the unalloyed inclination of the subject' and limits on 'the free and accurate external expression of internal choices'.[75] For Sadler, external actions were, under ideal circumstances, ways of expressing internal allegiance, but she argued that in practice this expression was compromised by external pressures.

Morrill and Sadler criticized the quantitative approach used by Blackwood, Underdown and Stoyle because it privileged actions over intentions.[76] This disagreement is not as big as it might seem. All of these historians implicitly accepted that allegiance was some kind of underlying essence. The only disputes were over how much it could change and how accurately it can be measured using records of external actions. Therefore all of the works on allegiance discussed so far can legitimately be described as essentialist, even if their authors would dispute that label. Many of these works can also be defined as intentionalist because they privileged people's intentions, motives and feelings over the effects of their actions.

In the last 15 years the traditional historiography has been increasingly challenged by new anti-essentialist arguments. Andy Wood showed that some Derbyshire lead miners agreed to join the King only after they had negotiated concessions, while others supported Parliament. Their decision could have gone either way and was influenced, but not determined, by external economic factors.[77] This groundbreaking article disturbed many old assumptions about allegiance. Their willingness to negotiate and choose suggests that the miners were not driven by deference, economic structures or fixed internal feelings, but their choice to support the King does not fit Morrill's model of reluctant neutrals being dragged into a war which they did not want. Wood was mostly arguing against Underdown's ecological determinism, but the example of the miners who fought for the King is just as big a problem for essentialism. Rather than essentially being royalists, the miners chose to become royalists; instead of expressing a pre-existing internal royalist allegiance through their external actions, they made themselves royalist by acting for the King.

---

[74] Ibid., 16.

[75] Ibid., 2, 6–7.

[76] Morrill, *Nature*, 208; Sadler, 'Cambridgeshire', 9.

[77] Andy Wood, 'Beyond Post-Revisionism? The Civil War Allegiances of the Miners of the Derbyshire "Peak Country"', *Historical Journal*, 40/1 (1997): 32–6.

In one of the most important articles ever to be published on the English Civil War, Rachel Weil set out a more explicit challenge to essentialist assumptions, stating that 'the idea that allegiance existed in a person's "heart of hearts" may be anachronistic with respect to early modern mentalités'.[78] Weil suggested that we can think about allegiance 'as something that exists on the boundary of the inside and outside of a person' and focus on public narratives instead of inner feelings to see how individuals and organizations constructed the terms of what allegiance was.[79] Her analysis of compounding cases showed that actions could be more important than feelings. The Committee for Compounding was concerned with outward conformance to Parliament, not with extracting sincere conversion narratives. The stories which compounders offered to the committee were ambiguous and often privileged actions (both what the petitioners had done, and what had been done to them) over convictions: 'the petitions do not make sense in modern terms as narratives of inward intention'.[80] Different committees received different kinds of narratives. Weil's article concluded that allegiance was more about external actions than internal beliefs.[81]

Andrew Hopper has added to the sophistication of anti-essentialism by bringing the theory of self-fashioning into the study of allegiance. His focus on officers who changed sides exposes one of the major weaknesses of essentialist approaches. Side-changers were neither as unusual nor as unpopular as essentialism needed them to be. They were derided by the side which they had deserted, but the vindications that they published could be valuable propaganda for the side which they joined. These narratives often claimed that it was the deserted faction rather than the man himself that had changed. The self-serving hypocrisy of some turncoat narratives shows that while the idea of constancy was an important aspect of masculine honour, it was not always achieved in practice.[82] Hopper's work on the Hothams suggests that even the most apparently sincere allegiances could change drastically. Sir John Hotham became one of the first men in England to take military action against Charles I on behalf of Parliament when he denied the King entry to Hull in April 1642. This action carried a huge risk of assassination or execution for treason. It seems implausible that Hotham was coerced into acting, or was reluctantly going along with Parliament, although Hopper suggested that he may have underestimated

---

[78]   Rachel Weil, 'Thinking About Allegiance in the English Civil War', *History Workshop Journal*, 61/1 (2006): 184.

[79]   Ibid., 185.

[80]   Ibid., 186–8.

[81]   Ibid., 189, 190.

[82]   Andrew J. Hopper, 'The Self-Fashioning of Gentry Turncoats during the English Civil Wars', *Journal of British Studies*, 49/2 (2010): 236–7, 241–2, 245, 249–50, 256.

the chances of Charles being able to fight back. In 1643 Hotham took another risk by changing sides, and this did lead to his execution.[83] Hotham is as close as we can get to knowing a person's sincere internal allegiance through outward actions, and yet he chose to change his allegiance.

Jason McElligott and David Smith have rightly pointed out that royalism has been neglected by many studies of allegiance and have tried to redress the balance.[84] They strongly argued that allegiance was not fixed:

> We might no longer be able to think of allegiance as a fixed, unchanging and unchangeable entity. This insight may explain why all attempts to find pre-determining factors for political allegiance during the Civil Wars have failed. There was, quite simply, no single, fixed, pre-determined allegiance but a conscious choice to adhere to one side or the other which was dependent on a whole series of entirely contingent factors which differed from time to time, from place to place, and from person to person.[85]

While the McElligott and Smith collection certainly is the important contribution that it claims to be, the emphasis on *conscious* choice reveals a problem. Unlike Sadler, they did not carefully discuss the distinction between internal and external, or acknowledge the difficulty of knowing inward thoughts and feelings. By defining a royalist as 'somebody who, by thought or deed, identified himself or herself as a royalist and was accepted as such by other individuals who defined themselves as royalists' they made thoughts and actions equivalent, or at least comparable, and equally knowable.[86] This intentionalism was found in more than one essay in the same volume. According to Ian Roy, 'country gentlemen *felt* a basic instinct of loyalty' (emphasis added).[87] Rachel Foxley was able to write about 'feelings within the army', 'deeply held beliefs' and 'expressing genuinely nostalgic and conservative views'.[88]

---

[83] Ibid., 253–5; Andrew J. Hopper, 'Fitted for Desperation: Honour and Treachery in Parliament's Yorkshire Command, 1642–1643', *History*, 86/282 (2001): 139, 146, 150–51.

[84] Jason McElligott and David L. Smith, 'Introduction: Rethinking Royalists and Royalism', in Jason McElligott and David L. Smith (eds), *Royalists and Royalism During the English Civil Wars* (Cambridge, 2007), p. 1. It should also be pointed out that 'not enough work on the royalists' is not quite the same thing as 'too much work on the parliamentarians'. More work is needed on both.

[85] Ibid., 15.

[86] Ibid., 12–13.

[87] Ian Roy, 'Royalist Reputations: the Cavalier Ideal and the Reality', in Jason McElligott and David L. Smith (eds), *Royalists and Royalism During the English Civil Wars* (Cambridge, 2007), p. 93.

[88] Rachel Foxley, 'Royalists and the New Model Army in 1647: Circumstance, Principle and Compromise', in Jason McElligott and David L. Smith (eds), *Royalists and Royalism During*

Most recently, Ann Hughes has stressed both the contingency of allegiance and the relevance of gender. 'It was painfully obvious that political obligation was not natural or innate, but a matter to be negotiated and constructed.'[89] In printed propaganda, 'rival allegiances or identities were given physical and active form', stressing the external and performative aspects of self-fashioning and the power of stereotypes.[90] Allegiance and masculinity were closely related, and neither was natural: 'at the heart of understandings of identity were different ways of being a man'.[91]

Doing Allegiance

Inspired by Weil, I have decided to focus on external aspects of allegiance, particularly actions and material contributions, which have been under-researched despite being much easier to discover than internal aspects. My book follows from the premise that other minds are largely unknowable. Even if we reject the postmodern assertion that other minds are completely unknowable, we have to accept that knowing them is very difficult.[92] Neuroscience has made some impressive advances. For example, scans of brain activity have been used to communicate with comatose patients and to partially reconstruct images perceived by subjects.[93] But these experiments cannot be applied to the seventeenth century because they depend on scanning a living brain using Magnetic Resonance Imaging, and their results fall a long way short of the claims which historians have routinely made about the motives and intentions of people in the past. Cromwell has a reputation as a sincere Godly man and as a self-serving hypocrite.[94] There is no objective way to choose between these two views. When Cromwell's writings and speeches make claims about

---

the English Civil Wars (Cambridge, 2007), pp. 157, 164, 167.

[89]   Hughes, *Gender*, 92.

[90]   Ibid., 94.

[91]   Ibid., 90, 96, 118.

[92]   Keith Jenkins, *Re-Thinking History* (Abingdon, 2003), p. 48.

[93]   Martin M. Monti et al., 'Willful Modulation of Brain Activity in Disorders of Consciousness', *New England Journal of Medicine*, 362/7 (2010): 579–89; Shinji Nishimoto et al., 'Reconstructing Visual Experiences from Brain Activity Evoked by Natural Movies', *Current Biology*, 21/19 (2011): 1641–6.

[94]   Patrick Little, 'Introduction', in Patrick Little (ed.), *Oliver Cromwell: New Perspectives* (Basingstoke, 2009), pp. 2–3, 13–14, 16–17; Ian Gentles, *Oliver Cromwell: God's Warrior and the English Revolution* (Basingstoke, 2011), pp. 85, 87, 89.

external reality they can be compared with other accounts and questioned.[95] Corroboration is an important part of empirical methodology, but it cannot help us with Cromwell's internal mental state. No text ever gives a direct insight into the author's mind. Public versus private writing is a false dichotomy. Letters are usually read by the recipient, and even writing a personal diary is an external act. If written sources can tell us anything about what people did and said in the past (and for the purposes of this work I am assuming that they can), they give us no reliable evidence of what people thought or felt. Minds are largely outside the scope of empirical history.

Admitting that we cannot know much about other minds opens up different ways of looking at identities. If we free ourselves from the old obligation to privilege internal feelings and the impossible task of finding out what people 'really' thought, we can analyse the construction of allegiance through external actions and material objects. Essentialist approaches to allegiance are paradoxical because they treat thoughts and feelings as more 'real' than external physical reality, and proceed from metaphysical foundations despite their ostensibly empirical methodology. Morrill suggested that 'militancy was a psychological condition not an intellectual proposition', but surely the defining characteristic of militancy is violent actions, not an internal mental state.[96] Actions made the war happen. Other minds were mostly unknowable to seventeenth-century people, and this gave them both problems and opportunities. Because it was not possible to be sure of anyone's sincerity it was possible to fashion royalist or parliamentarian identities out of expediency. This was a potential source of anxiety but it was not always a problem. As Weil suggested, sincerity was irrelevant to resource gathering.

Contemporary writings show a diverse range of available positions on the question of whether internal allegiance was knowable or important. Some writers certainly did privilege intentions. A newsbook published in August 1642 began, 'Sir, Now others Intentions are discovered by their actions'.[97] Others suggested that there could be a difference between what people wanted and what they did. Nehemiah Wharton, a relatively humble Londoner who served as a sergeant in the parliamentary army, heard from a friend in September 1642 that

---

[95] Malcolm Wanklyn, 'A General Much Maligned: The Earl of Manchester as Army Commander in the Second Newbury Campaign (July to November 1644)', *War in History*, 14/2 (2007): 133–56; S.L. Sadler, '"Lord of the Fens": Oliver Cromwell's Reputation and the First Civil War', in Patrick Little (ed.), *Oliver Cromwell: New Perspectives* (Basingstoke, 2009), pp. 64–89.

[96] Morrill, *Revolt in the Provinces*, 188–9.

[97] *Some Speciall Passages from Hull, Anlaby and Yorke*, TT E.108[33], p. 3.

'the whole city were now either real or constrained Roundheads'.[98] While this statement made a clear distinction between sincere and insincere, and claimed that the difference could be known, it did not present the latter as a problem. A constrained roundhead was apparently as good as a real one. Outward conformity alone was not good enough for some. Puritan preacher Stephen Marshall was obedient enough to avoid persecution by Archbishop Laud in the 1630s despite his apparently well-known opinions. For Laud's vicar general, Sir Nathaniel Brent, this was anything but a victory, writing that Marshall 'is held to be a dangerous person, but exceeding cunning. No man doubteth but he hath an inconformable heart, but externally he observeth all'.[99] Similar positions were found on the parliamentary side after the outbreak of civil war. In June 1643 Harbottle Grimston wrote of a man who 'hath but a poore purse but I am sure hee hath a malignant proud heart ... without question the man beares a mischeivous heart to the Towne and had hee power answerable to his will I am confident yee would find it'.[100] Making such confident predictions about a person's motives, intentions and future actions was a gamble which risked disappointment and embarrassment because these things were not always as certain as Grimston claimed. A list of subscriptions promised by MPs in June 1642 noted that 'Collonell Goring: will (as soone as his moneths pay due to him as Governor of Portsmouth Comes in) expresse what hee will doe in this service to w[hi]ch hee hath soe much affecc[i]on'.[101] Within a few weeks he declared for the King instead of contributing to Parliament.[102] According to Sir Simonds D'Ewes, 'This news so staggered the hot spirits in both houses as they scarce knew what counsel to take.'[103]

Recognizing that it was difficult to know other minds and predict future actions could provoke impractical measures to find out. In theory, oaths, vows and covenants were powerful instruments to make windows into men's (and sometimes women's) souls, since God was a witness to an oath and a party to a covenant.[104] John Pym described the Protestation as a shibboleth, referring to the

---

[98]   Nehemiah Wharton, *Letters of a Subaltern in the Earl of Essex's Army*, Henry Ellis (ed.) (London, 1854), p. 17.

[99]   William Hunt, *The Puritan Moment: The Coming of Revolution in an English County* (Cambridge, MA, 1983), p. 276.

[100]   ERO D/Y 2/8, p. 51, Harbottle Grimston to mayor of Colchester, 28 June 1643.

[101]   Bodleian Library, Tanner 63, fol. 59v.

[102]   John Webb, 'The Siege of Portsmouth in the Civil War', in R.C. Richardson (ed.), *The English Civil War: Local Aspects* (Stroud, 1997), p. 70.

[103]   Wilson Coates, Anne Steele Young and Vernon F. Snow (eds), *Private Journals of the Long Parliament, 2 June to 17 September 1642* (New Haven, 1982), p. 280.

[104]   Vallance, *Revolutionary England*, 84.

passage in the book of Judges in which idolaters were identified by their inability to say the word and then had their throats cut.[105] This strongly implied that Pym expected to discover true allegiance, but in practice the Protestation was open to many different interpretations.[106] Pym advocated one version of the true protestant religion but many other people acted as if it was something different. Not everyone was as confident as Pym about the power of oaths. The hostility directed against catholics who were found to have used mental reservations would be consistent with serious anxiety that taking an oath was not reliable proof of sincerity.[107] Some people were clearly prepared to swear completely false oaths. Nehemiah Wallington's journeyman unhesitatingly swore that he was innocent of the embezzlement which he had almost certainly committed.[108] By making oaths compulsory, Parliament further undermined their relevance to internal allegiance. If people had to take an oath or face a penalty they were much less likely to be sincere. Rather than discovering people's 'true' allegiance, the Negative Oath introduced in 1645 only controlled people's future actions by swearing that they would not 'directly or indirectly adhere unto or willingly assist the King in this war'.[109] A cavalier drinking song celebrated taking Parliament's oaths without meaning to keep them.[110] This was apparently derived from the position that illegal oaths were not binding.[111]

The 'heart of hearts' is not completely anachronistic but was overprivileged and misinterpreted by twentieth-century historians. Although some people were clearly concerned about internal allegiance, others accepted that they did not know or that they did not need to know. Weil has shown that sincerity was rarely an issue for the Committee for Compounding.[112] Using a wider range of sources than Weil's article, Chapters 1 to 3 will confirm that material resources were often Parliament's highest priority, and that extracting them never depended on a 'true' internal allegiance. Sir Thomas Barrington could describe possibly insincere contributions to Parliament as a 'good effect' rather than as hypocrisy

---

[105]   Ibid., 52–3.

[106]   Ibid., 53, 110, 113–14; David Cressy, 'The Protestation Protested, 1641 and 1642', *Historical Journal*, 45/2 (2002): 253, 257, 263, 269, 270, 277.

[107]   Vallance, *Revolutionary England*, 103–5.

[108]   Paul S. Seaver, *Wallington's World: A Puritan Artisan in Seventeenth-Century London* (London, 1985), p. 119.

[109]   Vallance, *Revolutionary England*, 59.

[110]   Hughes, *Gender*, 123.

[111]   Jones, *Conscience and Allegiance*, 138–9.

[112]   Weil, 'Thinking About Allegiance', 189–90.

or deception.[113] This is all the more significant because Barrington and Grimston had many things in common. Both were heirs to gentry estates, studied at the Inns of Court, supported puritan church reform, sat as MPs for Colchester in the Long Parliament and were appointed deputy lieutenants of Essex.[114] Despite these similarities they set out very different views of allegiance. Both must be taken seriously.

Although contemporaries took various positions on internal versus external allegiance, they were much less likely to represent allegiance as fixed. Parliament often referred to its supporters as 'well-affected' and to its enemies as 'ill-affected', which could imply that actions were expected to be motivated by underlying feelings (see Chapter 2). Similarly, in the summer of 1642 a royal declaration described sending horses and men to York as 'an acceptable expression of their particular good affection'.[115] But according to the theories of Galen of Pergamon, which were still widely read and reproduced in this period despite the arrival of the new Paracelsian model of disease, feelings were influenced by the four humours of the body, which were very changeable.[116] Table I.1 shows the relationship of the four humours to the four elements, bodily fluids and qualities.

Table I.1   The four humours of the body

Element	Characteristics	Bodily Fluid	Humour
Fire	Hot, dry	Yellow bile	Choleric
Air	Hot, wet	Blood	Sanguine
Earth	Cold, dry	Black bile	Melancholic
Water	Cold, wet	Phlegm	Phlegmatic

Source: Shepard, *Meanings of Manhood*, 51.

---

[113]   John Walter, *Understanding Popular Violence in the English Revolution: The Colchester Plunderers* (Cambridge, 1999), p. 156. This example will be discussed in more detail in Chapter 1.
[114]   Keeler, *Long Parliament*, 97–8, 199; Christopher W. Brooks, 'Grimston, Sir Harbottle, second baronet (1603–1685)', *ODNB*; Chris R. Kyle, 'Barrington, Sir Thomas, second baronet (c.1585–1644)', *ODNB*.
[115]   *Some Speciall Passages from Hull, Anlaby and Yorke*, TT E.108[33], p. 6.
[116]   Shepard, *Meanings of Manhood*, 50–53.

There were natural defaults in the humoral constitution. Men and horses were generally hotter than women, who were supposed to be cold and wet.[117] The colour of a horse's coat was linked to its constitution: black horses were hot and white horses cold.[118] Humoral theory was dualist, but in this model mind and body were closely related and could easily affect each other.[119] Henry Townshend described a dispute over negotiations of the surrender of Worcester in 1646 in distinctly humoral terms, writing that the governor, Colonel Henry Washington, 'fell into so great a passion (being much addicted to choler and ill commander of it)' that he attacked and threatened several men who were ostensibly on his own side.[120] The phrase 'fiery spirits', which D'Ewes used to refer to MPs whom he perceived as extremists, was not yet a dead metaphor and could easily have been understood at the time as a literal description and causal explanation of their physical characteristics and behaviour.

The environment was supposed to affect the defaults of the humoral constitution. Different climates tended to produce different characteristics in both humans and animals.[121] David Underdown's hypothesis that allegiance was determined by economic, social and cultural differences between chalk and cheese countries unquestioningly reproduced this geohumoral theory, echoing John Aubrey's blatantly Galenic description of the people of western Wiltshire: 'slow and dull, heavy of spirit ... they feed mainly on milk meats, which cools their brains too much'.[122] A body's humours could easily get out of balance, leading to changes in outward characteristics. Air, diet, seasons and even time of day were among the external factors which could cause imbalances.[123] A man whose humours got too cold and wet would become sluggish, lethargic and effeminate.[124] A woman whose humours became too hot could grow 'mannish', or even turn into a man, which was entirely plausible when female bodies were

---

[117] Fletcher, *Gender*, 33; Shepard, *Meanings of Manhood*, 51; Edwards, *Horse and Man*, 55; Hughes, *Gender*, 13.

[118] Louise Hill Curth, '"The Most Excellent of Animal Creatures": Health Care for Horses in Early Modern England', in Peter Edwards, Karl Enenkel and Elspeth Graham (eds), *The Horse as Cultural Icon: The Real and the Symbolic Horse in the Early Modern World* (Leiden, 2011), p. 221.

[119] Ibid., 225.

[120] C.D. Gilbert, 'The Catholics in Worcestershire, 1642–1651', *Recusant History*, 20/3 (1991): 348.

[121] Ian F. MacInnes, 'Altering a Race of Jades: Horse Breeding and Geohumoralism in Shakespeare', in Peter Edwards, Karl Enenkel and Elspeth Graham (eds), *The Horse as Cultural Icon: The Real and the Symbolic Horse in the Early Modern World* (Leiden, 2011), pp. 175–89.

[122] Daniel MacCannell, '"Dark Corners of the Land"? A New Approach to Regional Factors in the Civil Wars of England and Wales', *Cultural and Social History*, 7/2 (2010): 175.

[123] Shepard, *Meanings of Manhood*, 51; Curth, 'Most Excellent of Animal Creatures', 223.

[124] Shepard, *Meanings of Manhood*, 59.

often represented as imperfect male bodies whose genitals were the same but inverted.[125] Anger and drunkenness could both make a man bestial, 'having no more of a man but the shape'.[126] If the humoral body described in early-modern texts was so unstable that it could lead to changes of sex and species, it is unlikely that it could be the site of the fixed internal allegiance that twentieth-century essentialist historiography required. Humoral theory cannot be dismissed simply because it is scientifically untrue. Seventeenth-century people acted as if the four humours were real. Farriers and physicians were often paid to restore the humoral balance of animals and humans by letting blood.[127] Therefore humoral theory has to be taken seriously as an influence on people's perceptions and actions.

Puritan preachers railed against hypocrisy in their sermons, but even this does not fit easily with essentialist models of allegiance. While Godly preachers valued sincerity very highly, they also said that it was very difficult to achieve. Their sermons spoke of confusion, divided hearts, troubled or unstable minds and souls at war with themselves.[128] Puritans sometimes distrusted or disowned their feelings and attributed their actions to God or the Devil. Nehemiah Wallington considered committing suicide by jumping out of a window, 'but God of his great love and mercy caused me presently to go down the stairs as fast as I could'.[129] Obadiah Sedgwick warned that 'Your worst enemies lie in your own breasts ... None ought to be more carefully watched than the traitors within our own bosoms.' This implied that people could not even know their own minds, a claim made more explicitly by Richard Sibbes: 'Self hinders the knowledge of itself all it can.'[130] Furthermore, puritan preachers insisted that the only way to avoid hypocrisy was through a combination of sincere faith and sincere actions.[131] For Stephen Marshall, grieving for Ireland but failing to do anything was just as hypocritical as doing something insincerely.[132] When he rhetorically asked 'what Love is it?', he answered that Saint John:

---

[125]   Thomas Laqueur, *Making Sex: Body and Gender from the Greeks to Freud* (Cambridge, MA, 1992), pp. 126–8; Fletcher, *Gender*, 41, 44; Hughes, *Gender*, 13.

[126]   Shepard, *Meanings of Manhood*, 28.

[127]   Louise Hill Curth, 'English Almanacs and Animal Health Care in the Seventeenth Century', *Society and Animals*, 8/1 (2000): 8; Curth, 'Most Excellent of Animal Creatures', 225, 228.

[128]   Stephen K. Baskerville, *Not Peace but a Sword: The Political Theology of the English Revolution* (London, 1993), pp. 34–5, 43, 152.

[129]   Seaver, *Wallington's World*, 22.

[130]   Baskerville, *Not Peace*, 70, 97.

[131]   Seaver, *Wallington's World*, 42.

[132]   Stephen Marshall, *Meroz cursed, or, A sermon preached to the honourable House of Commons, at their late solemn fast, Febr. 23, 1641 by Stephen Marshall ...* (London, 1642), E.133[19], pp. 10, 50.

meanes it not of an inward affection only, to wish well to them, and so forth, but by love to serve our brethren, to lay out our selves, our lives, and parts, and all to serve them, To lay downe our lives for the Brethren, as Christ laid downe his life for us.[133]

Constancy could demonstrate sincerity, but rather than being a natural state, the elect had to struggle to achieve it. A Godly man had to 'overcome himself'.[134] Doing things was a necessary part of puritan militancy, as Stephen Baskerville argued: 'If anything was truly distinctive and innovative in Puritan ideas about revolution, therefore, it was not what they said about it but that they did it; they put their theory into practice, their thought into action'; 'To be a Christian was to be an activist, not believing only, but constantly doing'.[135] This included praying as well as physical acts.[136] Marshall insisted that 'though prayer be the great means, yet prayer is not all the means'.[137] Action was absolutely necessary for the construction of manliness as much as Godliness. Marshall derided 'neuters' who failed to help the church because of their 'sluggishnesse'.[138] This was heavily gendered language which questioned their manhood as well as their religious conviction. Sluggishness was supposed to be a characteristic of cold-humoured old men who lacked manly heat.[139] Classical republican writing also presented action for the public good as an important part of manhood.[140] Deeds were just as necessary for the King's cause. Clarendon later complained that 'they who wished well to him thought they had performed their duty in doing so and they had done enough for him in that they had done nothing against him'.[141] In 1644 Edward Bagshaw described allegiance in terms of a physical ritual, arguing that it could not be due to an impersonal state 'that is an invisible nothing, and can neither give nor take homage'.[142] Allegiance was very much about what people did. Like Clarendon, puritan and republican writing tended to imply that affections not expressed by actions did not count for much. From a historian's

---

[133]   Ibid., 28.

[134]   Baskerville, *Not Peace*, 57, 122.

[135]   Ibid., 10, 166.

[136]   Ibid., 165. Prayer is largely outside the scope of this book, but it deserves to be taken seriously as a way of participating in the war.

[137]   Marshall, *Meroz Cursed*, 47.

[138]   Ibid., 24.

[139]   Shepard, *Meanings of Manhood*, 51, 59.

[140]   Richard Cust, 'The "Public Man" in Late Tudor and Early Stuart England', in Peter Lake and Steven Pincus (eds), *Politics of the Public Sphere* (Manchester, 2007), pp. 117–18.

[141]   Holmes, *Why*, 91.

[142]   Howard Nenner, 'Loyalty and the Law: The Meaning of Trust and the Right of Resistance in Seventeenth-Century England', *Journal of British Studies*, 48/4 (2009): 861.

point of view, unexpressed affections may be interesting even though we have no way of knowing about them. But if we cannot know internal allegiance, why should we believe that it ever existed?

> The challenge for rethinking gender categories outside of the metaphysics of substance will have to consider the relevance of Nietzsche's claim in *On the Genealogy of Morals* that "there is no 'being' behind doing, effecting, becoming; 'the doer' is merely a fiction added to the deed – the deed is everything." In an application that Nietzsche himself would not have anticipated or condoned, we might state as a corollary: There is no gender identity behind the expressions of gender; that identity is performatively constituted by the very "'expressions'" that are said to be its results.[143]

In turn, the rethinking of civil war allegiance will have to consider the relevance of Judith Butler's radical rethinking of gender identities. The categories 'royalist' and 'parliamentarian' cannot be accepted uncritically. As Weil pointed out, 'allegiance itself is a category with a history'.[144] We must pay attention to how allegiance was constructed during the 1640s, and how it has been constructed by historians ever since. One thing about early-modern minds which we can infer from contemporary texts is that they thought very differently from ours. Seventeenth-century people seem to have represented allegiance as changeable rather than fixed, external as much as internal, and something that was done as much as felt. Early-modern writing often gives the impression that mind, body and soul were all inherently unstable rather than being the solid foundations of an authentic self. Parliament often valued outward conformance over inward sincerity, especially when there was a pressing need for material resources. Allegiance was constructed and contested rather than just there waiting to be discovered. The construction of allegiance was intimately connected with competition for resources. The act of providing material assistance to one side or the other could be used to fashion an identity based on that side, but as Morrill pointed out, unwilling acts could change the way that people were perceived and classified. The identities which people chose or had thrust upon them affected their property rights, since both sides were more likely to take the property of perceived enemies. By my definition, we could even begin to talk about animals having allegiance. This is not as absurd as it might sound at first. Horses actually did things which had real effects regardless of motives and intentions. The elite men who dominated Parliament could not have won the civil war without animals and common people, but neither could be completely controlled.

---

[143]   Judith Butler, *Gender Trouble* (Abingdon, 2006), p. 34.
[144]   Weil, 'Thinking About Allegiance', 183.

Language Barriers

I am all too aware that language limits what I can say and what I can think. One of the things which science can tell us about human minds in general is that perception is influenced by language, culture and built environments.[145] Essentialist assumptions about identity are so deeply embedded in the English language that they are difficult to challenge, or even recognize. It feels perfectly natural to say that a person was a royalist, and awkwardly unnatural to say that a person did royalism, even though that might be a more accurate way of describing how identities were formed and performed. In order to think differently about allegiance, I have found it necessary to fight against what feels most natural and force myself to use different language. Some scientists have advocated E-Prime, a form of English which challenges essentialist and naive-realist assumptions by excluding all forms of the verb 'to be'.[146] I am not willing or able to go that far, and I recognize that no language can be neutral, but I have taken extra care with language, avoiding some words and using others in specific, and perhaps unusual, ways.

From this point in the book I will be using the words 'royalist' and 'parliamentarian' as little as possible, and then only to criticize their use by other historians. This might appear eccentric, but it is absolutely necessary and not entirely unprecedented. Morrill has already objected to the use of the words on the grounds that they lump together people who did not necessarily have very much in common.[147] Sadler's thesis was 'not, however, concerned with counting people as Parliamentarians, Royalists or as neutrals, sidechangers and unclear cases'.[148] It might still be legitimate to use 'royalist' and 'parliamentarian' as adjectives to describe organizations such as armies and committees, but in these cases I prefer 'royal' and 'parliamentary' because they describe accurately enough and have less cultural baggage. Following Morrill, I have used 'militant' to describe people who were very active in making the war happen without much

[145] Joseph Henrich, Steven J. Heine and Ara Norenzayan, 'The Weirdest People in the World', *Behavioural and Brain Sciences*, 33/2–3 (2009): 8–9; Jonathan Winawer et al., 'Russian Blues Reveal Effects of Language on Color Discrimination', *Proceedings of the National Academy of Sciences*, 104/19 (2007): 7780–85; Lera Boroditsky, 'Sex, Syntax, and Semantics', in D. Gentner and S. Goldin-Meadow (eds), *Language in Mind: Advances in the Study of Language and Cognition* (Cambridge, MA, 2003), pp. 61–79.

[146] Robert Anton Wilson, 'Towards Understanding E-Prime', in D. David Bourland Jr. and Paul Dennithorne Johnston (eds), *To Be or Not: An E-Prime Anthology* (1991), pp. 23–6 http://nobeliefs.com/eprime.htm.

[147] Morrill, *Revolt in the Provinces*, 128, 189.

[148] Sadler, 'Cambridgeshire', 2.

obvious external coercion. This seems like a particularly appropriate word, even when used as a noun, because its origins in the present participle of the Latin verb *militare* emphasize doing rather than an underlying state of being.[149] The most problematic and most unavoidable word in this book is 'puritan'. While I prefer to use it as an adjective there are times when only the noun will succinctly get the idea across without rendering a sentence unreadable. In mitigation, the problems of defining 'puritans' are much more widely acknowledged and accepted than the problems of defining 'royalists' and 'parliamentarians'.[150] Using the word 'puritan' in the currently accepted way implicitly problematizes the word and the people it describes. While this book will mention 'puritan preachers', 'puritan sermons' and even 'puritans', I will avoid using 'puritanism' because it reifies a vague abstraction and denies the diversity of puritan speech, writing and other actions. I have sometimes used 'Godly' as a synonym for 'puritan' for the sake of variety.

Since this book works from the premise that other minds are unknowable, I have tried not to make claims about what people 'thought', 'felt', 'believed', 'wanted' or similar. While focusing on what people wrote it has been very difficult to avoid 'concept' or 'idea' because there is no alternative but 'meme', which has its own ideological baggage and will not necessarily be clear to all readers. When I write about 'ideas' I am referring to what is written in texts, not what is thought in minds. I use 'assumption' to refer to something which could have got onto the page without having been thought about very much. Another problematic word is 'support'. Essentialism and football fandom have given it connotations of intense emotional commitment, but I use it only to refer to acts which benefited one side without making claims about motives.

In line with Ashgate's house style I have used capitalization to distinguish between the specific and the general, but rather than unquestioningly following a dictionary or style manual I have thought carefully about the implications of capital letters and their absence. Capital letters tend to reify categories whereas lower case may help us to question them. I have capitalized specific people, places and organizations, for example 'the King', 'the Earl of Essex' and 'Parliament'. Groups of people are usually not capitalized, even if this appears unconventional. While I would capitalize 'the Catholic Church' I would not capitalize 'catholicism', 'catholics' or 'a catholic conspiracy'. In seventeenth-century England, catholicism was surprisingly diverse, contested and hard to define (Chapter 2). Clearly no use of 'protestant' can be capitalized because it refers to a wide variety of churches and doctrines. Since the nature of the true

---

[149]   *OED*, sv 'militant'.

[150]   John Coffey and Paul C.H. Lim, 'Introduction', in John Coffey and Paul C.H. Lim (eds), *The Cambridge Companion to Puritanism* (Cambridge, 2008), p. 1.

protestant church was violently contested in England in this period, 'the church' must be left in lower case too. In some places 'Royalist' and 'Parliamentarian' will appear in quotes because they have been capitalized by the historians against whom I am arguing. The main exception to this rule is when the label of a group is derived from a proper noun, for example 'Marxists', 'Calvinists' or 'Londoners'. I have also used 'Presbyterian' and 'Independent' to refer specifically to the two factions which dominated Parliament and its armies from 1644 onwards, but I have not assumed that these map easily onto the 'war' and 'peace' parties. Before the middle of 1644 I tend to agree with Morrill that a two- or three-party taxonomy is inadequate.[151]

The 'English Civil War' in the title of this book must be justified rather than accepted as the default. British, European and Atlantic perspectives have provided new ways of understanding what happened in England as well as being important in their own right. They show that the term 'English Civil War' is a false universal which erases the role of other countries. But if I used 'British' to describe my own work it would also be a false universal which promised more than I could deliver. I have chosen to specialize in England, particularly the southeast. While a narrow focus allows more attention to detail it also necessarily prevents breadth. I have tried to turn this problem into an opportunity. Since Mark Stoyle published his brilliant work on the ethnic dimensions of the civil wars it has been possible to see Englishness as a problem to be analysed rather than a default to be taken for granted.[152] 'English' is yet another constructed and contested identity. Chapter 1 will show that the Englishness of puritan militants was a false universal which privileged some parts of England over others, and that ideals of English puritan masculinity could be difficult to achieve in practice.

While 'Civil War' appears more neutral than 'English' it is one of many terms to describe what happened in the 1640s, and rejecting those other terms necessarily involves taking a position. The word 'revolution' will be used very little in this work because the problems of defining the term and deciding whether or when one occurred are too difficult and complex to deal with in the confines of a book which is mostly about other things. I generally accept the arguments of John Adamson and David Cressy that some revolutionary things happened in England before the outbreak of the First Civil War.[153] It could also be asked whether it was revolutionary for Parliament to take executive power and raise an army in defiance of the King. Chapter 1 will give a vague impression that it

---

[151] Morrill, *Revolt in the Provinces*, 199.

[152] Mark Stoyle, *Soldiers and Strangers: An Ethnic History of the English Civil War* (New Haven, 2005).

[153] John Adamson, *The Noble Revolt: The Overthrow of Charles I* (London, 2007); David Cressy, *England on Edge: Crisis and Revolution 1640–1642* (Oxford, 2007).

was, without pushing the point too far. While avoiding discussing revolutions, I have sometimes described Parliament's military action as a rebellion. Because Clarendon used the term to imply that the King's cause was legitimate and that Parliament's was not, many other historians have tended to avoid it.[154] Similarly, social-political historians sometimes prefer 'crowd action' because 'riot' can have so many negative connotations. But these words can also be used in positive ways. By putting 'riot' and 'rebellion' next to 'revel', David Underdown made the title of his famous book a celebration of disobedience.[155] The ordinary people whom he studied defied not only their social superiors but the Whig and revisionist historians who limited themselves to high politics or studies of county gentry. The horses, women and men in my book will not obey the categories, abstractions and assumptions which historians have tried to impose on them.

---

[154]   Edward Hyde, Earl of Clarendon, *The history of the Rebellion and civil wars in England begun in the year 1641*, William Dunn Macray (ed.) (Oxford, 1888).

[155]   Underdown, *Revel, Riot, and Rebellion.*

Chapter 1

The Propositions

Parliament

Attempts to explain the start and end of the First Civil War have suffered from a large hole in the historiography where the Earl of Essex's army should be. This omission is surprising to say the least. How could so many eminent historians have claimed that they understood the causes of the First Civil War when they had not even asked about the origins of one of the armies which fought the first campaign? Godfrey Davies published a brief article on its organization in 1934.[1] Military historians continued to study the army's campaigns and battles without adequately explaining how it was created or maintained. Peter Young's book on Edgehill devoted only five pages to raising the parliamentary army, while a more recent interpretation of the battle covered the recruitment of Essex's army in only half a page.[2] It is only in the last five years that academic publications have started to deal with the recruitment, finance and administration of Essex's army in sufficient detail.[3] This chapter will add to the new work on the origins of Essex's army.

Parliament started raising an army on 10 June 1642. This was one month before the Earl of Essex was appointed Lord General and nearly ten weeks before Charles I raised his standard at Nottingham. The process began with an ordinance inviting the public to contribute money, plate, horses and arms for the

---

[1]   Godfrey Davies, 'The Parliamentary Army under the Earl of Essex', *English Historical Review*, 49/193 (1934): 32–54.

[2]   Peter Young, *Edgehill 1642: The Campaign and the Battle* (Kineton, 1967), pp. 54–9; Christopher L. Scott, Alan Turton and Eric Gruber von Arni, *Edgehill: The Battle Reinterpreted* (Barnsley, 2004), p. 44.

[3]   Gavin Robinson, 'Horse Supply and the Development of the New Model Army, 1642–1646', *War in History*, 15/2 (2008): 121–40; Aaron Graham, 'Finance, Localism, and Military Representation in the Army of the Earl of Essex (June–December 1642)', *Historical Journal*, 52/04 (2009): 879–98; Aaron Graham, 'The Earl of Essex and Parliament's Army at the Battle of Edgehill: A Reassessment', *War in History*, 17/3 (2010): 276–93; Tom Crawshaw, 'Military Finance and the Earl of Essex's Infantry in 1642 – a Reinterpretation', *Historical Journal*, 53/04 (2010): 1037–48. Many important questions will be answered in forthcoming PhD theses by Tom Crawshaw and Jeff Hoppes.

defence of Parliament.⁴ This system of public subscriptions was often referred
to as the Propositions. John Smith and Thomas Richardson were appointed
commissaries to receive and value horses and arms in London. They kept detailed
records containing descriptions and values of the horses, along with the name,
and sometimes the address and status, of the owner. The original lists have not
survived, but the commissaries made copies in 1644 when they were required to
account for everything they had received. These books, which were handed in to
the Committee for Taking Accounts of the Whole Kingdom, have survived and
provide a reliable account of horses which were actually brought in.⁵ By the time
of the battle of Edgehill on 23 October 1642, just over 3,200 cavalry horses with
a total value of over £48,500 had been listed.

Resistance Practice

Parliament's official words and actions in 1642 did not depend heavily on
resistance theory. Debates with Charles I over the theory of the king's two bodies
were about who had the right to exercise royal authority rather than who had the
right to resist it.⁶ The ordinances by which Parliament took control of the militia
and raised new forces to fight against the King offered no explicit theoretical
justification for these actions. The preambles of the Militia Ordinance and
Propositions Ordinance concentrated on why action needed to be taken rather
than on why Parliament was allowed to take it. They relied on fear more than
constitutional principle.⁷ The Propositions Ordinance began by creating a strong
impression of approaching disaster:

> Whereas it appears that the King (seduced by wicked Counsel) intends to make
> War against His Parliament, and, in Pursuance thereof, under Pretence of a Guard
> for His Person, hath actually begun to levy Forces both of Horse and Foot, and sent
> out Summons throughout the County of Yorke, for the calling together of greater
> Numbers; and some ill-affected Persons have been employed in other Parts, to raise
> Troops, under the Colour of His Majesty's Service, making large Offers of Reward
> and Preferment to such as will come in; and that His Majesty doth, with a high and
> forcible Hand, protect and keep away Delinquents, not permitting them to make their
> Appearance, to answer such Affronts and Injuries as have been by them offered unto
> the Parliament; and those Messengers which have been sent from the Houses for them,
> have been abused, beaten, and imprisoned; so as the Orders of Parliament (which is

⁴   *A & O*, vol. 1, 6–9.
⁵   TNA: PRO, SP 28/131, parts 3, 4, and 5.
⁶   Conrad Russell, *The Fall of the British Monarchies 1637–1642* (Oxford, 1991), pp. 507–9.
⁷   Ibid., 499–500.

the highest Court of Justice in this Realm) are not obeyed, and the Authority of it is altogether scorned and vilified, and such Persons as stand well affected to it, and declare themselves sensible of these Public Calamities, and of the Violations of the Privileges of Parliament, and Common Liberty of the Subject, are baffled and injured, by several Sorts of malignant Men, who are about the King: some whereof, under the Name of Cavaliers, without having Respect to the Laws of the Land, or any Fear either of God or Man, are ready to commit all Manner of Outrage and Violence, which must needs tend to the Dissolution of this Government, the destroying of our Religion, Laws, Liberty, and Propriety; all which will be exposed to the Malice and Violence of such desperate Persons as must be employed in so horrid and unnatural an Act as the overthrowing of a Parliament by Force, which is the Support and Preservation of them all; which being duly considered by the Lords and Commons, and how great an Obligation lies upon them, in Honour, Conscience and Duty, according to the high Trust reposed in them, to use all possible Means in such Cases for the timely Prevention of so great and irrecoverable Evils, they have thought fit to publish their Sense and Apprehension of this imminent Danger ...[8]

This was an argument from necessity, not from constitutional principles. By Glenn Burgess's definition it is arbitrary government, and by Johann Sommerville's definition it is absolutism.[9] The Earl of Dorset wrote, probably in August 1642, that there was 'an arbitrary government even on both sides'.[10] The preamble was so controversial that it was omitted when the Propositions Ordinance was read at subscription meetings in Norfolk.[11] Sir Simonds D'Ewes had spoken against it before the ordinance passed the Commons, saying that 'I did conceive this expression might prove of dangerous consequence because it would fill men's hearts with the fear and expectation of a civil war.'[12]

By asserting that Charles I was controlled by a popish conspiracy and incapable of ruling, Parliament claimed the right to resist in theory and suggested ways of resisting in practice. The methods used to raise forces against the King in 1642 drew on Elizabethan plans to defend the protestant commonwealth from catholic conspiracies in the absence of a monarch. The 1584 oath of association committed protestants to material action. In an emergency the

---

[8]   *A & O*, vol. 1, 6–7.

[9]   Glenn Burgess, *Absolute Monarchy and the Stuart Constitution* (New Haven, 1996), p. 212; Johann P. Sommerville, *Royalists and Patriots: Politics and Ideology in England, 1603–1640* (London, 1999), pp. 228–9, 233.

[10]   Russell, *Fall*, 498.

[11]   Clive Holmes, *The Eastern Association in the English Civil War* (Cambridge, 2007), p. 59.

[12]   Wilson Coates, Anne Steele Young and Vernon F. Snow (eds), *Private Journals of the Long Parliament, 2 June to 17 September 1642* (New Haven, 1982), p. 43.

associations were to raise armed forces, with money and weapons subscribed by the swearers.[13] This idea was put into practice in 1642 with the creation of the Earl of Essex's army. Material contributions were linked to the Protestation, which was often compared to the 1584 bond of association.[14] The ordinance stated that its purpose was 'to excite all well-affected Persons to contribute their best Assistance, according to their solemn Vow and Protestation'.[15] People who took the Protestation potentially committed themselves to providing resources and to fighting, as they promised to defend the King, Parliament, the protestant religion and the liberty of the subject 'with my Life, Power, and Estate'.[16] The Protestation was closely associated with threats of violence. It was drawn up around the time of the first Army Plot in May 1641 and imposed on the whole kingdom after the attempt on the five members in January 1642.[17] It countered these threats from the supposed popish conspiracy with more threats, binding those who took it to 'by good Ways and Means, endeavour to bring to condign Punishment, all such as shall, either by Force, Practice, Counsel, Plots, Conspiracies, or otherwise, do any thing to the contrary in this present Protestation contained'.[18] This threat of violence was made even more explicit by John Pym's description of the vow as a 'shibboleth', recalling the bloodthirsty passage in the book of Judges in which idolaters had their throats cut if they could not say the word.[19] The Propositions Ordinance interpreted the Protestation as a very literal call to arms and attempted to put it into practice.

Stephen Marshall's fast sermon *Meroz Cursed* insisted that 'All people are cursed or blessed according as they do or do not joyne their strength and give their best assistance to the Lords people against their enemies.'[20] This sermon was preached to Parliament on 23 February 1642 and subsequently printed by order of the Commons. Marshall exhorted the listening MPs and peers to take action, particularly in putting down the Irish rebellion. He did not explicitly mention the possibility of fighting a civil war in England, but it would have been easy for listeners and readers to make connections with problems closer

---

[13]   Edward Vallance, *Revolutionary England and the National Covenant: State Oaths, Protestantism and the Political Nation, 1553–1682* (Woodbridge, 2005), pp. 21–4.

[14]   Ibid., 61.

[15]   *A & O*, vol. 1, 7.

[16]   *CJ*, vol. 2, 132.

[17]   Vallance, *Revolutionary England*, 51, 53.

[18]   *CJ*, vol. 2, 132.

[19]   Vallance, *Revolutionary England*, 52–3.

[20]   Stephen Marshall, *Meroz cursed, or, A sermon preached to the honourable House of Commons, at their late solemn fast, Febr. 23, 1641 by Stephen Marshall* ... (London, 1642), TT E.133[19], p. 9.

to home. *Meroz Cursed* was delivered only seven weeks after the King's attempt on the five members, and around the time when the Protestation was being tendered throughout the kingdom. Marshall's insistence that 'Gods meanest servants must not be afraid to oppose the Mighty' could have been taken as a threat to Charles I, since he defined the mighty as 'all, of what ranke or quality soever, who are eminent in wisdom, strength, authority or riches, and mannage an ill cause against the Lord or against his Church'.[21] This was more or less an explicit resistance theory based on religion: everyone had not only a right but a duty to resist any enemies of the church.[22] Furthermore, the sermon fits into what Ethan Shagan defined as the Foxean view of the Irish rebellion, a strongly anti-catholic interpretation associated with opposition to the King.[23] Like Pym's shibboleth, *Meroz Cursed* drew a line between those who were with the Lord and those who were against him. Those who did not come to the aid of the church would be cursed. The sermon was particularly apt for the Propositions, as Marshall stated that members of Parliament 'all should be as the Lord: their Horses as his Horses'.[24]

Marshall's words were much more extreme than the vague and pragmatic justifications in official ordinances. This may have been a consequence of the need to gain the approval of moderates in order to pass an ordinance. Sermons and ostensibly unofficial tracts could be used to avoid the delays and compromises of official channels and to increase tension.[25] While militants were pressing ahead with military preparations in the summer of 1642, moderates were still attempting to avoid violence by negotiating a compromise.[26] On 6 July the Earls of Leicester and Portland, and Lord Spencer dissented to several resolutions of the Lords concerning spending Proposition money, raising infantry and sending reinforcements to Hull.[27] Later that day they were added to a committee to draw up peace terms, after which their protests stopped. It was easy for men in this position to change sides or be perceived as enemies. In August Spencer joined

---

[21]   Ibid., 7–8. This was Marshall's own gloss. The text of Judges 5 does not define the 'mighty'. It cannot be assumed that the 'all' in Marshall's definition necessarily included women. Hilda L. Smith, *All Men and Both Sexes: Gender, Politics, and the False Universal in England, 1640–1832* (University Park, PA, 2002), p. 3.

[22]   William Hunt, *The Puritan Moment: The Coming of Revolution in an English County* (Cambridge, MA, 1983), p. 296. Marshall simply ignored the problem of Romans 13.

[23]   Ethan Shagan, 'Constructing Discord: Ideology, Propaganda, and English Responses to the Irish Rebellion of 1641', *Journal of British Studies*, 36/1 (1997): 7, 15–16, 27–8.

[24]   Marshall, *Meroz Cursed*, 4.

[25]   Jason Peacey, *Politicians and Pamphleteers: Propaganda During the English Civil Wars and Interregnum* (Aldershot, 2004), pp. 56, 58, 310.

[26]   Anthony Fletcher, *The Outbreak of the English Civil War* (London, 1981), pp. 273–4.

[27]   *LJ*, vol. 5, 186.

the King, while Portland was sent to the Tower on suspicion of involvement in the plot to betray Portsmouth.[28]

Although Parliament claimed to be fighting a defensive war, the army it created was capable of aggressive war right from the start. When the Commons voted to raise 10,000 volunteers on 9 July 1642, it was explicitly stated that 'this Body shall be ready to march into any Part of the Kingdom, where both Houses of Parliament shall direct'.[29] The Militia Ordinance was not a mechanism for fighting a war.[30] It soon became an end in itself as both sides had to raise regular armies in order to enforce the rights which they claimed over the militia. The implementation of the Propositions from June 1642 onwards, and the commissioning of Essex as Lord General in July, were the beginnings of Parliament's field army. They made it possible to fight if the King would not back down.

Public Rebellion

One of the most striking things about Parliament's preparations to fight in 1642 is that they were carried out in the open. Unlike many previous English rebellions, this was no secret conspiracy. As Conrad Russell pointed out, it was clear that Parliament was getting ready to fight for several months before the fighting started. Russell also argued that private rebellion by barons was no longer viable in seventeenth-century England and was not seriously attempted after 1601.[31] The peers did not have the resources to raise armies on their own. John Adamson has shown that noble leadership was a central part of opposition to Charles I in the early 1640s, but also acknowledged that the dissident peers lacked military power and had to appeal to the public for support.[32] This support required more than favourable opinions, since 'public opinion in the seventeenth century did not constitute a power base unless it was translated into action by some other force'.[33] If the parliamentary leaders were to raise an army, they would need many more people to act with them.

---

[28]   S.L. Sadler, 'Spencer, Henry, first earl of Sunderland (bap. 1620, d. 1643)', *ODNB*; Sean Kelsey, 'Weston, Jerome, second earl of Portland (1605–1663)', *ODNB*.

[29]   *CJ*, vol. 2, 663.

[30]   Fletcher, *Outbreak*, 334, 348.

[31]   Conrad Russell, 'The Scottish Party in English Parliaments, 1640–1642', *Historical Research*, 66 (1993): 43, 46.

[32]   John Adamson, *The Noble Revolt: The Overthrow of Charles I* (London, 2007), pp. 32–3, 44–5.

[33]   Russell, 'Scottish Party', 37.

Parliament claimed to be acting for the public good and portrayed the King's supporters as a malignant minority. The Propositions Ordinance described the actions of the 'malignants' as 'these Public Calamities'.[34] Parliament claimed to be 'the Support and Preservation' of 'Religion, Laws, Liberty, and Propriety'. This paternalist view was partly undermined because the junto needed to appeal for material support from outside Parliament.[35] Action for the public required action by the public, but these two publics were not quite the same. According to Hughes, 'all men were invited to become political actors' by Parliament in 1642, but this needs to be qualified because some actions were not equally open to all men.[36] The Propositions Ordinance was necessarily aimed at property owners. The Protestation's promise to defend King, Parliament and protestantism 'with my Life, Power, and Estate' potentially provided as much excuse for inaction as the reservation 'as far as lawfully I may', since people with no estate could not be obliged to give what they did not have.[37] Therefore the Propositions Ordinance's 'all well-affected Persons' was a false universal which excluded the poor, and even less-wealthy members of the middling sort. The ordinance used ambiguous language which did not explicitly include or exclude women, stating that 'because every *Person* may not be provided with present Money, or with Horse, or not have *his* Plate with *him* which *he* means to bring in, and yet resolves to contribute *his* Part' (emphasis added).[38] In this sentence it must be the case that either 'person' excludes women or that 'he' and 'his' include women. In practice, women were less likely than men to be able to contribute because they were less likely to be financially independent. In legal theory, a married woman under coverture could not normally have an estate of her own and therefore could not use it to defend the commonwealth, even if she was one of the relatively few women who had taken the Protestation.[39] Widows could be financially independent if their husbands left them a sufficient estate free from debt, but more often widows were poor.[40] Surviving records show that only a minority was capable of contributing to the Propositions. In Childerditch, Essex, 35 people took the Protestation on 23 January 1642 (all with apparently male forenames,

---

34 *A & O*, vol. 1, 7.

35 Ann Hughes, *Gender and the English Revolution* (Abingdon, 2011), p. 7.

36 Ibid., 109.

37 *CJ*, vol. 2, 132.

38 *A & O*, vol. 1, 8–9.

39 Amy Louise Erickson, *Women and Property in Early Modern England* (London, 1995), pp. 24–5, 100; Vallance, *Revolutionary England*, 110. A husband could not dispose of freehold land without his wife's consent but he was automatically entitled to the rents and profits.

40 Erickson, *Women and Property*, 178, 196, 201.

but no gender-specific statuses are given).[41] The minister Daniel Duckfield lent over £36 in money to the Propositions, Nicholas Thresher sent in two horses worth £24, and only five other men were assessed for not having contributed, including one who had not taken the Protestation.[42]

Because Parliament required action by some of the public, it was necessary to communicate with that section of the public. One of the purposes of propaganda was to persuade people to provide resources.[43] As soon as the ordinance had been approved on 10 June, the Lords ordered 'That the Propositions shall be printed and published forthwith.'[44] In July, Hertfordshire MPs were ordered to advance the Propositions at the quarter sessions and assizes in Hertford.[45] Preparing for war in public was not just a side effect of appealing for contributions of resources. Openly acting on behalf of the public made Parliament's actions appear more legitimate. The junto fashioned a public image by appearing to act like a government, not like rebels conspiring in secret, although the creation of this image may well have been the result of a secret conspiracy.

Charles I was well aware of Parliament's public attempt to raise an army and made similarly public attempts to stop it. He must have been informed of the Propositions Ordinance by 14 June, when he wrote a letter to the Lord Mayor of London, Sir Richard Gurney, stating that although it was acceptable to raise money and forces to suppress the Irish rebellion, anyone complicit in raising forces for use in England would be proceeded against.[46] The letter also included a vague threat to revoke the City's charter if its citizens did not comply. According to the King's instructions, the Lord Mayor was to circulate the letter to the masters and wardens of the London livery companies. This suggests an authoritarian approach using traditional hierarchies. In any case, the strategy failed because the letter was reported to Parliament and both houses agreed that it should not be published. The following week, the Lord Mayor received a royal proclamation against the Propositions and ordered it to be published in the City immediately without asking Parliament.[47] This soon came to the attention of the House of Lords, and the officials responsible were summoned to explain themselves. William Hall, the sword bearer of the City, deposed that he had published the proclamation on the Lord Mayor's orders 'but the

---

[41]   'Childerditch protestation return', *Essex Review*, 26 (1916): 93.

[42]   TNA: PRO, SP 28/153, part 6, Account of John Fenning; TNA: PRO, SP 28/131, part 3, fol. 55r.

[43]   Peacey, *Politicians and Pamphleteers*, 62, 318, 323.

[44]   *LJ*, vol. 5, 123.

[45]   *CJ*, vol. 2, 654, 671.

[46]   *LJ*, vol. 5, 148.

[47]   *LJ*, vol. 5, 160, 163, 167–8.

same did not belong unto his Place; but to the Carvers and Water-Bailiffs, &c. who were out of the Way at this Time'.[48] Hall also stated that 'the Lord Mayor commanded the said Proclamation to be pasted up upon Doors, and other usual Places, where Proclamations are pasted up', implying the existence of a number of printed copies. Royal declarations were usually printed in runs of 1,400, and £40 was paid for printing them in June 1642.[49] The proclamation was clearly contested, as Hall said, 'That he being interrupted, that he could proclaim but Six or Seven Lines of the Proclamation, he returned, and acquainted the Lord Mayor therewith; and he said, it was enough.'

King and Parliament competed to take control of communication with the public and deny the other access to an audience. Orders of Parliament to deputy lieutenants often included instructions for taking control of the post, ensuring that letters were not intercepted, punishing people who spoke against Parliament, clearing Parliament from aspersions, making Parliament's justifications for war clear, and publishing and executing orders of Parliament.[50] This could imply that neither side assumed that the obvious rightness of their own cause would automatically win public support. Parliament attempted to suppress royal proclamations in London rather than arguing against them, but these attempts were not always successful. In one provocative act of defiance, a royal proclamation was posted on a maypole in Southwark.[51] While this demonstrated that Parliament did not have unanimous support and could not fully control discourse, it also showed that with London dominated by Parliament, royal proclamations had been reduced to the status of libels.

What happened in 1642 was not a private rebellion but a public rebellion. Parliament claimed to be acting for the public and used published communications to solicit actions from some members of the public, and so preparations were carried out in public. Membership of 'the public' varied according to circumstances, and was not equally open to all people. The public which was expected to act was more exclusive than the public which was to be defended, and neither was universal. Parliament's words and actions suggest that 'the public' privileged wealthy protestant English men over women, catholics, poor people and racial Others, who were reduced to the status of dependants or enemies. By acting as public defenders, elite men effectively disguised their privilege as a burden.

---

[48]   *LJ*, vol. 5, 160.

[49]   Peacey, *Politicians and Pamphleteers*, 46–8. Parliament preferred bigger print runs of up to 12,000.

[50]   For example, *LJ*, vol. 5, 128–9, 134–5, 252–3, 260–61, 291–3, 382–4.

[51]   Russell, *Fall*, 520.

That 'the public' was a false universal is just one of the problems with the concept of the public sphere.[52] Habermas imagined an ideal of the rational-critical bourgeois public sphere in which individuals would come together as a public in opposition to the state and reach a consensus about truth through rational debate in which arguments were judged on their own merits rather than by the status of the people making them.[53] Freist has argued that the role and nature of public opinion was transformed in the 1640s, but made it clear that it was more diverse and complex, and less intellectual, than Habermas's ideal. While public discourse was often well informed, it relied heavily on gender stereotypes, sexual slander, familiar rituals and traditional folk heroes.[54] The boundary between public and private was blurred as 'politics spilled over into everyday life'.[55] More recently, Peacey has cautioned that while there was clearly an increasing need for politicians to appeal to the public, 'it would be a mistake to confuse this with the emergence of a public sphere', and that politicians used propaganda to advance their agendas rather than encouraging a search for truth.[56] Public debate in 1642 privileged some people and excluded others. Rather than being independent from or opposed to the state, public men were asked to choose between two rival states. Both made demands for obedience backed up by tradition and fear as much as by rational arguments. Religious bigotry, whether against popery or puritans, played a large part in their rhetoric.[57] These rival governments sought to control discourse rather than encourage rational and open debate. While Parliament was more willing and able than the King's supporters to use print for propaganda, it was no more committed to a free press than Archbishop Laud had been. There was de facto press freedom in 1642 only because Parliament's attempts at censorship failed to cope with the increased volume of publications.[58] If any kind of public sphere emerged in the 1640s, it was despite rather than because of Parliament. Both governments made exclusive claims that they had authority over the state and were acting for the public good,

---

[52]   Rachel Weil, 'Matthew Smith Versus the "Great Men": Plot-Talk, the Public Sphere and the Problem of Credibility in the 1690s', in Peter Lake and Steven Pincus (eds), *The Politics of the Public Sphere* (Manchester, 2007), p. 234; Mark Knights, 'How Rational Was the Later Stuart Public Sphere?', in Peter Lake and Steven Pincus (eds), *The Politics of the Public Sphere* (Manchester, 2007), pp. 253–4.

[53]   Weil, 'Matthew Smith', 247; Knights, 'How Rational', 252–4, 257; Dagmar Freist, *Governed by Opinion: Politics, Religion and the Dynamics of Communication in Stuart London, 1637–45* (London, 1997), p. 13.

[54]   Freist, *Governed by Opinion*, 2–4, 19–21, 79, 198–9, 201–4, 300–301.

[55]   Ibid., 21–2, 305.

[56]   Peacey, *Politicians and Pamphleteers*, 331–2.

[57]   Ibid., 311.

[58]   Ibid., 135–8, 142–3; 330–31; Freist, *Governed by Opinion*, 47.

but neither was entirely legitimate in theory and neither achieved supremacy in practice until the issue had been decided by war. Both had to ask the public for support in order to fight. Whenever one side demanded allegiance and insisted on the illegitimacy of the other side, more debate was provoked, and people were reminded that they had a choice.[59] The justifications offered were ostensibly self-evident, but the fact that any justification had to be offered admitted that the public needed to be persuaded.[60] Rather than building consensus, 'public opinion is characterized by division'.[61] King and Parliament were playing a language game with very real consequences. The results of the discourse were manifested not as nebulous public opinion, but as armies which fought each other at Edgehill. As Venetian historian Paolo Sarpi had earlier written, 'they are words that draw armies behind them'.[62] Public debate did not lead to rational consensus over truth, but to violence and death.

Voluntary or Compulsory?

The question of whether Propositions contributions were voluntary or compulsory does not have a simple answer. Even leaving aside the problems of individual motivation, the system outlined by ordinances of Parliament was ambiguous and changed over time. The original Propositions Ordinance of June 1642 presented the contributions as more-or-less voluntary. The stated aim was 'to excite all well-affected Persons to contribute their best Assistance, according to their solemn Vow and Protestation'.[63] This implied an assumption that the majority would want to contribute because they were well-affected to Parliament, the commonwealth and the protestant religion, but it also suggested that people were bound by the Protestation to contribute. This is not necessarily what people had been expecting when they took the vow. The intentions of the MPs and peers who drafted and approved the text could not control the meanings which other people found in it.[64] In practice, the Protestation was interpreted in many different ways. Some people took it with extra reservations or omitted some parts of it, including catholics who did not promise to defend

59   Russell, *Fall*, 499–500; Freist, *Governed by Opinion*, 31, 303.
60   Peacey, *Politicians and Pamphleteers*, 38, 310.
61   Freist, *Governed by Opinion*, 305.
62   Peacey, *Politicians and Pamphleteers*, 39.
63   *A & O*, vol. 1, 7.
64   David Cressy, 'The Protestation Protested, 1641 and 1642', *Historical Journal*, 45/2 (2002): 253, 263.

the protestant religion.[65] The official text included the reservation 'as far as lawfully I may'.[66] Charles I's proclamations that the Propositions were unlawful made it easy to claim that the Protestation did not bind people to contribute.[67] When a non-contributor called Fletcher was examined by the Commons on 15 October 1642, he answered that 'the Doubt that remained with him was, the Command of the King did lie upon him, not to lend upon those Propositions'.[68] Sir Robert Cooke declared that contributing to the Propositions was against his conscience, and refused to take the Protestation.[69] When MPs were asked to subscribe on 10 June, William Pleydell 'stood up and showed that he could not give or lend any money or find any horses because he had given his No to all the propositions and so desired to be excused'.[70] Evasion seems to have been more common than appeals to principles. An account book from the parish of St Clement Danes in the western suburbs of London recorded a total of around £900 in money and plate subscribed by 140 individuals, whose contributions ranged from a few shillings up to £500.[71] Another 21 did not contribute anything. Some of them claimed that they could not afford it, including Lady Penelope Spenser, 'in regard of her greate Charge of Children and smalnes of meanes'. Three other men and one widow were not even asked because they could not be found. William Owten delayed by saying he would 'first consider of the matter'. Hughe Gamblin, 'a blind man, but of good [financial] ability', and three other men simply refused to lend without giving any excuse.[72]

Parliament's official interpretation of the Protestation given in the Propositions Ordinance, and Stephen Marshall's exhortation in *Meroz Cursed*, implied that people would have broken their vow if they subsequently failed to make any material contribution to the parliamentary war effort. Whatever the spiritual consequences of this, the original ordinance did not mention any punishments for not contributing, or any powers of distraint for Parliament's officials. It explicitly stated that contributors would not be judged by the size of their contribution:

---

[65]   Vallance, *Revolutionary England*, 53, 110, 113–14; Cressy, 'Protestation Protested', 257, 269, 270, 277; Peter Newman, 'Roman Catholics in Pre-Civil War England: The Problem of Definition', *Recusant History*, 15 (1979): 149.

[66]   *CJ*, vol. 2, 132.

[67]   *LJ*, vol. 5, 148, 160.

[68]   *CJ*, vol. 2, 810.

[69]   TNA: PRO, SP 23/173, p. 65.

[70]   Coates, Young and Snow, *Private Journals*, 58.

[71]   TNA: PRO, SP 16/492/47, fols 112r–117v.

[72]   TNA: PRO, SP 16/492/47, fols 118r–119r.

And because a considerable Aid cannot be raised by few Hands, and the Condition of all Men's Estates and Occasions is not always proportionable to their affection, the Lords and Commons do declare, That no Man's Affection shall be measured according to the Proportion of his Offer, so that he express his goodwill to this Service in any Proportion whatsoever.[73]

As a further incentive, Parliament promised that the value of horses would be paid back, and that interest would be given for money (see Chapter 5). The Propositions Ordinance gives the impression of confidence that sufficient resources could be raised from the well-affected without too much trouble. For a few months this prediction appeared to be correct.

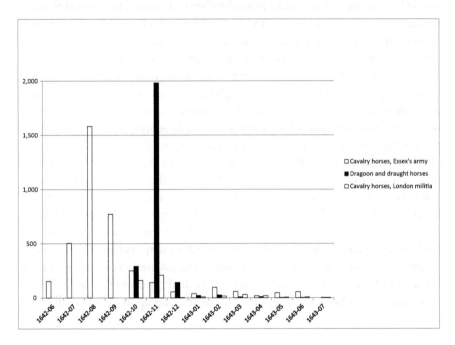

Figure 1.1   Horses listed on the Propositions, monthly totals 1642–43

Figure 1.1 shows that after a slow start, contributions of cavalry horses took off in July and August. Although hundreds of horses were brought in during September, they were only around half of the number that had been contributed in August. The supply of money was still adequate at this time as infantry

---

[73]   *A & O*, vol. 1, 7–8.

regiments continued to be well paid throughout September and October.[74] Parliament started looking into potential problems with the system well before contributions became inadequate. On 12 September the Commons ordered a committee to draw up a list of members who had subscribed to the Propositions but not brought in what they had promised, or who had not even declared what they would subscribe.[75] A week later it was ordered that all MPs who had not yet done so should declare what horses, money or plate they were prepared to bring in.[76] Further orders, declarations and excuses concerning MPs' contributions continued throughout October.

The first known mention of concern about non-contributors outside Westminster occurred in late August. An order of Parliament on 26 August, asking for further contributions from the City of London, mentioned that the names of non-contributors were to be entered in a book in addition to records of subscriptions.[77] This instruction seems to have been put into practice in St Clement Danes, where Robert Braswell, 'a very able man and hath only given fyve shillings', and John Howe, 'a man very able hath given but ten shillings', were listed alongside the 21 refusers.[78] Although their names were to be recorded there is no mention of any action to be taken against them. Similarly, instructions issued by Parliament on 19 September for implementing the Propositions in the counties included orders to 'certify the Names of all such Persons as are of Ability, and do absent themselves out of the County and repair to the City of London, or other Parts of the Kingdom; or otherwise absent themselves from the said Service or Contribution'.[79] A committee had been appointed to 'receive the Answers of such as refuse to contribute upon the Propositions' by 10 October, when Sir William Armyn was ordered to bring a report from it so that the Commons could 'consider what is fit to be done with such as refuse'.[80] On 12 October the Committee for the Propositions was ordered to draft a declaration 'That this Demanding of Contribution, upon the Propositions, is according to Law; and to set a Mark of Malignity and Disaffection upon such as shall refuse

---

[74]   Crawshaw, 'Military Finance', 1037, 1044. Crawshaw has conclusively disproved the traditional assumption that there was a financial crisis in September. Graham, 'Finance', 895; Vernon F. Snow, *Essex the Rebel: the Life of Robert Devereux, the Third Earl of Essex 1591–1646* (Lincoln, NE, 1970), p. 326.

[75]   *CJ*, vol. 2, 763.

[76]   *CJ*, vol. 2, 772.

[77]   *CJ*, vol. 2, 738–9; Graham, 'Finance', 896.

[78]   TNA: PRO, SP 16/492/47, fols 118r, 119r.

[79]   *CJ*, vol. 2, 773.

[80]   *CJ*, vol. 2, 802.

to contribute, in this Time of common Danger.'[81] The original Propositions Ordinance had only vaguely implied this. If contributors were the well-affected then it logically followed that non-contributors were not, but this was not pushed very far until contributions started to go down. The need to insist that the Propositions were lawful shows that this question was still being contested. The mark of malignity echoes Pym's interpretation of the Protestation as a shibboleth, and Stephen Marshall's sermon on the cursing of Meroz. According to Marshall, the *Song of Deborah* in Judges 5 'proceeds to Stigmatize and brand with reproach, and marke out for punishment all such companies, as had played either the Traitours or the Cowards, or were otherwise wanting to their duty in this great expedition'.[82] The mark to be set on refusers was not just symbolic: as with the curse on Meroz and the slaughter of the idolaters who could not say shibboleth, it had very real consequences. The Commons resolved on 14 October that non-contributors should be secured and disarmed. This was immediately followed by an order of the Lords and Commons to arrest ten named individuals from London 'as it appears by the Report from the Committee, they have not contributed as they ought, to the Charge of the Commonwealth, in this Time of imminent Necessity'.[83] The word 'ought' confirms a shift from voluntary to compulsory contributions: people were now obliged to contribute and would face earthly punishment if they refused. Making an example of a few prominent men by arresting and disarming them did not necessarily encourage the others. Contributions of cavalry horses for Essex's army continued to fall, and from December onwards never exceeded 100 per month, which was almost certainly lower than the rate of attrition. There was still no official minimum contribution until the end of November 1642, when non-contributors in and near London were assessed at a twentieth of their estate. By the middle of 1643 this had developed into the fifth and twentieth assessment, which was imposed on all counties (see Chapter 5).

In early October 1642 Parliament began new collections of dragoon and draught horses. Previously these had not been supplied directly by the Propositions. An order of the Lords on 3 October invited subscriptions to raise 1,000 dragoons for Lancashire.[84] Shortly after this date the second account book of the London commissaries starts to record horses listed for dragoons.[85] In the short term the collection appeared to be a spectacular success, with just over 2,000 horses listed in November. Some of these appear to be cart horses as they

[81] *CJ*, vol. 2, 805.
[82] Marshall, *Meroz Cursed*, 3.
[83] *CJ*, vol. 2, 808.
[84] *LJ*, vol. 5, 376–7, 382.
[85] TNA: PRO, SP 28/131, part 4.

were brought in complete with draught harnesses, and probably correspond to the 524 draught horses delivered to Essex's artillery train by the commissaries from November 1642 to January 1643.[86] The Lord General had appealed directly to county authorities to provide him with more horses after Edgehill. Horses collected at Boston on 7 November 1642 were sent directly to Essex's army at Northampton, 'upon the proposic[i]ons & desire of his Excellencie menc[i]oned in his l[ette]re to [th]e Deputy Lieutenn[an]ts & others of this Countie'.[87] Around the same time the Committee of Safety demanded 2,000 dragoon horses from Essex and Suffolk to reinforce the army.[88] In response, the mayor of Colchester started collecting horses from the town and surrounding hundreds on 1 November.[89] Just over 500 horses in this list came from addresses that can be identified in Essex, more than from any other county but a long way short of the quota. Suffolk managed only 255. From the end of November, contributions of dragoon and draught horses fell off even more drastically than cavalry horses. It is hard to tell whether the spike in November was a response to the threat of punishment or whether these cheaper horses were listed by people who had always been willing to contribute but could not afford cavalry horses and equipment. Either could explain why there is so little overlap between names in the first and second account books. Only 42 people can be proved to appear in both lists by matching their names, addresses and social status. Even allowing for uncertain cases, the overlap must be lower than 401. It is also likely that the agricultural year influenced the availability of horses. Parliament may have deliberately avoided collecting draught horses until the harvest was over. This did not affect the listing of expensive saddle horses for the cavalry, which was at its height around harvest time.

Places

Propositions contributions began in London. Ben Coates suggested that the majority of horses came from London, but this is a false impression.[90] The early pages of the first list are full of London addresses, but this pattern changed in August as the system spread out from London. Table 1.1 shows that only a minority of the

[86]   TNA: PRO, SP 28/143, Account of Anthony Fastolfe, fol. 30.

[87]   TNA: PRO, SP 28/131, part 4, fols 20v, 22v.

[88]   ERO, D/Y 2/9, p. 347; ERO, D/Y 2/9, p. 71.

[89]   TNA: PRO, SP 28/131, part 4, fol. 8r.

[90]   Ben Coates, *The Impact of the English Civil War on the Economy of London, 1642–50* (Aldershot, 2004), p. 55.

horses in each list can be assigned to London, even using a very broad definition which includes all suburban parishes within the Bills of Mortality.[91]

Table 1.1   Horses listed on the Propositions, London and elsewhere, 1642–43

Address	Part 3 horses	%	Part 4 horses	%
London	935	25	202	8
Not London	1,743	46	1,376	55
Unidentified	29	1	14	1
Unstated	1,068	28	897	36

Source: TNA: PRO, SP 28/131, parts 3–4

The account books of the London commissaries incorporated lists of local commissaries. Some of these were clearly indicated, but others have been silently merged with the main lists.[92] Parish accounts suggest that many people in Hertfordshire took horses and money to London in person since they named the treasurers and commissaries, and sometimes specified that they were valued in London.[93] Some inhabitants of Wigginton and Tring claimed to have delivered horses to Smith and Richardson at Dunstable on 4 November.[94] Patterns of addresses in the main lists suggest that in other counties horses were collected by local commissaries from a certain area and then delivered to London or directly to the army. The second account book of the London commissaries explicitly stated that it listed dragoon horses, 'many whereof were [brou]ght uppe with lists of their valuac[i]ons from [d]eputye lieuetan[a]nts

---

[91]   Vanessa Harding, 'The Population of London, 1550–1700: A Review of the Published Evidence', *London Journal*, 15/2 (1990): 113, 125.

[92]   Clearly separate lists are: TNA: PRO, SP 28/131, part 3, fols 45–8, 99, 121; TNA: PRO, SP 28/131, part 4, fols 8–9, 20–24, 33–6, 43–4.

[93]   Alan Thomson (ed.), *The Impact of the First Civil War on Hertfordshire 1642–1647*, Hertfordshire Record Society 23 (2007), p. xxxvi; TNA: PRO, SP 28/155, unfol.

[94]   TNA: PRO, SP 28/353, part 2, fols 249r, 253r. These contributions do not appear in Smith and Richardson's surviving accounts. It is not certain whether the parish accounts are inaccurate or the commissaries' surviving accounts are incomplete.

of sev[er]all Counties and were entred with us and ticketts by us d[elivere]d accordinglye'.[95] The dates given in the account books are almost certainly the dates when the horses were first received by local commissaries, not the dates when they were delivered to London. This is made clear by a list from Suffolk in which Richardson noted that two of the horses listed had been lost on the way to London.[96] Most contributions from outside London were probably not spontaneous or solely a result of direct engagement between Parliament and individual members of the public. Even when people went to London themselves, this was usually only after Parliament had given specific orders to the deputy lieutenants to start taking subscriptions. Success depended on county authorities taking control and implementing the system. A cluster of entries from Cambridgeshire on 30 August 1642 coincides with 500 dragoons under Cromwell occupying Cambridge.[97] Although this shows that there could be informal pressure, it does not necessarily mean that all contributors were unwilling. Starting a civil war required enthusiasm *and* organization.

The Propositions outside London

The Watford troop   There were exceptions to the general rule that the Propositions were implemented outside London from the top down by deputy lieutenants following an ordinance of Parliament. On 30 June 1642, a week before Parliament issued formal instructions to execute the Propositions Ordinance in Hertfordshire, the Commons received a petition from a group of people from Watford, led by their vicar Cornelius Burges, offering to provide £1,270 and 50 horses with riders for a troop of cavalry.[98] The petition requested that John Bird be appointed captain of the troop and that he should be allowed to nominate the rest of the troop officers.[99] Although it did not say so directly, this implied that the petition placed conditions on the contributions. Nevertheless, both houses accepted the five propositions offered by the petitioners.[100] The Commons

---

[95]   TNA: PRO, SP 28/131, part 4, fol. 3r.

[96]   TNA: PRO, SP 28/131, part 4, fol. 37r.

[97]   TNA: PRO, SP 28/131, part 3, fols 76r–77v; Ian Gentles, *Oliver Cromwell: God's Warrior and the English Revolution* (Basingstoke, 2011), p. 23; Holmes, *Eastern Association*, 55.

[98]   *CJ*, vol. 2, 644, 646–8, 654; *LJ*, vol. 5, 172–3.

[99]   *LJ*, vol. 5, 173.

[100]   A list annexed to a manuscript copy of the petition has a sixth article crossed out, asking for neighbouring parishes to be included in the petition if Watford could not raise enough horses and riders. It is not certain whether this was struck out because it was unacceptable to Parliament or because it was unnecessary, enough horses having come in from Watford. PA, HL/PO/JO/10/1/126, House of Lords Main Papers, 1 July 1642, Petition of inhabitants of Watford.

ordered the petition to be printed, making it into a public demonstration rather than a private deal.[101] The published petition confirmed that the petitioners were not afraid to declare their allegiance to Parliament in public and were willing and able to back up this declaration with material contributions. Their actions conferred legitimacy on Parliament and its military preparations, the petition's preamble stating that they were

> assured that whatsoever shall be so brought in shall not be employed upon any other Occasion than to maintain the Protestant Religion, the King's Authority, and His Person, in His Royal Dignity, the free Course of Justice, the Laws of the Land, the Peace of the Kingdom, and the Privilege of Parliament, against any Force which shall oppose them.[102]

These words echoed the Protestation, which was given a very militant interpretation:

> not intending to rest in these Propositions, but resolving to part with all they have, if Need be, in Pursuit of their said Protestation; which as they seriously considered of before they took it, so they resolutely prepare themselves to make it good, to the last Drop of their Blood.[103]

A majority in Parliament must have accepted this interpretation. Publication of the petition, which in its printed form included the thanks of the Commons and their order that it be printed, made it appear official, and encouraged others to interpret the Protestation in the same way.[104] The petitioners' words were soon translated into action. The London commissaries recorded 44 horses brought in from Watford on 2 July 1642, and another 13 came in on 20 July.[105] Later in July, the Propositions treasurers paid £500 to Stephen Estwicke to buy arms for the troop, and £350 to pay the troopers.[106]

Aaron Graham suggested that the Watford petition was an example of localism because the petitioners placed conditions on their contributions and

[101] *CJ*, vol. 2, 646.

[102] *LJ*, vol. 5, 173; Anon., *To the honorable the House of Commons, now assembled in Parliament. The humble petition of the inhabitants of Watford, in the county of Hertford.* (London, 1642) TT 669.f.5[52].

[103] *LJ*, vol. 5, 173.

[104] *Humble Petition.*

[105] TNA: PRO, SP 28/131, part 3, fols 8–10, 21.

[106] TNA: PRO, SP 28/170, Account of Guildhall treasurers. I am grateful to Tom Crawshaw for supplying me with a copy of this document.

demanded control over the appointment of officers.[107] This is not the only possible interpretation. We cannot assume that Bird was appointed captain because he was a local man, or because he was popular in Watford. Currently, little is known of his background other than that he was a gentleman. He does not appear in the lists of horses contributed to the troop. The cornet and quartermaster of the troop, Ambrose Rooke and Jonathan Finch, were almost certainly local men as similar names with Watford addresses appear in the horse lists.[108] The petition stated that the lieutenant and a corporal were to be appointed for their military experience. The lieutenant was probably Samuel Bosa or Boza, who was probably not English, although he had been replaced by Rooke by the end of 1642. Similarly, the lieutenant of Richard Grenville's Buckinghamshire troop was Carlo Fantom, a Croatian mercenary.[109] Even Burges was not entirely local. Although he had been vicar of Watford since 1618, he was born in Somerset, educated at Oxford, and held the London parish of St Magnus in plurality from 1626. In 1640 he had a house in London as well as one in Watford, and his children were baptized in London from 1641 onwards.[110] He only contributed one horse to Parliament, on 31 October 1642, and although the commissaries recorded his address as Watford, the horse was for the London militia.[111] Given all this, it would be difficult to argue that Burges had an identity strongly focused on Watford.

The records of horse contributions suggest that the rest of the petitioners did live in Watford, but this was not necessarily the most important thing about them. They did not explicitly claim to represent the whole town. It is impossible to be sure how many people signed the petition because the surviving manuscript copy does not contain any signatures.[112] The petitioners referred to themselves as 'but a small Handful'.[113] While the petition linked contributions to the Protestation, there was a very important difference between the two texts: 'the Protestant Religion' was not qualified by 'expressed in the Doctrine of the

---

[107]　Graham, 'Finance', 883–4, 887.

[108]　Alan Turton, *Chief Strength of the Army: Cavalry in the Earl of Essex's Army* (Leigh-on-Sea, c. 1992), p. 20; TNA: PRO, SP 28/131, part 3, fols 9r, 21v.

[109]　Turton, *Chief Strength*, 20, 30, 45; Mark Stoyle, *Soldiers and Strangers: An Ethnic History of the English Civil War* (New Haven, 2005), pp. 94, 214; TNA: PRO, SP 28/149, part 1, fol. 178v.

[110]　Tai Liu, 'Burges, Cornelius (d. 1665)', *ODNB*.

[111]　TNA: PRO, SP 28/131, part 5, fol. 6v.

[112]　PA, HL/PO/JO/10/1/126, House of Lords Main Papers, 1 July 1642, Petition of inhabitants of Watford.

[113]　*LJ*, vol. 5, 173.

Church of England'.[114] Combined with their promise to make the Protestation good 'to the last Drop of their Blood', this could easily imply a militant puritan clique.[115] The prominent involvement of Cornelius Burges makes this all the more likely. Although he supported primitive episcopacy and later had reservations about taking the Covenant, Burges was clearly one of the hotter protestants. Along with Stephen Marshall, he preached a sermon on the Long Parliament's first fast day in 1640. As well as reinforcing his Godly credentials, this is evidence of his close links with the parliamentary junto. He was a long-standing client of the earls of Bedford, announced the Protestation to the crowd outside Parliament in May 1641, and was appointed chaplain to the Earl of Essex's cavalry regiment in 1642.[116] Burges was involved in parliamentary committees for religious reform, and had possibly been on secret missions to Scotland.[117] Because of these links, it has to be suspected that the Watford petition was no surprise to the junto. It is even possible that the terms had been discussed in private before the petition was presented. It was not unusual for politicians to collaborate with writers and printers in order to produce propaganda which did not appear to be official, or for petitions to be organized from the centre to give an impression of spontaneous support.[118] Burges was ideally placed to orchestrate the Watford petition, and had previously organized other petitioning campaigns.[119] Perhaps it is significant that while the *Commons Journal*, which was not written for public consumption, explicitly stated that 'Doctor Burgesse, who preferred the Petition of Watford, and the Propositions, was called in: And Mr. Speaker, by Command of the House, told him, "Your Petition hath been read, and accepted ...", the published version omitted his name and referred to him only as 'one of the Petitioners'.[120] This may have been an attempt to create a false impression of spontaneity by disguising the role of a man who was well known to be in with the junto. Collusion between the junto and Burges's friends in Watford could have been a stratagem to outflank moderate MPs who opposed military preparations.

Even the request of the petitioners that the troop should stay in Watford cannot automatically be interpreted as a desire to protect the local community from outsiders. It is at least as likely that the intention was to protect the Godly from enemies within the local community. Over the summer of 1642

---

114   *CJ*, vol. 2, 132.
115   *LJ*, vol. 5, 173. Thomson, *Impact*, xxii, identified the group as radicals, not localists.
116   Liu, 'Burges, Cornelius'.
117   Peacey, *Politicians and Pamphleteers*, 306.
118   Ibid., 61, 112–3, 185, 205, 220, 237, 251–2, 312.
119   Ibid., 252.
120   *CJ*, vol. 2, 646; *Humble Petition*.

military control of Hertfordshire was contested between local militants as well as by outside forces. Members of a company of parliamentary volunteers were prosecuted at the June quarter sessions by JPs who supported the King. The mayor of St Albans published the royal proclamation against the Propositions in July. On 18 August an attempt to execute the Commission of Array was prevented by the arrival of the Earl of Bedford's cuirassier troop from London, and it was only after this that Parliament secured control of the county and the Militia Ordinance was executed.[121] In this context, the petition looks like part of a conflict between extremists. The Watford troop was recruited before there was any official parliamentary attempt to implement the Propositions in the county. This does not fit with the image of moderates reluctantly mobilizing forces to avoid trouble. From August 1642 Bird's troop was paid as part of the army by Essex's warrant, and in early September it went to Portsmouth.[122]

Buckinghamshire and Hertfordshire   In most places, people waited to be asked for contributions rather than petitioning Parliament with an offer. The original Propositions Ordinance was not explicitly limited to any geographical area, and the link to the Protestation suggested that it applied to the whole kingdom. In practice, contributions were mostly from London in the first few weeks. A few horses came in from the surrounding counties in the early weeks, but London dominated the lists for a while. On 16 June, Parliament ordered that all MPs who were deputy lieutenants were authorized to tender the Propositions to the other deputy lieutenants of the county, and that any who subscribed were then authorized to take subscriptions from the rest of the county.[123] In practice, granting permission was not enough. If county authorities acted at all, it was not until they had received specific orders. On 1 July the Lords issued an order similar to the one issued by the Commons on 16 June, but added 'That the Knights, Citizens, and Burgesses of the several Counties, Cities, and Boroughs, within this Realm, be *required* with all Speed to recommend these Propositions to their several Counties, Cities, and Boroughs respectively, to be put in Execution' (emphasis added).[124] General instructions to county committees issued in July and August did not usually mention the Propositions.[125] In the same period, Parliament issued specific instructions to the MPs and deputy lieutenants of several counties to implement the Propositions. Quantifying the response is difficult because so many entries in the horse lists have no address,

---

121   Holmes, *Eastern Association*, 53.
122   Turton, *Chief Strength*, 20.
123   *CJ*, vol. 2, 627.
124   *LJ*, vol. 5, 175.
125   Fletcher, *Outbreak*, 337.

some horse troops were kept for local defence, and there is no similar record of money and plate contributions. Nevertheless, repeated instructions to the same county imply that Parliament had not yet received a satisfactory response.

Formal instructions were not sent to Hertfordshire until after the Watford petition was accepted. On Tuesday 5 July, Sir Thomas Dacres and Sir William Litton were ordered to announce the Propositions at the quarter sessions on the following Monday.[126] Then on 12 July a further order named 48 men to tender the Propositions in the county and gave them more detailed instructions.[127] They were authorized to appoint receivers and were to send records of contributions to the treasurers in London, but were given no instructions specific to collecting horses. These orders did not have an immediate effect on contributions of horses. People with Hertfordshire addresses brought in 57 horses in July 1642, but these were all associated with the Watford petition, and most were listed before the Hertfordshire orders were issued. This does not necessarily demonstrate a lack of enthusiasm. By the end of August a further 167 horses had been brought in from the county without any further prompting from Parliament. Implementing the system needed time, an absence of active opposition and leadership to organize collection. On 3 August, 38 horses were listed, all from addresses in Dacorum hundred. Another 76 were listed on 6 August, many from Cashio hundred but a few from Dacorum and others.

There was a similar pattern in Buckinghamshire. On 5 July the Buckinghamshire MPs John Hampden, Arthur Goodwin, Bulstrode Whitelocke and Richard Winwood were ordered to go into their county 'to further the Propositions for Raising of Horse'.[128] On 12 July Buckinghamshire received the same instructions as Hertfordshire, this time naming 46 men.[129] Despite these orders no horses from Buckinghamshire addresses were listed in July. It took a further order to make things happen. An order of Parliament on 9 August appointed Thomas Sanders and Thomas Westall commissaries to value horses and arms.[130] Both men had already been named in the order of 12 July, which could suggest that the earlier order was only for collecting money and plate, not for horses and arms. The final order produced an immediate response. On 11 and 13 August, Sanders and Westall received and issued enough horses to mount four troops of Arthur Goodwin's cavalry regiment.[131] All of the identifiable

---

126   *CJ*, vol. 2, 654.
127   *LJ*, vol. 5, 207.
128   *CJ*, vol. 2, 654.
129   *LJ*, vol. 5, 207–8.
130   *CJ*, vol. 2, 711.
131   TNA: PRO, SP 28/127, part 4, fol. 40r; TNA: PRO, SP 28/131, part 3, fols 45–8.

addresses were in Newport hundred on 13 August and other hundreds on 11 August, again suggesting highly organized collections.

Essex   Like Buckinghamshire, the county of Essex had a slow start, but contributions took off in August. The Earl of Warwick's faction was more active and successful in taking control of the county for Parliament than local elites in Hertfordshire had been, implementing the Militia Ordinance in June and suppressing dissent without the help of forces from London.[132] Parliament first ordered the Essex authorities to implement the Propositions on 11 July.[133] The order mentioned that the Essex deputy lieutenants had nominated men who were considered to be well-affected to Parliament and willing to advance the Propositions. These men were to be appointed as receivers of money and plate, but there was no mention of commissaries to receive horses. Collections of horses seem to have been carried out separately from collections of money and plate. Ralph Josselin, minister of Earls Colne in Lexden hundred, attended a meeting in Colchester in early August at which he subscribed £10.[134] Only two horses were listed in Lexden hundred before 25 August, and most did not come in until September. John Fenning was named as treasurer for the southern division. His account book records that he began receiving money in late July but does not contain any horses.[135] The order of 11 July was clearly not acted on immediately, as on 19 July the Commons ordered that 'the Deputy Lieutenants of the County of Essex be injoined to go into the County of Essex, to put in Execution the Instructions for the Proposition for Raising of Horse, Money, and Plate'.[136] There were no more reminders after this, but very few horses came in from Essex parishes until August.

Getting the MPs and deputy lieutenants to execute the orders of Parliament was only part of the problem. The county authorities then had to implement the system at county level and below. Most of the contributions were concentrated on a few days rather than evenly spread over August and September. More than half of the horses were listed on five days: 9, 11, 16 and 17 August, and 9 September. This suggests that collections were organized on specific days. The contributions in Essex were concentrated by place as well as time. People from Lexden hundred provided only 12 horses in August but 47 in September. There was a similar pattern in the borough of Colchester, whereas horse contributions in southern

---

[132]   Holmes, *Eastern Association*, 34–5.

[133]   *CJ*, vol. 2, 666.

[134]   Ralph Josselin, *The Diary of Ralph Josselin 1616–1683*, Alan MacFarlane (ed.) (London, 1976), pp. 12–13.

[135]   TNA: PRO, SP 28/153, part 6, Account book of John Fenning.

[136]   *CJ*, vol. 2, 681.

and western Essex peaked in August. This pattern again suggests that collections by local commissaries were highly organized and that contributions were not entirely spontaneous. The order of Parliament of 11 July listed commissioners and receivers of money by divisions and boroughs.[137] Collections in the Colchester area were probably delayed by the Stour Valley riots which broke out in late August. Horses listed in September were concentrated in the period 7–9 September, after the trouble had died down.

By the end of September Essex proved to be one of the most important sources of horses for Parliament's army. Of the 3,014 horses listed by the end of September, 214 were explicitly stated to be from Essex, more than any other county. Including places where no county is given but which can be inferred to be in Essex brings the figure up to 570. The next highest county figure is 269 for Hertfordshire. Even allowing for the 742 horses from unknown places, Essex must have had one of the highest totals. Relative to the size of the population, Essex's contributions were higher than London's. The population of Essex was around 85,000, which gives one horse per 149 people (roughly equivalent to 0.7 per cent of the population, since most horses in this period were listed by single individuals).[138] London's population was between 200,000 and 400,000, giving one horse for 244 to 489 people, or 0.2 to 0.4 per cent of the population (see Table 1.2 below).[139]

Local Sentiment?

Essex people provided many horses for Parliament's army, but this does not make Essex a 'parliamentarian' county. Although horse contributors were more numerous in Essex than in most other counties, they were a very small minority of the county's population. Very few of the 85,000 people who lived in Essex could afford to part with a riding horse, but the contributors were probably a minority of this group too. There were 3,200 Essex people on the 1640 subsidy roll, and 14,500 were assessed for ship money.[140] In the southern division around 2,400 names appear on the 1637 ship money assessment, far more than the 800 who were considered liable for the Propositions.[141] Around 48 per cent of these 800

---

[137] *LJ*, vol. 5, 203–4.

[138] John Walter, *Understanding Popular Violence in the English Revolution: The Colchester Plunderers* (Cambridge, 1999), p. 207.

[139] Harding, 'Population of London', 112.

[140] John Morrill, *Revolt in the Provinces: The People of England and the Tragedies of War, 1630–1648* (London, 1998), p. 43.

[141] TNA: PRO, SP 16/358, fols 10r–12r, 46v–52r, 76v–81v. The figure for ship money does not include out dwellers.

Table 1.2   Horses listed on the Propositions, county totals 21 June to 30 September 1642

County	Horses
London (City and suburbs)	818
Unknown	767
Essex	570
Hertfordshire	269
Buckinghamshire	115
Huntingdon	92
Middlesex	82
Bedfordshire	78
Oxfordshire	65
Cambridgeshire	65
Other	93
Total	3,014

Source: TNA: PRO, SP 28/131, part 3

people were assessed for the fifth and twentieth because they had not contributed any money to the Propositions, and a further 8 per cent had contributed too little.[142] Since there were many possible reasons for not contributing, it cannot be assumed that non-payers were 'royalists'. In southern Essex the Propositions and the fifth and twentieth assessment brought in similar amounts of money (about £3,900 each), but the balance was different in the western division of

---

142   TNA: PRO, SP 28/153, part 6, Account of John Fenning.

Surrey, where money, plate and horses lent and given on the Propositions were worth £1,511 but £4,269 was assessed for the fifth and twentieth.[143]

Too many historians have tried to classify geographical areas according to how 'royalist' or 'parliamentarian' they were. This is best summed up by Gerald Aylmer's statements that while 'very few regions were solidly for King or Parliament', 'some counties and towns, and some districts within counties, were more or less Royalist or Parliamentarian than others'.[144] The problems with applying the categories 'royalist' and 'parliamentarian' to geographical areas are even greater than with individual people. Blackwood concluded: 'The combatant gentry were predominantly Royalist in twelve English counties, including Lancashire, fairly evenly divided in Norfolk and West Suffolk, and largely Parliamentarian only in East Suffolk.'[145] The word 'combatant' is crucial here, as Blackwood actually classified a large majority of the gentry in Lancashire (58.4 per cent), Norfolk (70.6 per cent) and Suffolk (72.4 per cent) as 'Neutral/Unknown'.[146] Underdown argued that 'Blackmore Vale was impressively royalist' but at most could only identify 5.3 per cent of the population as 'royalists'.[147] The statistics presented by Blackwood and Underdown do not prove that areas can or should be classified as 'Royalist' or 'Parliamentarian'. Attempting to classify areas by the allegiance of the largest group to take up arms erases the people who did nothing and denies the diversity of the groups and individuals who made up local populations. The 'map of allegiance' privileges some people and excludes others. All that lists of Propositions contributors show is that a minority in some places was bigger than a minority in other places. Nobody has rigorously proved that 'patterns of allegiance' are not just random. Daniel MacCannell has recently speculated that mapping the clergy of the Church of England may reveal and explain patterns but has not yet produced any results. His article assumed the conclusion that there must be patterns of allegiance to be found and did not address the questions of what allegiance was, how it can be

---

[143]   TNA: PRO, SP 28/334, Account book of Richard Wither, fols 6v, 19v.

[144]   Gerald Aylmer, *Rebellion or Revolution? England 1640–1660* (Oxford, 1987), pp. 50, 43, cited in Mark Stoyle, *Loyalty and Locality: Popular Allegiance in Devon During the English Civil War* (Exeter, 1994), p. 231.

[145]   B.G. Blackwood, 'Parties and Issues in the Civil War in Lancashire and East Anglia', in R.C. Richardson (ed.), *The English Civil War: Local Aspects* (Stroud, 1997), p. 278.

[146]   Ibid., 265–7.

[147]   David Underdown, *Revel, Riot, and Rebellion: Popular Politics and Culture in England 1603–1660* (Oxford, 1985), pp. 197–8.

measured, what counts as a pattern or what we should do about minorities who did not belong to the dominant group in a particular place.[148]

Many historians once assumed that the English 'county community' was a greater focus of loyalty than King or Parliament, but this paradigm has been completely destroyed by Clive Holmes.[149] Graham recently suggested that many people wanted military representation for their local communities in Essex's army. According to this argument, some people demanded that military resources be kept for local defence, while others demanded local influence over army regiments, including the right to nominate officers. When they were not given the representation they wanted, they held back from contributing to the Propositions.[150] This is a very ambitious claim about the motives of a large number of people, based mostly on what they did not do rather than on what they explicitly said. While there was no financial crisis in September 1642, it is true that horse contributions dropped off in October 1642 and that around the same time Parliament started paying more attention to local defence. But some people contributed regardless of local representation, some would only contribute for local defence, and many others refused to contribute even when threatened with disarmament and imprisonment.

Counties were established administrative units which were conveniently available when Parliament imposed its war administration from the top down. The Propositions relied on MPs and deputy lieutenants to organize collections in their counties. Because of this it was common for large numbers of horses to come in from the same area at the same time, but county boundaries did not impose rigid limits on the behaviour or identities of individual people. Arthur Goodwin's cavalry regiment was very strongly associated with Buckinghamshire, but two of its horses were brought in from Stratton Audley, a village which was partly in Buckinghamshire and partly in Oxfordshire.[151] The idea of local identities is further complicated by the group of six men 'all of Crawley [Husborne Crawley] in the County of Bedford' and one man 'of Wavenden [Wavendon] in Com Bucks' who jointly listed a horse worth £16 on 24 March 1643.[152] The two parishes were close to each other but on opposite sides of the

---

[148]   Daniel MacCannell, "'Dark Corners of the Land'? A New Approach to Regional Factors in the Civil Wars of England and Wales', *Cultural and Social History*, 7/2 (2010): 175, 179–83.

[149]   Clive Holmes, 'The County Community in Stuart Historiography', *Journal of British Studies*, 19/2 (1980): 54–73; Clive Holmes, 'Centre and Locality in Civil-War England', in John Adamson (ed.), *The English Civil War: Conflict and Contexts, 1640–1649* (Basingstoke, 2009), pp. 153–74.

[150]   Graham, 'Finance', 880, 883, 889.

[151]   TNA: PRO, SP 28/131, part 3, fol. 47v; *VCH Oxfordshire*, vol. 6, 324–33.

[152]   TNA: PRO, SP 28/131, part 3, fol. 127r.

county boundary. All seven men had different surnames, and the relationship between them is unknown. People from Herefordshire brought in 15 cavalry horses on 16 September 1642, but they are recorded in a list compiled by the deputy lieutenants in Gloucester, which suggests that the system had not been implemented in Herefordshire.[153] More Herefordshire addresses occurred on 22 September.[154] It is not clear where these were listed because they are incorporated into the main list of the London commissaries, but the fact that they are clustered together in the list and mixed in with Gloucestershire addresses suggests that they were also listed in Gloucester. The Earl of Stamford did not arrive in Hereford until 2 October and found the local people largely hostile.[155]

Many people from south-eastern England sent their horses up to London to be used for Essex's army, but inhabitants of some other areas were much more particular. In Cheshire most gentlemen would only agree to subscribe to the Propositions if their contributions were used for local defence.[156] Sir Walter Erle's cavalry troop was raised in Dorset in 1642 and did not join Essex's army.[157] Whether the Watford petition was about local control or a Godly minority, it was still unusual. Contributions from the rest of Hertfordshire were not tied to any explicit conditions. Even in Watford, not all contributions were conditional. On 25 November 1642, commissaries in Watford listed dragoon and draught horses brought in from several places in Hertfordshire, including many from Watford itself.[158] Some of the owners were people who had previously listed horses for Bird's troop, and others had not previously listed any horses. There is no evidence of any petition placing conditions on these contributions, and the dragoons to be sent into Lancashire were clearly not for local defence. This all suggests that local identities could intersect with other aspects of identity and influence people's actions in different ways. The diversity of reactions to the Propositions does not easily fit into the false dichotomy of 'local' and 'national'.

There were enough wealthy militants in Watford and elsewhere to provide the horses and money needed to create Essex's army, but they could not afford to supply the army indefinitely. Although they were committed to aggressive war, they were relatively few in number and their wealth was finite. The figures above show that they were a small minority of the population, even in London and Essex where they were most numerous. If they did want any representation for their communities, this would have been a false universal which excluded

---

[153]   TNA: PRO, SP 28/131, part 3, fol. 99.
[154]   TNA: PRO, SP 28/131, part 3, fol. 102.
[155]   Andrew J. Hopper, 'Grey, Henry, first earl of Stamford (c.1599–1673)', *ODNB*.
[156]   Fletcher, *Outbreak*, 338.
[157]   Turton, *Chief Strength*, 29; Underdown, *Revel, Riot, and Rebellion*, 190–91.
[158]   TNA: PRO, SP 28/131, part 4, fols 43–4.

the majority of the local population. By the end of November militants had a further reason for not contributing: they were losing confidence in the Earl of Essex. In December Henry Marten and Thomas Hoyle alleged in the Commons that Essex was deliberately delaying and that his lack of aggression would lose the war.[159] Over the winter of 1642–43 radical Londoners sought to replace Essex and raise their own army.[160] Around the same time the focus of Parliament's strategy shifted from a single field army to taking control of territory. This was not a drastic break as Essex had already left garrisons in several towns before Edgehill, and field armies continued to be an important part of parliamentary strategy throughout the war, but there was a change of emphasis in late 1642. Many Propositions orders from June to October 1642 specified that contributions collected in the counties were to be sent up to London.[161] John Fenning recorded that nearly all of the money he collected in 1642 was paid to the central treasury at Guildhall in London.[162] During the summer, even money for local defence sometimes went to London and back. For example, on 16 August the Lords ordered that money sent to London from Dorset should be paid to Denzil Holles and Sir Walter Erle for the defence of Dorset.[163] Even when MPs used the rhetoric of local defence, they left themselves enough room to ignore it in practice. The order of 19 September to implement the Propositions in each county required local collectors to send their money up to London, qualified by the ambiguous statement that what they raised 'shall be employed in or for the Safety of that County'.[164]

In mid-October, local defence became a higher priority. Parliament ordered the deputy lieutenants of Devon to take subscriptions to raise a troop which was to remain at Exeter, with officers chosen locally.[165] This was probably a specific response to the rising in Cornwall, which threatened the security of Devon.[166] On 28 October the Surrey committee was allowed to keep back money to pay local forces.[167] An order of the Lords on 24 November required all money, plate

---

[159]   Ian Gentles, *The English Revolution and the Wars in the Three Kingdoms, 1638–1652* (London, 2007), p. 159; BL, Harleian 164, fol. 248r.

[160]   Robert Brenner, *Merchants and Revolution: Commercial Change, Political Conflict and London's Overseas Traders 1550–1653* (Cambridge, 1993), p. 427.

[161]   *CJ*, vol. 2, 627, 730, 763, 806, 808.

[162]   TNA: PRO, SP 28/153, part 6, Account of John Fenning.

[163]   *LJ*, vol. 5, 297.

[164]   *CJ*, vol. 2, 773. An example of the order was initially drawn up for Sussex, but it was stated to be general for all counties.

[165]   *CJ*, vol. 2, 812; *LJ*, vol. 5, 408–9.

[166]   Stoyle, *Soldiers and Strangers*, 40.

[167]   *CJ*, vol. 2, 826.

and horses raised on the Propositions in the northern counties of Cumberland, Durham, Northumberland, Westmorland and Yorkshire to be given to Lord Fairfax, probably to counter the growing threat from Newcastle's 'popish' army.[168] It is doubtful whether very much came of this, since Fairfax's army was short of money and had particular problems raising cavalry.[169] After Edgehill and Turnham Green had failed to end the war, controlling territory became a much higher priority. At the same time, Parliament's attempts to compel Propositions contributions were increasing polarization. These two trends came together in the plans for the Eastern Association. As well as an association of counties, this was to be an association of people bound together by an oath. Like the Protestation, Pym and his radical allies referred to it as a shibboleth, but this time the oath was to be 'not subject to equivocation' so that they could discover 'who are for us and who are against us'.[170] Parliament passed an ordinance on 20 December grouping Cambridgeshire, Essex, Hertfordshire, Norfolk and Suffolk together for mutual defence and ordering the county committees to impose the association oath. In another echo of 1584, the oath required swearers to subscribe arms and money.[171] The militants in Parliament imposed the new association from the top down despite opposition from the moderate gentlemen who had kept Norfolk and Suffolk largely neutral and isolated from the effects of war. Even in Hertfordshire, where the Propositions had been implemented relatively early and successfully, nothing was done about the association until February 1643.[172] Most people did nothing to encourage a civil war.

People

The Elite and the Middle Sort

Parliament's military and political leadership in 1642 was overwhelmingly elite, but leaders could achieve nothing without an army to lead. The Propositions lists, especially for cavalry horses, are heavily biased towards the upper end of society because they only include people who could afford to give away valuable horses. They can tell us nothing about plebeian actions. The average value of cavalry horses listed before October 1642, including equipment, was £15, 6s. In

---

[168]   *LJ*, vol. 5, 458.

[169]   Andrew J. Hopper, *'Black Tom': Sir Thomas Fairfax and the English Revolution* (Manchester, 2007), pp. 37, 43, 210.

[170]   Holmes, *Eastern Association*, 63.

[171]   Ibid., 63–5; *A & O*, vol. 1, 51–2.

[172]   Holmes, *Eastern Association*, 62–5, 68.

London, where wages were unusually high, a construction labourer could earn 16d per day in 1642, and allowing for Sundays and other holidays could work a maximum of 279 days in a year, but in practice labourers could be unemployed for several months.[173] Therefore the value of one of these horses was about as much as, or more than, most labourers were likely to earn in a year. Only four individuals are listed as husbandmen in the first account book, and none of these occurs before October 1642.[174] This makes it all the more significant that contributions were not limited to the elite.

Table 1.3   Horses listed on the Propositions by social status, 21 June to 30 September 1642

Group	Horses	Average value
Tradesmen	734	£18, 12s
Gentry	649	£14, 18s
Unstated	614	£11, 16s
Yeomen	383	£10, 8s
Professionals	225	£14, 4s
Merchants	119	£18, 4s
MPs	89	£23, 18s
Peers	66	£35
Women	55	£13, 12s
Other	80	£13, 8s
Total	3,014	

Source: TNA: PRO, SP 28/131, part 3

---

[173]   Jeremy Boulton, 'Wage Labour in Seventeenth-Century London', *The Economic History Review*, 49/2, New Series (1996): 273, 287, 288. In the north, labourers were usually paid half as much as in London.

[174]   TNA: PRO, SP 28/131, part 3, fols 117v, 127v, 131v.

Table 1.3 shows that the middling sort were at least as important as the elite. If the nobles had revolted on their own they would only have had enough horses to mount one troop. They also supplied money and plate, but this was still not enough to start a war. Less than one third of the horses can be assigned to peers, MPs and gentlemen. Twice as many tradesmen and yeomen contributed, and they brought in more than one third of the horses. These horses were not necessarily inferior to those of the gentry.

Because contributions were not officially compulsory from June to September 1642, and because there was no official minimum contribution, it cannot be assumed that contributions are directly proportional to wealth. What people gave was necessarily limited by what they could afford to give, but it was also influenced by how much they wanted to give. The horse lists do not tell the whole story because they do not include money and plate. Nevertheless, the figures suggest that the upper middling sort, particularly in London, had access to substantial resources and that the distribution of wealth did not always reflect traditional social hierarchies. Some of these people were prepared to risk their fortunes by backing Parliament's war effort. None of this evidence supports old Marxist assumptions that the English Civil War was a class conflict. The middling and gentry contributors were minorities of their social groups. For the whole of the list in the period up to the end of September 1642 the maximum number of individuals identified as gentry is 482, with no more than 382 yeomen. Blackwood identified 774 gentry families in Lancashire, 689 in Suffolk and 633 in Norfolk.[175] The 1593 Bedfordshire subsidy roll named 250 gentlemen and 1,177 yeomen and husbandmen.[176] There were 309 armigerous families in Essex.[177] More people contributed money than horses, but they were often a minority or narrow majority of their social groups. The accounts of the southern division of Essex include 74 knights, esquires and gentlemen. Of these men, 35 contributed at least some money to the Propositions and 39 were assessed for the fifth and twentieth having contributed no money.[178] The surviving records of the Propositions fit with John Morrill's argument that the First Civil War was started by militant minorities and that the majority avoided taking part at first.[179] Parliament's attempts to compel contributions from October 1642 onwards suggest a perception that there were many more people who could contribute but who had not.

---

[175] Blackwood, 'Parties and Issues', 265–7.

[176] Mildred Campbell, *The English Yeoman Under Elizabeth and the Early Stuarts* (London, 1960), pp. 358–9.

[177] Hunt, *Puritan Moment*, 309.

[178] TNA: PRO, SP 28/153, part 6, Account of John Fenning.

[179] Morrill, *Revolt in the Provinces*, 178.

The term 'middling sort' was more commonly used in the 1640s than before, and came to be associated with allegiance to Parliament.[180] Hostile speech and writing often made a point of this. The name 'roundhead' came from the hairstyles of London apprentices, associating the rebels with youth, dependency and non-elite status.[181] Major-General Richard Browne, a wealthy London merchant who was free of the Woodmongers' Company, was condescendingly referred to as 'the woodmonger'.[182] The narrative of the battle of Brentford in John Gwynne's memoirs poured scorn on 'Holles his butchers and dyers'.[183] There was clearly some truth in these stereotypes, since more cavalry horses were brought in by tradesmen than by gentlemen. But for these tradesmen their social rank was not necessarily the source of shame that their elitist enemies said it should be. Nehemiah Wallington and Nehemiah Wharton, both from a middling London background, sometimes used 'roundhead' in positive ways in their writings.[184] For supporters of Parliament, middling status tended to connote respectability. John Corbet described the middle sort of Bristol, who opposed the elite and poor supporters of the King, as 'the true and best citizens'.[185] Puritan preachers Richard and John Rogers usually aimed their sermons at a middling audience, using the first person for the middle sort but the third person for the rich and the poor.[186]

The term 'middling sort' is notoriously hard to define. It can be misleading because it lumps together very diverse and unequal groups, or because it is too narrow and exclusive.[187] Some London citizens had limited financial means, but were still a long way from being poor. Nehemiah Wallington was admitted to the freedom of the Turners' Company by patrimony and was set up in his own shop and household at an unusually early age, thanks to his father, who

---

[180]   Keith Wrightson, '"Sorts of People" in Tudor and Stuart England', in Jonathan Barry and Christopher Brooks (eds), *The Middling Sort of People: Culture, Society and Politics in England, 1550–1800* (Basingstoke, 1994), pp. 41–6.

[181]   Michael Braddick, *God's Fury, England's Fire: A New History of the English Civil Wars* (London, 2008), p. 407.

[182]   Keith Lindley, 'Browne, Sir Richard, first baronet (c.1602–1669)', *ODNB*.

[183]   John Gwynne, *Military Memoirs of the Great Civil War* (Edinburgh, 1822), p. 24.

[184]   Paul S. Seaver, *Wallington's World: A Puritan Artisan in Seventeenth-Century London* (London, 1985), p. 104; Nehemiah Wharton, *Letters of a Subaltern in the Earl of Essex's Army*, Henry Ellis (ed.) (London, 1854), p. 24.

[185]   Underdown, *Revel, Riot, and Rebellion*, 169; Wrightson, 'Sorts of People', 46.

[186]   Hunt, *Puritan Moment*, 124.

[187]   Jonathan Barry and Christopher Brooks, 'Introduction', in Jonathan Barry and Christopher Brooks (eds), *The Middling Sort of People: Culture, Society and Politics in England, 1550–1800* (Basingstoke, 1994), pp. 12–17, 24; Peter Earle, 'The Middling Sort in London', in Jonathan Barry and Christopher Brooks (eds), *The Middling Sort of People: Culture, Society and Politics in England, 1550–1800* (Basingstoke, 1994), pp. 141–8.

was a warden of the company. Despite these privileges, Nehemiah was never very successful at his trade and was often short of money.[188] It is unlikely that he was able to contribute very much money to the Propositions, and he certainly did not provide any horses. He does not appear to have owned a horse, as he usually travelled on foot or by boat.[189] Nehemiah's brother, John, was much more successful in business and contributed two horses on the Propositions with a combined value of nearly £30.[190] This shows that wealth could vary within the same social rank, and that advantages at birth could lead to different outcomes.

Men and Women

The gentlemen, yeomen and tradesmen who listed horses proved their manhood as well as their social status. To be a man was to be the financially independent head of a household, in full control of his own body, his wife, his children, his servants and his animals.[191] He was to dominate and discipline his household as well as provide resources. A man who could not provide for and control his family failed to be a man and could be considered unfit for public office.[192] Men who could afford to give away valuable horses, even if they were expecting repayment, must have been independently wealthy. The vast majority of cavalry horses brought in before October 1642 were attributed to a single owner.[193] These men were able to contribute because they had achieved the financial independence of full manhood, and their conspicuous display of wealth reinforced their masculinity. Patriarchal manhood depended on age, wealth, marital status and social rank. It could not be achieved by young, unmarried men who were dependent on other men.[194] Calling a man a 'roundhead' denied his manhood by insinuating that he was a young, dependent apprentice.[195] Providing a horse for Parliament was proof of manliness which challenged this stereotype. Financial independence was perhaps more manly than fighting. Many of the horses

---

[188]   Seaver, *Wallington's World*, 1, 14, 74, 76, 78, 112–13, 115–6, 118, 121–4.

[189]   Ibid., 97–8.

[190]   TNA: PRO, SP 28/131, part 3, fol. 8v; TNA: PRO, SP 28/131, part 4, fol. 29v.

[191]   Alexandra Shepard, *Meanings of Manhood in Early Modern England* (Oxford, 2006), pp. 70, 186–7, 210; Anthony Fletcher, *Gender, Sex and Subordination in England 1500–1800* (New Haven, 1995), pp. 204–5; Hughes, *Gender*, 16–17, 19.

[192]   Hopper, *Black Tom*, 190, 198; Hughes, *Gender*, 111.

[193]   TNA: PRO, SP 28/131, part 3. Only 41 entries in this period include more than one donor.

[194]   Shepard, *Meanings of Manhood*, 21, 33–4, 70, 74, 206, 246.

[195]   Braddick, *God's Fury*, 407; Shepard, *Meanings of Manhood*, 180; Steven R. Smith, 'The London Apprentices as Seventeenth-Century Adolescents', *Past and Present*, 61 (1973): 151.

listed on the Propositions came with a rider, but only one gentleman and four tradesmen rode their own horses.[196] George Willingham sent his servant David Avys to ride the horse which he contributed.[197] This suggests that troopers could be younger and less independent than the horse owners. Fathers and masters could influence the allegiance of sons and servants who were set out in this way, as family loyalty and financial dependence limited the freedom of young men.

Financial independence alone did not guarantee manhood. A man was required to demonstrate his manhood by serving the public, even more so in times of war, and this was particularly emphasized on the parliamentary side.[198] Men who avoided these responsibilities by putting their private interests before the public good risked losing their privileged status. Action for the public was manly.[199] It followed from this that preferring private interests could be seen as effeminate. These ideological assumptions were manipulated in exhortations to act for what was supposedly the public good. Stephen Marshall railed against 'neuters' who failed to help the church out of 'meere sluggishnesse and desire of ease or basenes of spirit: loving only their worldly profits and sensuall pleasures', insinuating that their inactivity was a sign of cold humours and effeminacy.[200] These men had attended to their own private business instead of working for the common good.[201] Marshall contrasted them with the women who did fight against the Canaanites: Deborah, Israel's only female judge, commanded Barak to fight and played a leading role in the battle; Jael killed the enemy general Sisera in defiance of her husband, who was an ally of the King of Canaan.[202] This threatened men with the shame of being outdone by women.[203]

In the summer of 1642 the threat of women outperforming men in public service was very real, because a few of the people who listed horses on the Propositions were female. The word 'men' continued to be ambiguous in the

---

[196] TNA: PRO, SP 28/131, part 3, fols 5, 6v, 27r, 34r.

[197] TNA: PRO, SP 28/131, part 3, fol. 19r; Wharton, *Letters*, 9, 11, 12, 16; TNA: PRO, PROB 11/218, Will of George Willingham, Painter Stainer of Saint Swithin, City of London, proved 27 October 1651.

[198] Richard Cust, 'The "Public Man" in Late Tudor and Early Stuart England', in Peter Lake and Steven Pincus (eds), *Politics of the Public Sphere* (Manchester, 2007), pp. 117–18; Ann Hughes, 'Men, the "Public" and the "Private" in the English Revolution', in Peter Lake and Steven Pincus (eds), *Politics of the Public Sphere* (Manchester, 2007), p. 192; Hughes, *Gender*, 27, 97, 142–3.

[199] Hughes, 'Men', 193, 195, 197–8.

[200] Marshall, *Meroz Cursed*, 23–4; Shepard, *Meanings of Manhood*, 51, 59.

[201] Marshall, *Meroz Cursed*, 9–10, 24, 26.

[202] Ibid., 2, 9; Judges 4:6–22; 24–27 (AV).

[203] Ann M. Little, *Abraham in Arms: War and Gender in Colonial New England* (Philadelphia, 2007), p. 89.

commissaries' account books. In a list dated 1 October 1642 and headed 'Horses sent in by severall *men* whose names are underwritten to the right hon[or] able the Lord viscount Say and Seale, for the use and service both of Kinge and Parliament' (emphasis added) the first name is Lady Leye of Dichley![204] By the end of September 1642, 55 cavalry horses worth £748 had been listed by people whose status identifies them as women. The vast majority of these female contributors were stated to be widows, although two horses were listed by Joan Martin, described as the wife of Robert Martin, coachman.[205] The total for all three lists is 176 horses from donors explicitly given female statuses. The maximum number of individual female donors before October 1642 is 49, but by the same standards of proof only 634 can be shown to be male, and the other 1,831 are unknown. Two London widows, Ann Sacheverell and Elizabeth Fant, contributed 21 horses worth £575 to the London militia in October and November 1642.[206] These women must have been wealthy and financially independent. Although coverture placed married women at a severe disadvantage, and widows were often poor, a few women managed to achieve financial independence. Some widows inherited valuable estates and became heads of households, taking on aspects of manhood.[207] Many ordinary married women made settlements which gave them more rights than the theory of coverture allowed, and informal conventions sometimes treated the resources a woman brought into a marriage as her own even though they legally belonged to her husband.[208]

Morrill suggested that 'it is often less of a political act to obey an order than to disobey it, especially when the person making the order has the power of arrest or the ability to plunder your property'.[209] Before October 1642 this overt pressure to contribute to the Propositions did not exist. For women, contributing was arguably a more political act than doing nothing. Women usually had to justify their interventions in politics to an extent that men did not, but there is surprisingly little evidence of this in relation to the Propositions.[210] Official orders did not specifically exclude women, and their money and horses were accepted in practice. At a less formal level women's contributions were openly

---

[204] TNA: PRO, SP 28/131, part 3, fol. 121r.

[205] TNA: PRO, SP 28/131, part 3, fol. 42v.

[206] John Tincey, 'Armed Complete', *English Civil War Times* 55 (1998): 19; TNA: PRO, SP 28/131, part 5, fols 3v, 4r, 5r, 6r, 6v, 9r, 10v, 11r.

[207] Erickson, *Women and Property*, 24–5, 178, 187–8, 196, 201–2. Up to a fifth of households were headed by women: Hughes, *Gender*, 17.

[208] Erickson, *Women and Property*, 104–7, 129–30, 184.

[209] Morrill, *Revolt in the Provinces*, 189.

[210] Hughes, *Gender*, 60.

encouraged. An undated ballad which advocated bringing money and plate to Guildhall specifically addressed women as well as men, urging seamstresses to donate their silver thimbles to help depose the King.[211] Leveller women later emphasized their own contributions to the Propositions in order to validate their political activities, citing the examples of Jael and Deborah just as Stephen Marshall had.[212] Once the Propositions became compulsory, women who had not contributed were assessed even in places where the Protestation was exclusively male. No women took the Protestation in Wanstead, Essex, but in the fifth and twentieth assessment Dame Elizabeth Cooke was charged with £5 and Mary Cox with £3.[213]

The outbreak of civil war gave financially independent women an opportunity to get involved in war and national politics. Although these women were exercising agency and demonstrating their independence, they were also necessarily helping patriarchy. They gave material support to a parliament which excluded women. Its members all had a vested interest in the continued domination of women by men. The Long Parliament overturned many parts of the established order in the early 1640s, but it did nothing to give women any more political rights. Although there were differences between royal and parliamentary ideologies of order, hierarchy and gender, they both assumed that men should rule and that women should not. As Hughes has recently pointed out, 'at one level the civil war was a struggle among (largely male) elites'.[214] A decisive victory for Parliament might have changed many things, but would not have ended patriarchal equilibrium. Although some women contributed, the Propositions system was mostly gendered as male. The process of building Essex's army was dominated by men and served the interests of men. The rhetoric which encouraged contributions drew on and reinforced ideologies of masculinity.

The Godly and the Ungodly

The Protestation and the Propositions Ordinance required the public to defend the protestant religion, only vaguely defined, and were open to a wide range of interpretations. Some people used the Protestation as an excuse to avoid fighting

---

[211]   Freist, *Governed by Opinion*, 153.

[212]   Hughes, *Gender*, 59.

[213]   J.S.W. Gibson and Alan Dell, *Protestation Returns, 1641–42 and Other Contemporary Listings* (2004), p. 34; TNA: PRO, SP 28/153, part 6, Account of John Fenning. Neither woman had contributed money on the Propositions but a Lady Elizabeth Coote of Wanstead, probably the same person, listed a horse worth £15: TNA: PRO, SP 28/131, part 3, fol. 65r.

[214]   Hughes, *Gender*, 6, 60.

for Parliament.[215] The Propositions Ordinance asked all 'well-affected' people to contribute to the defence of the commonwealth and suggested that the King's supporters were a malignant minority.[216] This all suggests that the junto were trying to make their rebellion appear as inclusive as possible. The vagueness of the Protestation created the illusion that consensus had been achieved, but when Parliament tried to turn this apparent agreement into action with the Propositions, the consensus evaporated. Stephen Marshall's *Meroz Cursed* insisted that those who did not come to help the Lord would be cursed. Most property owners did not come to help in the summer of 1642. By October Parliament had decided that exhortations and curses were not enough, and that worldly sanctions were necessary to extract worldly goods. No more than 2,500 individuals listed horses before the end of September 1642. Even allowing for the unequal distribution of wealth in early-modern England, Parliament's contention that only a minority of those able to contribute to the war effort actually had contributed seems to be justified.

In practical terms, the absence of consensus in favour of a war against the King, and the diminishing Propositions contributions were failures for Parliament. But for puritan militants this was likely to reinforce their own Godly identities and millenarian rhetoric. Because the activists were a minority they could easily see themselves as the elect, separating from the damned and fighting against anti-Christ. The Godly often represented themselves as being apart from, and hated by, the ungodly majority, and 'were expected to shun, as far as possible, the company of the people of the world'.[217] The Watford petitioners referred to themselves as 'but a small Handful'.[218] It was the actions of people like Cornelius Burges and his Watford friends which made the war possible. According to Calvinist doctrine they could not be saved by good works, but by listing a horse they could demonstrate their faith and convince themselves that they were destined to be saved. As Hunt put it, 'Godly behavior was a consequence rather than a cause of regeneration'.[219] By actively resisting the King, puritan militants could reinforce their own belief that they were God's instruments. Nehemiah Wharton emphasized this role in his letters, which described Essex's soldiers burning altar rails, plundering catholics and ducking a woman whom they identified as a whore.[220] Diane Purkiss has pointed out

---

[215]   Vallance, *Revolutionary England*, 108–10, 112–14.

[216]   *A & O*, vol. 1, 7.

[217]   Hunt, *Puritan Moment*, 231–2.

[218]   *LJ*, vol. 5, 173.

[219]   Hunt, *Puritan Moment*, 122.

[220]   Wharton, *Letters*, 4–7, 11.

that for Wharton this was all part of the war against anti-Christ.[221] These acts of destruction and misogynistic violence were also likely to be seen as God's work by the intended audience of the letters. By writing them, Wharton was performing a puritan identity. With their army, the Godly could seek God's judgement in battle. Wharton looked forward to combat, writing from Worcester on 30 September 1642, 'I am confident the Lord of Hoasts will in the end triumph gloriously over these horses and all their cursed riders.'[222] In the same month the Earl of Warwick wrote to Lord Mandeville, 'stand well upon your garde both military and politicke, for you will never gett the like oportunity if you slip this which god hath put into your hands.'[223] Patrick Little has made it clear that taking this opportunity was a very risky gamble. When Cromwell sold his property and used the capital to contribute £600 to the Irish Adventure and £500 to the Propositions, he was 'making a religious statement, almost putting his financial survival into the hands of God'.[224] Quick victory would bring the financial reward of a substantial return on investment, and the spiritual reward of greater certainty about elect status.

As it turned out, the battle of Edgehill was an anti-climax which failed to decide the war. The stand-off at Turnham Green was even more disappointing. Neither God nor the Earl of Essex had brought the victory that Parliament desperately needed.[225] This had very serious implications. Parliament's war machine was only adequate for a short war. At the time of Turnham Green there was no system in place to provide the resources necessary for a long war. Voluntary contributions were already running out. It was not until late November that Parliament started to build taxation systems, and it took more than two years of trial and error to make them work satisfactorily. Just as serious were the spiritual consequences. God had not passed unequivocal judgement in favour of Essex's army. The Godly militants who had gambled their fortunes and their souls on a quick victory now had to confront the possibility that they were destined to be financially ruined in this life and damned in the next. This may have contributed to the increasing polarization between war and peace factions as parliament men drew different conclusions about the meaning and consequences of their failure to win the war.

---

[221]   Diane Purkiss, *The English Civil War: A People's History* (London, 2006), p. 186.

[222]   Wharton, *Letters*, 22.

[223]   Holmes, *Eastern Association*, 37.

[224]   Patrick Little, 'Cromwell and Ireland before 1649', in Patrick Little (ed.), *Oliver Cromwell: New Perspectives* (Basingstoke, 2009), pp. 118–19.

[225]   Clive Holmes, *Why Was Charles I Executed?* (London, 2006), p. 71.

Englishmen and Strangers

Essex's army was the first English army to fight against Charles I and was often represented as 'an army for the defence of the English nation'.[226] In terms of personnel it was much less English than the New Model Army. The reforms of 1645 removed nearly all of the Scots and continental mercenaries who had played a major role in Essex's army.[227] Parliament also relied heavily on arms imports from the continent in the early years of the war.[228] In other respects Essex commanded an English army. It was raised by the English Parliament for service in England, although it included some English troops diverted from the Irish Adventure. For the first time, the English rebels had the military power to resist Charles I themselves without relying on the Scots Covenanter government. In the second half of 1642 the English parliamentary cause was less dependent on Scotland than it had been before, and than it would be again until 1645. Russell claimed that 'the whole of Pym's strategy from the Scots' withdrawal in September 1641 to their return in December 1643, was dominated by the desire to get them back', but this argument completely ignored the existence of Essex's army.[229]

The Propositions contributions which created Essex's army were mostly English. Nearly all of the horse contributors who gave addresses lived in England. Daniel Floyd, a Denbighshire yeoman, is the only Welshman mentioned in the lists, out of several thousand contributors.[230] Parliament never gave an explicit order to implement the Propositions in Cornwall, and no Cornish addresses appear in the horse lists. Valentine Stuckly, a vintner, gave his address as 'The white Beare in Cornwall', but this almost certainly means Cornhill in London.[231] By 8 October 1642 armed Cornishmen had taken control of Cornwall on behalf of the King, making it impossible for Parliament to gather any resources in the county.[232] On 11 October the Commons ordered that 'such Members of this House, or others of the Counties of Devon, Cornwall, and Sommersett, that have subscribed upon the Propositions to bring in Horses, and have not yet

---

[226] Stoyle, *Soldiers and Strangers*, 116.

[227] Ibid., 132, 92–7, 102–9.

[228] Peter Edwards, *Dealing in Death: The Arms Trade and the British Civil Wars* (Stroud, 2000), p. 175.

[229] Russell, 'Scottish Party', 51.

[230] TNA: PRO, SP 28/131, part 4, fol. 38v.

[231] TNA: PRO SP 28/131 part 3 f. 55r. Records of the 1641 poll tax mention Val Stucky of the White Bear in Cornhill, freeman of the Vintners' Company: Thomas Cyril Dale (ed.), *The Members of the City Companies in 1641 as Set Forth in the Return for the Poll Tax* (London, 1934), p. 164.

[232] Stoyle, *Soldiers and Strangers*, 40.

sent them in, shall send them to be employed in those Parts'.[233] This suggests assumptions by MPs that people who had subscribed horses for Parliament would not be present in Cornwall, that Cornwall was enemy territory which forces needed to be sent into, and that the Cornish were a threat to the security of Devon and Somerset. As Mark Stoyle has insisted, Englishness was a major factor in the civil wars which deserves more attention. The outbreak of civil war in England was accompanied by fears of foreign invasion.[234] Non-English people were often represented as barbarous and inhuman.[235] When parliament men acted for the public good, they acted in the interests of the *English* commonwealth. Patriotism and patriarchy were closely linked. Godly public service and Godly Englishness were represented as masculine, whereas racial and religious Others were represented as effeminate, godless and servile.[236] An ordinance of Parliament passed in December 1642 described joining with Essex's army as 'an Act well becoming all true-hearted Englishmen, and Lovers of their Country and Religion'.[237]

Essex's army did not represent Wales and Cornwall, but it did not represent all of England either. Most of the horses for Essex's cavalry came from south-east England. Between them Bedfordshire, Buckinghamshire, Cambridgeshire, Essex, Hertfordshire, Huntingdon, London, Middlesex and Oxfordshire accounted for more than two thirds of the cavalry horses listed before October 1642 (see Table 1.2). It is impossible to be certain of which counties did not send horses to London because 742 horses listed in the same period (25 per cent of the total) have no address. This leaves open the possibility that significant numbers of people from several other counties listed horses, but it also eliminates the possibility that all counties contributed to the same degree as the southern and eastern counties listed above. England north of the Trent is mostly absent from Propositions records relating to horses. It is not always clear whether horses listed in the north were kept for local defence or whether none were brought in. Very little seems to have happened in the West Riding of Yorkshire in the summer of 1642 when militants in the south-east were busy raising Essex's army. Lord Fairfax agreed to a neutrality pact in September and did not start raising an army until

---

233   *CJ*, vol. 2, 803.

234   Mark Stoyle, 'English "Nationalism", Celtic Particularism, and the English Civil War', *Historical Journal*, 43/4 (2000): 1116.

235   Mark Stoyle, 'Caricaturing Cymru: Images of the Welsh in the London Press 1642–46', in Diana Dunn (ed.), *War and Society in Medieval and Early Modern Britain* (Liverpool, 2000), p. 167; Stoyle, *Soldiers and Strangers*, 74–5, 101; Shagan, 'Constructing Discord', 12.

236   Shagan, 'Constructing Discord', 9; Hughes, 'Men', 192, 195; Little, *Abraham in Arms*, 20, 177–8.

237   *A & O*, vol. 1, 47.

October.[238] Parliament did not give specific orders to implement the Propositions in Yorkshire until 4 October, and no Yorkshire addresses appear in the lists of the London commissaries.[239] Orders were sent to Cheshire on 8 July, but on 8 August Sir William Brereton reported that subscriptions could only be got on condition that they were used for local defence.[240] The Mayor and aldermen of Derby received orders on 6 July, but Derbyshire is not mentioned in the cavalry horse list.[241] George Grisly, a gentleman of Drakelow, is the only person with a Derbyshire address in the list of dragoon and draught horses.[242] Parliament issued no specific instructions to implement the Propositions in Lancashire. The orders to raise 1,000 dragoons for Lancashire in London and the south-east imply that by October 1642 Lancashire was effectively treated as enemy or occupied territory which had to be suppressed or liberated.[243] Horses listed in the second account book were probably used for the Lancashire regiment as well as for Essex's army, since the start of the list on 5 October came just after the Lancashire order was agreed on 3 October. Although around 900 horses in this list have no address, the ones which do are overwhelmingly from southern and eastern England. Most came from Essex, Hertfordshire, London, Lincolnshire and Suffolk. It is not the case that the south-east was a 'parliamentarian' area. The activists were probably a minority even where they were most numerous. But the fact that they were more prevalent in the south-east than the north-west does have implications for their identities. The Englishness of the parliament men was a false universal which was heavily biased towards the south-east. Even if this was not consciously intended, it was necessarily reinforced by the creation of Essex's army.

'The Royalists' and 'The Parliamentarians'?

The headings in this section have suggested a number of binary oppositions between kinds of people, but have also undermined those oppositions. If identity could be reduced to five aspects (class, gender, religion, race and wartime allegiance), and if each of those aspects could be reduced to a simple binary, there would still be up to 32 possible combinations. Even working from such an oversimplified premise we have to conclude that identity must be very complex. In the text of each section, categories have spilled into each other,

---

[238] Hopper, *Black Tom*, 26–8.
[239] *LJ*, vol. 5, 386.
[240] *CJ*, vol. 2, 660; Fletcher, *Outbreak*, 338.
[241] *CJ*, vol. 2, 656.
[242] TNA: PRO, SP 28/131, part 4, fol. 40r.
[243] *LJ*, vol. 5, 376–7, 380, 382.

disturbing the neat distinctions claimed by the section titles. For parliament *men*, Godliness and manliness were inseparable, and full manhood depended on the financial independence of an elite or middling householder. But in practice Parliament relied on many people who did not live up to this ideal of the Godly English commonwealthsman. Crowds, which could include poor or dependent men and women, made crucial interventions in Westminster politics, helped to disarm delinquents in Essex, stopped the Commission of Array in Somerset and Gloucestershire, and mobilized against the Earl of Newcastle in Yorkshire.[244] Financially independent women supplied some of the resources for Parliament's war effort. The army that they helped to put into the field included many dependent young men and foreign mercenaries, and was led by a general who had failed to achieve full manhood despite his privileged social status because the failure of his marriages left him with a reputation as an impotent cuckold.[245] The Lord General's harshest critics in Parliament included Henry Marten, an adulterer and reputed atheist.[246] All this was before hostility between Presbyterians and Independents added new complications. Furthermore, the parliamentary army depended on several thousand horses which were not even human. It should be clear by now that there was not one shared 'parliamentarian' identity. The parliamentary war machine was a disparate coalition which included people from different groups whose identities were defined in many different ways. As Morrill recognized, if we classify people as 'parliamentarian' or 'royalist' according to some arbitrary criteria, the groups we find in each box will by very diverse in other ways.[247]

One thing that many people had in common was that they acted in the interests of Parliament and against the interests of the King. But this does not mean that they were 'parliamentarians'. The attempt to change Propositions contributions from voluntary to compulsory confirms that definitions of allegiance could change rapidly and arbitrarily. This privileged action over sincerity. If Parliament was prepared to use threats and punishment to make people contribute, then their underlying feelings and opinions cannot have been very important. After the Stour Valley riots, Sir Thomas Barrington reportedly told the Commons that 'this miscarriage of the people proceeding from their

---

244   Braddick, *God's Fury*, 137–8, 215–16; Walter, *Understanding Popular Violence*; Nick Poyntz, 'The Attack on Lord Chandos: Popular Politics in Cirencester in 1642', *Midland History*, 35/1 (2010): 71–88; Hopper, *Black Tom*, 37.

245   Snow, *Essex*, 42, 52–3, 67, 192–4, 343; Bruce Boehrer, *Shakespeare Among the Animals: Nature and Society in the Drama of Early Modern England* (New York, 2002), pp. 79–83.

246   Sarah Barber, *A Revolutionary Rogue: Henry Marten and the English Republic* (Stroud, 2000), pp. x, 83.

247   Morrill, *Revolt in the Provinces*, 189.

zeale to the Parliament did yet wrought this good effect that divers persons who were esteemed malignant before and refused to contribute monie horse or plate to Parliament did now bring in some monie or plate and others horses'.[248] Because the only record of this speech was written by D'Ewes in his diary, we cannot be certain that Barrington used these exact words, but it is probably a fairly accurate paraphrase, and at the very least D'Ewes must have considered it plausible. Suspected enemies contributing out of fear could be seen as an example of dual transcripts. This theory, developed by anthropologist James C. Scott, suggests that oppressed people act and speak differently in different circumstances. In the presence of their social superiors they perform the public transcript, acting out the required rituals of deference in order to avoid punishment or gain concessions. But when superiors are not present the hidden transcript comes into play. In safe places, resentment at inequality can be expressed openly and it can be revealed that the public transcript was not meant sincerely.[249] If we accept that knowing other minds is problematic, then there is no reason to believe that one transcript is any more 'real' than the other. Systems of power could function without anyone needing to know which transcript, if any, was authentic. The performance of the public transcript had effects regardless of the motives and intentions behind it. If suspected delinquents listed horses on the Propositions as part of an insincere public transcript, Parliament still got horses from them and these horses were still militarily useful. Mental reservations would change nothing. D'Ewes did not represent Barrington as saying anything to imply that insincerity was a problem, referring to it as 'this good effect'. Barrington's speech adds even more weight to Rachel Weil's argument that allegiance was conceived as being more external than internal. He represented allegiance as being based on reputation and actions rather than on feelings or opinions, and as being changeable rather than a fixed essence. He did not say that these people *were* malignants but that they 'were *esteemed* malignant' (emphasis added) but then they did something for Parliament. They were acting in both senses: performing an action and performing a role.

Barrington's view of allegiance was effectively made official on 14 October 1642, when Parliament made Propositions contributions compulsory. This change was not accepted by all MPs. D'Ewes opposed the order,

conceiving it to be of most dangerous consequence because it was a kinde of inforcement of people to that which ought not to bee enforced without the generall

---

[248] Walter, *Understanding Popular Violence*, 156; Coates, Young and Snow, *Private Journals*, 326.

[249] Andy Wood, 'Fear, Hatred and the Hidden Injuries of Class in Early Modern England', *Journal of Social History*, 39/3 (2006): 808–9.

consent of the kingdome declared by an Act of Parliament & I feared that if the two
Houses did gaine mens purses in a compulsorie way they would lose their hearts.[250]

This privileging of affection over action shows that definitions of allegiance were
strongly contested at the time and that there was no consensus. The majority in
Parliament preferred obedience to sincerity, and in practice they even failed to
achieve much of that. The people who did obey by listing horses constructed
a 'parliamentarian' identity for themselves. This is just as true of contributors
who were not suspected of insincerity. Their actions created and reinforced an
identity which was written in the commissaries' account books and in the tickets
which they issued. These documents created allegiance as much as recording it.
Meanwhile, people who did nothing had the identity of enemy imposed on
them by ordinance of Parliament. Allegiance existed outside people in words,
actions and objects. The Propositions lists are valuable sources, but they cannot
and should not be used to find out who was 'a parliamentarian'.

Horses

The official records of the Propositions treated horses as objects to be owned,
exchanged and used for the benefit of humans. The Propositions Ordinance
made no mention of the liberties, affections or public good of horses.[251] Whether
or not the phrase 'all well-affected Persons' included women, it certainly did not
include animals. Horses were lumped together with arms, money and plate as
resources to be priced and exploited. Although humans might have exercised
agency by constructing their own allegiance, they did this partly by using horses
as tokens of exchange, denying the horse's own agency and identity. The Long
Parliament privileged men above both women and beasts, but without horses,
Parliament could not win the war.

In practice, anthropocentric assumptions did not always stand up. The
exchange of property when people contributed horses was meticulously recorded
by the commissaries. The lists included a description of each horse giving its sex
and colour, and sometimes details of its markings. For example, on 28 June 1642
Captain George Thompson of Dice Key in London listed two horses, 'the one
blacke w[i]th two white feete and a blase downe his face, the other a bright bay'.[252]
It was not unusual to keep such descriptions of horses in early-modern England

---

[250]   BL, Harleian 164, fol. 31v.
[251]   *A & O*, vol. 1, 6–9.
[252]   TNA: PRO, SP 28/131, part 3, fol. 6r.

as they were necessary to identify the animals in case of legal disputes. The law required transactions at horse fairs and markets to be recorded in toll books, and stolen horses could be tracked down by their descriptions.[253] While this was all ostensibly about protecting human property rights, it necessarily acknowledged an uncomfortable fact: no two horses are the same. Just like humans, every horse has a unique appearance. Treating horses as property necessarily involved treating them as individuals: 'to own an animal the owner has to know the animal'.[254] While the Propositions lists required and reinforced this knowing, they did not go as far as naming the horses. It was usual for owners to give their horses names, although horse names were distinct from human names.[255] These names were very rarely recorded by parliamentary administrators. The names of seven horses sent in by the Earl of Lincoln on 14 November 1642 were recorded on a separate piece of paper: Litchfeild, Horncastle, Gunpowder, Palmer, Sparks, Edward Jennings mare and Woodward.[256] There is no record of the names of any more of the thousands of horses listed on the Propositions. This did not quite enforce a rigid boundary between animals and humans, as some people were mentioned in the lists without being named. While the names of many of the riders were given, some were simply referred to as 'rider'.[257] This may have followed from, and reinforced, the fact that riders had lower status than owners. Sometimes even the owners were not named, particularly if a horse was jointly listed by a large group, which became more common in late 1642. For example, the list of cavalry horses recorded that on 14 November 1642, 'The Inh[ab]itants of Bowden magna in Lestershire listed 5 horses vizt one gray geldinge valued at 5li one bay geldinge at 5li one bay bald horse at 5li one gray mare at 4li and one white geldinge at 4li.'[258] In this case the horses were given more individuality than their owners.

The identities recorded in the Propositions lists allowed some individuality to the horses, but these identities were imposed by humans. If their owners treated them like objects or slaves, the horses themselves sometimes refused to be passive and compliant. Even this can only be glimpsed through texts written by humans, but the writers had to admit that the horses had done things that they were not supposed to do. Thomas Richardson submitted a bill to the Committee of Safety for charges incurred in sending 80 draught horses to the

---

[253]   Peter Edwards, *The Horse Trade of Tudor and Stuart England* (Cambridge, 2004), pp. 56, 111.

[254]   Erica Fudge, *Perceiving Animals: Humans and Beasts in Early Modern English Culture* (Urbana, 2002), p. 117.

[255]   Peter Edwards, *Horse and Man in Early Modern England* (London, 2007), pp. 24–5.

[256]   TNA: PRO, SP 28/3A, part 2, fol. 187r.

[257]   For example, TNA: PRO, SP 28/131, part 3, fols 3, 4r, 6.

[258]   TNA: PRO, SP 28/131 part 3, fol. 116r.

army at Worcester. These included sixpence paid on the way to Acton on 28 September 1642 for 'helpe on the hyway ... when the horses broke loose'. The following day a shilling was paid 'for hireing a man to seeke two horses that were lost', and then on 1 and 2 October another two shillings 'for two men to helpe seeke horses that were lost'.[259] Horses were clearly very difficult to control, especially in large numbers. The noise and stress of battle could make horses even more uncontrollable. Sir Richard Bulstrode's memoirs described this happening at Powicke Bridge in 1642: 'This was the first Action I was ever in, and being upon an unruly Horse, he ran away with me amongst the Enemy.'[260] The behaviour of horses had a crucial impact on the outcome of battles. The most decisive battles of the First Civil War were won by infantry and cavalry working together, since neither could easily win on their own.[261] Victory often went to the side whose cavalry could rout their opposite numbers and then re-form for another charge against the remainder of the enemy cavalry or infantry, or which had enough cavalry in reserve to launch another charge without having to re-form the first wave. For this to work, both horses and men had to be kept under control. Both sides failed to win at Edgehill because they were let down by their cavalry: Essex's cavalry wings ran away without putting up much resistance, and all of the King's cavalry, including the reserves, pursued them off the field and failed to return until it was too late. Meanwhile, Essex's cavalry reserves under Sir William Balfour and Sir Philip Stapleton took advantage of the absence of enemy cavalry by charging the King's infantry, turning what could have been a disaster into a draw.[262] It has to be suspected that inability to control their horses contributed to the failures of both sides, but this possibility has not been explored in detail. Contemporaries did admit that horses could be difficult to control. Horses were said to have very hot humours.[263] The ability to master a horse could be an important aspect of manhood, particularly for members of the elite who practised manège and commissioned equestrian portraits.[264] The symbolic importance of dominating and controlling horses depended on the knowledge that horses were not naturally compliant.[265]

---

[259]   TNA: PRO, SP 28/262, part 4, fols 438–9.

[260]   Richard Bulstrode, *Memoirs and reflections on the reign and government of King Charles Ist and king Charles IId* (London, 1721), pp. 73–4.

[261]   Malcolm Wanklyn, *Decisive Battles of the English Civil War* (Barnsley, 2006), pp. 202–3.

[262]   Ibid., 46–52, 55.

[263]   Edwards, *Horse and Man*, 55.

[264]   Ibid., 27–30; Karen L. Raber and Treva J. Tucker, 'Introduction', in Karen L. Raber and Treva J. Tucker (eds), *The Culture of the Horse* (Basingstoke, 2005), pp. 22–3.

[265]   Bruce Boehrer, 'Shakespeare and the Social Devaluation of the Horse', in Karen L. Raber and Treva J. Tucker (eds), *The Culture of the Horse* (Basingstoke, 2005), pp. 94–5; Pia Cuneo, 'Just

Conclusion

The Propositions system was a crucial part of the outbreak of the First Civil War. Public contributions built a field army and allowed Parliament to fight. Despite this, many historians have ignored or dismissed it. James Scott Wheeler's narrative of progress towards Britain's great power status acknowledged that contributions of money and plate were 'impressive' to begin with, but was still able to dismiss the whole system in only three sentences.[266] According to Robert Brenner, the Propositions brought in 'insufficient funds' because contributions were voluntary.[267] Graham has given the Propositions and the creation of Essex's army much more attention than most historians, but still concluded that the system was flawed and that the potential of the army was unfulfilled.[268] These assumptions that failure was inevitable logically depend on the result of the battle of Edgehill being either inevitable or irrelevant to the continuation of the war, but Wanklyn and Jones have rightly insisted that we need to put tactical and operational contingency back into the history of the English Civil War.[269] It was possible for the Civil War to be decided in one battle in 1642 because King and Parliament each concentrated most of their resources into a single field army. If either army had been completely destroyed at Edgehill, as later armies were at Roundway Down and Naseby, it is difficult to imagine the war continuing as it did until 1646. The Propositions contributions served their immediate purpose: to create an army capable of fighting and defeating the King's army. The failure to destroy the King's army in 1642 can be attributed largely to tactical factors. Graham has recently calculated that the size of Essex's army has been overestimated and that it was similar in numbers, but not in quality, to the royal army, concluding that Essex deserves credit for avoiding a likely defeat and that parliamentary victory may have been impossible.[270] The conclusion that roughly equal numbers led to an unequal chance of victory depends on the circular argument that Rupert's cavalry beat Essex's because they were better, and that we know they were better because they beat their opponents. In fact the

---

a Bit of Control: The Historical Significance of Sixteenth- and Seventeenth-Century German Bit-Books', in Karen L. Raber and Treva J. Tucker (eds), *The Culture of the Horse* (Basingstoke, 2005), pp. 154–6; Edwards, *Horse and Man*, 28.

[266]   James Scott Wheeler, *The Making of a World Power: War and the Military Revolution in Seventeenth Century England* (Stroud, 1999), p. 102.

[267]   Brenner, *Merchants and Revolution*, 430.

[268]   Graham, 'Finance', 880.

[269]   Malcolm Wanklyn and Frank Jones, *A Military History of the English Civil War* (Harlow, 2005), pp. x, 24.

[270]   Graham, 'Earl of Essex', 289, 293.

performance of cavalry units varied wildly, which is not consistent with having an essential quality which made them always better or worse than the enemy. Essex's lifeguard ran away at Powicke Bridge but made a crucial charge against the King's infantry at Edgehill a few weeks later.[271] Both sides had the numbers to make a decisive victory possible. A greater imbalance of forces might have made victory more likely but could never guarantee it, because battles were inherently unpredictable. More cavalry on the field at the start of the battle of Edgehill might only have resulted in more cavalry leaving the field in disorder shortly afterwards. Parliament's military and administrative system was designed for a short war.[272] The Propositions gave Essex the chance to win (or lose) the war in a single campaign. If he had succeeded, the system would have served its purpose perfectly and historians would not have dismissed it, while if he had lost his whole army it is unlikely that inadequate resources would have been accepted as an excuse for defeat.

Michael Braddick has suggested that the destruction of Essex's army at Edgehill would not have ended the war because 'it is very unlikely that resistance elsewhere would have ceased, or that the Scots would have stood by while the royalists imposed terms on Parliament'.[273] It does seem likely that a royal victory in England would have led to another war with the Scots, although the covenanters had already disbanded the army which had invaded England in 1640 and would have needed time to build another. It is also true that the war would not have ended instantly, but the English rebels would have very little chance of winning without Essex's army. Parliament's victories at Naseby and Langport in 1645 did not end resistance elsewhere, and the war continued for more than a year afterwards, but there was no chance of the King winning once he had run out of field armies (see Chapter 5). A decisive victory for either side at Edgehill would have drastically changed the balance of forces. Most of the local and regional forces which played an increasingly important role in the fighting in later years were only in the early stages of creation, or did not exist at all. The King's most viable second force was Newcastle's northern army, which invaded Yorkshire on 1 December with 8,000 men.[274] Hopton's Cornish army tried and failed to invade Devon in November, and by the end of the year had only grown to 3,000 men.[275] Parliament still had the London trained bands, which

---

[271]　Wharton, *Letters*, 19, 21; Wanklyn, *Decisive Battles*, 50–52.
[272]　Morrill, *Revolt in the Provinces*, 86–7.
[273]　Braddick, *God's Fury*, 247.
[274]　Hopper, *Black Tom*, 36.
[275]　Stoyle, *Soldiers and Strangers*, 43.

had mustered 8,000 infantry in May 1642.[276] The Ordnance Office in the Tower and the draught horses coming in on the Propositions from East Anglia could provide a new artillery train if Essex lost his. The biggest problem was cavalry. Propositions contributions for the London Militia only provided enough horses for one regiment of 450 by the end of November, and at the time of Edgehill fewer than 70 horses had been brought in.[277] Meanwhile, cavalry horse contributions for Essex's army were in terminal decline, amounting to only 136 in November 1642.[278] Without an adequate cavalry screen, the Trained Bands would be very vulnerable to enemy cavalry and artillery, and might not have been able to march out of London if they were opposed by the King's main army. A second chance would depend on how many of Essex's cavalry troops – many of which had been detached from the army before Edgehill – could regroup in London, how many horses could be requisitioned without provoking resistance, and whether new troopers could be recruited and trained in time. Other forces were even less viable. Lord Fairfax did not start raising his army until October. By 1 December it was only 2,000 strong, and was always short of cavalry.[279] Sir John Hotham had the forces to hold Hull, but was not strong enough to prevent Newcastle's advance into Yorkshire. The Earl of Stamford only had a small force in Hereford, was unable to get enough recruits or resources from the local population, and abandoned the city on 14 December.[280] The Eastern Association was not formed even on paper until December 1642, and its army was not comparable to Essex's until much later. In October Waller was still a colonel under Essex rather than an independent general. If one of the major field armies had been destroyed at Edgehill, the other would have been free to wipe out at least one of the enemy's embryonic regional armies, further changing the balance of forces.

It was because Edgehill was not a decisive victory for either side that the Propositions became inadequate. The traditional view placed the decline of contributions too early – Crawshaw has shown that Essex's army was still well paid at the time of Edgehill[281] – but the system was unable to finance a second campaign or support multiple armies. Horse contributions were already falling before Edgehill, and Parliament's attempts to force contributions in mid-October would be consistent with increasing anxiety that resources would run out too soon. The indecisive result at Edgehill did not cause the decline in contributions

276 Lawson Chase Nagel, 'The Militia of London 1641–1649' (PhD, University of London, 1982), p. 62.
277 TNA: PRO, SP 28/131, part 5; Tincey, 'Armed Complete', 22.
278 TNA: PRO, SP 28/131, part 3.
279 Hopper, *Black Tom*, 28, 36–7, 43, 210.
280 Hopper, 'Grey, Henry'.
281 Crawshaw, 'Military Finance', 1037, 1044.

but it made the problem more urgent. An army supplied mostly by voluntary contributions was a one-shot weapon because only a minority gave material support. These people did not necessarily all become less enthusiastic about fighting after Edgehill. While Denzil Holles started advocating peace instead of war, Cromwell continued to pursue victory but had given all the money he could and had nothing left. Meanwhile, the majority remained just as inactive as ever, despite the threat of being treated as enemies. Parliament could not carry on fighting without the support of wealthy gentlemen, yeomen, tradesmen, merchants and widows: not just a vague feeling of allegiance but actual material support. The challenge faced by Parliament and its administrators was to extract resources from the uncommitted majority. Aggressive polarization and coercion failed in late 1642. Parliament would have to develop new systems and make them work in order to win war.

Chapter 2

The Other Side

Identifying the Enemy

This book is primarily about how identities were defined in relation to Parliament, but this does not mean that it is exclusively about people who supported Parliament. Before Parliament could take action against enemies, they had to be identified. This was not simply a case of uncovering 'true' allegiance to find out who was 'a royalist'. Parliament created identities and imposed them on people before doing anything else. Essentialist historiography treated these identities as less authentic and therefore less important than what people 'really' thought, but labels assigned by Parliament had very real consequences. They need to be taken just as seriously as the allegiances which people chose for themselves. The outbreak of civil war complicated the identities which were already available and made possible completely new identities.

Catholic Threats

Parliament's official justification for its unprecedented actions was based on popular anti-popery, which was much more widespread than puritanism, however they are defined.[1] Popery was a convenient foreign Other against which English protestants could potentially be united, although this did not always work in practice.[2] When the Grand Remonstrance listed England's calamities, it blamed Jesuits first, then wicked counsellors and bishops.[3] The Propositions Ordinance did not explicitly mention catholics, either as malignant or well-affected persons. The preamble emphasized the actions of the King and his wicked counsellors in preparing to wage war on Parliament. Although overthrowing religion was alleged to be one of their aims, the plot was not specifically described as

---

[1]   Peter Lake, 'Anti-Popery: The Structure of a Prejudice', in Richard Cust and Ann Hughes (eds), *The English Civil War* (London, 1997), pp. 201–2; Anthony Fletcher, *The Outbreak of the English Civil War* (London, 1981), p. 415; Andrew J. Hopper, *"Black Tom": Sir Thomas Fairfax and the English Revolution* (Manchester, 2007), pp. 136–8.

[2]   Lake, 'Anti-Popery', 190, 199–200; Frances E. Dolan, *Whores of Babylon Catholicism, Gender, and Seventeenth-Century Print Culture* (Notre Dame, 2005), pp. 22, 37–8.

[3]   Clive Holmes, *Why Was Charles I Executed?* (London, 2006), p. 38.

popish. It seems likely that the conventions of popish plot rhetoric were so well established that the preamble connoted 'the catholic threat' without having to use the words 'popery' or 'popish'. Wicked counsellors, tyranny and anti-religion were all conventionally associated with popery in English protestant discourse.[4] In practice, Parliament tended to treat catholics as enemies by default, denying them the choice of sides which was available to protestants. Puritan anti-popery perhaps gave English catholics an interest in Parliament losing the war, even if they did nothing to make it happen. Although English protestants routinely blamed the pope for their troubles, the papacy remained uncommitted to either the protestant Parliament or the protestant King, waiting to see what would happen before intervening.[5]

When wicked counsel was mentioned, Queen Henrietta Maria was probably one of the most likely suspects.[6] Parliament's *Declaration of Fears and Jealousies*, published in March 1642 and probably drafted by John Pym, described the Queen as 'a dangerous and ill-affected person'.[7] Anti-catholic propaganda often gendered catholicism as female and catholic men as effeminate.[8] The ambiguity of the words 'men' and 'persons' made the gender of the enemy fluid. The assertion in the Propositions Ordinance that 'some ill-affected Persons have been employed in other Parts, to raise Troops, under the Colour of His Majesty's Service' seems to refer mostly to men, but it could also include the Queen.[9] The mention of 'several Sorts of malignant Men, who are about the King; some whereof, under the Name of Cavaliers' is likely to mean men, but the ordinance goes on to describe 'the Malice and Violence of such desperate Persons as must be employed in so horrid and unnatural an Act as the overthrowing of a Parliament by Force'. It might be assumed that violence was associated with men, but use of the word 'unnatural' could also imply anxiety about gender roles and patriarchal order being disturbed. What could be more unnatural than women using violence to overthrow Parliament? Again, the Queen would be a chief

---

[4]   Lake, 'Anti-Popery', 182, 184, 199.

[5]   Stefania Tutino, 'The Catholic Church and the English Civil War : The Case of Thomas White', *Journal of Ecclesiastical History*, 58/2 (2007): 243–5.

[6]   Ann Hughes, *Gender and the English Revolution* (Abingdon, 2011), pp. 61–2; Dolan, *Whores of Babylon*, 124.

[7]   Dolan, *Whores of Babylon*, 123.

[8]   David Cressy, *Agnes Bowker's Cat: Travesties and Transgressions in Tudor and Stuart England* (Oxford, 2001), p. 235; Cynthia B. Herrup, 'The King's Two Genders', *Journal of British Studies*, 45/3 (2006): 500; Ann M. Little, *Abraham in Arms: War and Gender in Colonial New England* (Philadelphia, 2007), pp. 20, 129, 137; Dolan, *Whores of Babylon*, 6, 8, 75, 85.

[9]   *A & O*, vol. 1, 6.

suspect, and Irish women were often represented as unnaturally violent.[10] When the Elizabethan association oath referred to 'any person that may pretend title', it strongly implied that it was chiefly aimed at Mary Stuart.[11] These connotations potentially made acting against the supposed popish plot all the more masculine.

The stereotype of 'papist' was already well established, and protestants conventionally associated it with treason.[12] This did not make catholics easy to find. Frances Dolan has pointed out that catholics were an amorphous group, and that 'historians cannot determine exactly what it meant to be a "Catholic" in early modern England'.[13] There was no catholic essence: rather than naturally being catholics, people had to become catholics by repeatedly performing catholicism. This required attending church and participating in rituals conducted by ordained priests. Puritans tended to exaggerate this aspect, deriding it as superstitious idolatry and hypocritical outward action without inward faith.[14] Like puritans, catholics had to combine faith with action, but the necessary actions were not easy to carry out in an aggressively protestant state. Because of the threat of imprisonment, torture and execution, priests were not always available and mass had to be conducted in secret.[15] Although 'papists' were defined in relation to the Roman Catholic Church, the official hierarchy was largely absent from England.[16] Richard Smith, bishop of Chalcedon, had responsibility for the whole of England, Scotland and Wales, and he was away from 1631 until his death in 1655.[17] The chapter, which was the highest catholic authority in England during the bishop's absence, was divided between two factions.[18] Different orders of catholic priests came into conflict with each other and with the secular clergy.[19] As P.R. Newman pointed out, 'the only uniformity of interest which the Catholic community possessed, cutting across social divisions, was that which the pamphleteers imposed upon it'.[20] Hostility

---

[10]   Barbara Donagan, *War in England 1642–1649* (Oxford, 2008), pp. 208–9; Mark Stoyle, *Soldiers and Strangers: An Ethnic History of the English Civil War* (New Haven, 2005), p. 67.

[11]   Mary Leys, *Catholics in England, 1559–1829: A Social History* (London, 1961), pp. 35–6.

[12]   Ibid., 36, 78.

[13]   Dolan, *Whores of Babylon*, 1, 3.

[14]   Lake, 'Anti-Popery', 183.

[15]   Leys, *Catholics in England*, 44, 67–9, 74, 83, 85; Dolan, *Whores of Babylon*, 50.

[16]   Sally Anne Jordan, 'Catholic Identity, Ideology and Culture: The Thames Valley Catholic Gentry from the Restoration to the Relief Acts' (PhD, Reading University, 2002), p. 10.

[17]   Leys, *Catholics in England*, 70, 80.

[18]   Tutino, 'Catholic Church', 234, 248.

[19]   Ibid., 234; Leys, *Catholics in England*, 69–70, 80.

[20]   Peter Newman, 'Roman Catholic Royalists: Papist Commanders under Charles I and Charles II, 1642–1660', *Recusant History*, 15 (1981): 399.

to catholics drove them underground and made them harder to discover, reinforcing the image of a hidden enemy. The bishop and his chapter could find it difficult to know who their own priests were.[21] Even the priests themselves could lose their distinctive identities, since they had to disguise themselves to avoid capture and often took on roles as stewards or tutors in elite households.[22]

Catholics could also be partly defined in relation to the Church of England. If they were convicted for failing to attend services and take communion they were labelled as 'recusants', but this could also cover protestant nonconformists, and perhaps even atheists.[23] Some people were identified as 'church papists', because they occasionally attended Church of England services and rejected the authority of foreign powers but were still suspected of preferring catholic doctrine and ceremonies.[24] The law of recusancy was 'more about public observance than private belief' and only captured a subset of the people who practised catholicism; 'Both laws and polemic struggled to identify and vilify Catholics. But neither succeeded in drawing an indisputable or uncrossable line between Catholics and everyone else.'[25]

Oaths were regularly used to identify and control catholics. This method took advantage of the fact that catholic faith depended on a relationship between an individual's conscience and external structures. Oaths were constructed to conflict with well-known points of doctrine which catholics were required by their church and conscience to defend. The oath of supremacy required swearers to deny that the Pope or any other foreign power had jurisdiction in England. When catholics were tried in court, and therefore already sworn to tell the truth, they could be forced to incriminate themselves by the 'bloody question': would they fight against the Pope if he invaded England? In 1606 a new oath of loyalty rejected the Pope's power to excommunicate a ruler and required reporting of any conspiracies. The power of this oath was only increased when a papal bull banned catholics from taking it. At the same time, a new law made it compulsory to take communion in the Church of England at least once per year, forcing church papists to conform or become recusants.[26] Just like puritans, catholics had to bend their individual will to the will of God. In this period, faith was rarely represented as the spontaneous expression of a pre-existing authentic self. Because religion was defined in external terms as much as by inward conviction, anti-catholic oaths could partly overcome the problem of not knowing other

---

[21]   Leys, *Catholics in England*, 80.
[22]   Dolan, *Whores of Babylon*, 87–8.
[23]   Ibid., 19.
[24]   Leys, *Catholics in England*, 6–7; Dolan, *Whores of Babylon*, 19.
[25]   Dolan, *Whores of Babylon*, 5, 19.
[26]   Leys, *Catholics in England*, 16, 42, 59.

minds. Refusing an oath could be interpreted as an outward sign of a catholic conscience, while taking an oath could impose obedience. This effect was weakened in practice because catholic casuistry could sometimes justify mental reservations.[27] An ordinance of Parliament passed in August 1643 claimed the property of anyone who refused the following oath, denying both catholic doctrine and mental reservations:

> I A. B. Do abjure and renounce the Popes Supremacy and Authority over the Catholick Church in General, and over my self in Particular; And I do believe that there is not any Transubstantiation in the Sacrament of the Lords Supper, or in the Elements of Bread and Wine after Consecration thereof, by any Person whatsoever; And I do also believe, that there is not any Purgatory, Or that the consecrated Hoast, Crucifixes, or Images, ought to be worshipped, or that any worship is due unto any of them; And I also believe that Salvation cannot be Merited by Works, and all Doctrines in affirmation of the said Points; I do abjure and renounce, without any Equivocation, Mental Reservation, or secret Evasion whatsoever, taking the words by me spoken, according to the common and usual meaning of them. So help me God.[28]

Manipulating catholics in this way required and acknowledged that they must have a conscience, but some protestant propaganda insisted that they did not. James VI and I wrote of Jesuits that 'their consciences must ever be commanded and overruled by their Romish god', admitting that internal feelings and motivation could be influenced from outside even if this was a bad thing.[29]

Anti-popery was about an imagined enemy as much as, or more than, about real people.[30] The vague idea of a popish plot was convenient precisely because it did not focus on specific individuals.[31] In practice, protestants had often treated their catholic neighbours and relatives kindly and helped to protect them from harsh laws. English catholics themselves did not necessarily define themselves in opposition to the established order. They often insisted that they were English as much as catholic and that they were not enemies of the monarch. Catholic plots were sometimes represented as mistakes which would have bad consequences for the majority of catholics who were not involved.[32] Rather than dispelling

---

[27]   Edward Vallance, *Revolutionary England and the National Covenant: State Oaths, Protestantism and the Political Nation, 1553–1682* (Woodbridge, 2005), p. 103.

[28]   *A & O*, vol. 1, 255–6.

[29]   Dolan, *Whores of Babylon*, 16, 77, 85.

[30]   Ibid., 3.

[31]   Lake, 'Anti-Popery', 199.

[32]   Leys, *Catholics in England*, 36, 38–9, 56, 61–3, 78; Donagan, *War in England*, 199; Andrew J. Hopper, '"The Popish Army of the North": Anti-Catholicism and Parliamentarian

stereotypes and prejudice, the familiarity and Englishness of local catholics fed the idea of a threatening enemy within, provoking more polemic and harsher laws.[33] The outbreak of the British Civil Wars posed serious problems for English catholics. They had a tradition of offering to serve the monarchy to signify loyalty and prove that they were not traitors, but in the new context of the First Civil War this would reinforce Parliament's prejudice that they were dangerous traitors.[34] English catholics had subscribed money to help Charles I fight the Scots in 1639.[35] While this only brought in £14,000, which was trivial compared to the cost of the war and the sums later raised by the Propositions, it probably helped to confirm suspicions that the King was being manipulated by a popish plot.

Ultimately, catholic identities were never stable or easy to define. Even the narrow legal status of 'recusant' was contingent, since conforming to the Church of England would remove it and the legal disabilities which went with it and restore confiscated property. Anti-catholic polemicists had to deal with the problem that protestants could just as easily convert to catholicism. This was represented as a particular danger to women, whose feelings were supposed to be more easily influenced: 'the Emissaries of Rome ... steale away the hearts of the weaker sort', wrote John Gee in 1624.[36] Religion was not a fixed essence.

Naming

The generalizations and stereotypes of popish plot rhetoric were useful for inciting people to help Parliament, but less useful for dealing with real enemies. It was an awkward fact that many of these enemies were protestant.[37] Parliament needed words to describe them before it could define them and take action against them. The proceedings of both houses provide a large body of text which can be mined to produce statistical evidence of the vocabulary used to describe enemies and friends. It is important to note that this vocabulary is specific to the formal language of the Lords and Commons journals. These sources do not

---

Allegiance in Civil War Yorkshire, 1642–46', *Recusant History*, 25/1 (2000): 22–3; Dolan, *Whores of Babylon*, 5, 32; Peter Newman, 'Roman Catholics in Pre-Civil War England: The Problem of Definition', *Recusant History*, 15 (1979): 149.

[33]   Dolan, *Whores of Babylon*, 1–2, 5, 32, 34–5.

[34]   Leys, *Catholics in England*, 36, 41; Newman, 'Roman Catholic Royalists: Papist Commanders Under Charles I and Charles II, 1642–1660', 399.

[35]   Leys, *Catholics in England*, 84.

[36]   Dolan, *Whores of Babylon*, 41, 73, 90.

[37]   Rachel Weil, 'Thinking About Allegiance in the English Civil War', *History Workshop Journal*, 61/1 (2006): 184.

contain the full text of speeches and debates and so cannot be used to make claims about the words used by individual members. It will also be obvious that fast sermons and other printed propaganda used very different language, even if they were approved or encouraged by Parliament. Despite these limitations, the results of this analysis are important because they are very much about what Parliament did and how it officially classified people. Table 2.1 shows counts of words which could be used as nouns or adjectives to describe people who were for or against Parliament, taken from the Lords and Commons journals covering the period November 1640 to December 1646.

Table 2.1   Word counts in *Lords Journal and Commons Journal*, November 1640 to December 1646

Enemy words	Count	Friendly words	Count
delinquent	2,900	protestant	900
enemy	1,700	well-affected	600
papist	1,300	friend	500
rebel	1,200	godly	400
malignant	500	loyal	200
ill-affected	400	honest	100
traitor	300	–	–
Jesuit	100	–	–
cavalier	100	–	–
Catholic	100	–	–
Total	8,600		2,700

Note: Variant forms and spellings are included for each word. All totals are rounded to the nearest hundred.

Sources: *Commons Journal*, vols 2–4; *Lords Journal*, vols 4–8.

The most striking thing about the word counts is that there is a much greater variety and frequency of words for enemies than of words for friends. This seems to be a clear case of Othering: 'they' are different and need to be labelled, but 'we' are 'just normal'. There is not always such a large disparity between words which are definite opposites. 'Well-affected' is significantly more common than 'ill-affected', while 'protestant' and 'godly' together equal 'papist' and are not far behind if 'catholic' and 'Jesuit' are added. But 'enemy' outnumbers 'friend' by more than three times. The greatest imbalance is caused by 'delinquent', which is by far the most common enemy word and has no obvious opposite. In addition to this, there are just over 1,100 occurrences of the noun 'delinquency', and this is not matched by similar forms of other words, such as 'malignancy', which is negligible. Only 'treason' and 'treachery' are comparable, making 800 together. The figures clearly demonstrate the problem of dealing with a new protestant enemy. Less than a quarter of the negative words explicitly refer to catholics; and even allowing for the probability that many occurrences of 'rebel' are collocated with 'Irish', the total must still be less than a third.

The word 'party' was sometimes used to describe groups, but much less frequently than the words in the table. It was mostly collocated with neutral words such as 'the', 'that' or 'a'. The only negative word which comes before 'party' more than 50 times is 'malignant' at 111, but the most frequent positive word is 'well-affected', which occurs only 26 times. Again this seems to be a case of Othering: parties were more often represented as bad than good and very rarely referred to in the first person. 'Our party' occurs only five times, as do 'parliament party' and 'parliament's party', averaging less than once per year.

Words for neutrals have not been included in the table because they appear so infrequently that they would all round down to zero: 'neuter', 'neuters', 'neutral' and 'neutrals' only have 12 appearances between them. This is surprising, because the uncommitted majority were certainly a cause for concern. Stephen Marshall used the word 'neuter' very heavily in his sermons, emphasizing its negative connotations. Perhaps it is because Parliament tended to describe these people in more roundabout ways, but this reluctance to name them could still be significant. Even 'non-contributor' and 'not-contributor' are exceptionally rare. The existence of many people who were not active for either side was a problem for the parliamentary war effort. Sometimes they were treated as enemies and sometimes as friends, but they were not always clearly defined.

The word 'royalist' is very uncommon at 15 occurrences, and 'parliamentarian' is not found at all. While it is certainly not the case that we can or should only discuss the 1640s using words which were available at the time, these statistics should at least make us think about why 'royalist' and 'parliamentarian' have become so dominant in modern historiography and what we have gained or lost by using them more than other possible words. The name and image of the cavalier were clearly very widespread in popular print and speech at the time but largely absent from the formal language of Parliament. The word was used sometimes in the internal business of Parliament, but seems to have been more frequent in ordinances which were intended to be published. The Propositions Ordinance made 'some whereof, under the Name of Cavaliers' the worst kind of the 'several Sorts of malignant Men' who were allegedly about to destroy religion, law and liberty.[38] The relative infrequency of 'Jesuit' is probably a realistic reflection of the order's small numbers compared to secular priests and lay catholics, but is perhaps surprising considering their prominence in supposed popish plots. Again, this may be a word which was used more when addressing the public than in routine proceedings. It is probably not surprising that 'roundhead' was not used much in this context, appearing only 12 times in all variants, nine of them in 1642 and none earlier. These are all reports of scandalous speeches or pamphlets, and all but one were dealt with by the Lords.[39] While middling Londoners were able to reclaim the term, it was perhaps too insulting for peers and gentlemen to tolerate.

Parliament overwhelmingly preferred 'delinquent' to describe its enemies in the First Civil War. While it increasingly signified a new identity which was specific to the civil war in England, the word itself had a longer history. It had traditionally been used to denote an enemy of Parliament before it was conceivable that a parliament would fight a war against the King. The word was often used for people who were summoned to kneel before the bar of either house because they were accused of breaching parliamentary privilege or speaking scandalous words. For example, in April 1624 the Commons had a Dr Harrys 'brought to the Bar, kneeling, charged by Mr. Speaker with indiscreet Carriage about the Election of Blechingley, and with venting his Spleen in the Pulpit'.[40] In April 1628 Anthony Lamplugh was brought before the Lords as a delinquent for his 'unjust and scandalous Petition against the Lord Keeper and Bishop of Lincoln'.[41] The tradition seems to have been well established by 1614, when the *Commons Journal* noted Sir Thomas Hobby saying 'never any Man called to the Bar, as a Delinquent, but must kneel'.[42] From the start of the Long Parliament, many individuals were sent for and punished as delinquents. For example, on 10 November 1640 Sir William Beecher was summoned because he had breached privilege by searching the studies and pockets of the Earl of Warwick and Lord

---

[38]   *A & O*, vol. 1, 7. See Chapter 1 for a longer quotation.

[39]   *CJ*, vol. 2, 408; *LJ*, vol. 5, 220, 239, 241, 246, 302, 309; *LJ*, vol. 6, 24, 60; *LJ*, vol. 8, 88.

[40]   *CJ*, vol. 1, 695. Note the humoral connotations of 'venting his spleen'.

[41]   *LJ*, vol. 3, 742–3.

[42]   *CJ*, vol. 1, 488.

Brooke.[43] The Propositions Ordinance seems to have still used the word in this limited and technical sense when it alleged that 'His Majesty doth, with a high and forcible Hand, protect and keep away Delinquents, not permitting them to make their Appearance, to answer such Affronts and Injuries as have been by them offered unto the Parliament', although it implied that these delinquents were the same as the malignant men and cavaliers.[44] During the First Civil War, even parliamentary officers were sent for as delinquents if they were accused of breaching privilege (see Chapter 3). Therefore 'delinquent' was never completely synonymous with 'royalist' and was not a distinct or stable category. The term seems to have been extended to supporters of the King because they were enemies of both houses of Parliament. Before 1642 delinquents were usually named individuals, but during the war the term became a generalization and was closely associated with disarmament, sequestration and compounding (see below).

By the sixteenth century 'malignant' was being used in English as both a noun and an adjective to refer to evil people or, more specifically, people who rebelled against God, the established church or other authorities.[45] The journals of the Long Parliament first used it to refer to people in November 1641, when pardons were offered to Irish rebels 'the greatest Part whereof they conceive have been seduced upon false Grounds, by the cunning and subtle Practices of some of the most malignant Rebels, Enemies to this State, and to the Reformed Religion'.[46] Soon after this, the Grand Remonstrance blamed England's troubles on 'the malignant party'.[47] The word continued to be used mostly as an adjective to describe a group, but on 27 January 1642 the Commons voted that the Duke of Richmond was 'one of the malignant Party, and an ill Counsellor unto his Majesty'.[48] In August the Lords referred back to this vote, citing the fact that Richmond was 'a Person voted to be a Malignant' as a reason why his brother-in-law, the Earl of Portland, should no longer be in charge of the Isle of Wight.[49] Richmond was probably the first individual to be labelled as 'a malignant' by the Long Parliament. The first occurrence of the plural noun 'malignants' is in a petition from Kent read in the Commons on 30 August 1642, which referred

---

43 *LJ*, vol. 4, 86.

44 *A & O*, vol. 1, 6–7.

45 *OED*, sv 'malignant', A1a, A2, A4a, B1a.

46 *LJ*, vol. 4, 422.

47 Samuel Rawson Gardiner, *The Constitutional Documents of the Puritan Revolution 1625–1660* (Oxford, 1899), p. 224.

48 *CJ*, vol. 2, 400.

49 *LJ*, vol. 5, 261; Sean Kelsey, 'Weston, Jerome, second earl of Portland (1605–1663)', *ODNB*; David L. Smith, 'Stuart, James, fourth duke of Lennox and first duke of Richmond (1612–1655)', *ODNB*.

to 'an ill-affected Party of Malignants and Cavaliers'.[50] On 18 October 1642 the Committee of Safety drafted a letter which described the King's army as 'Papists, and all Sorts of Malignants', making a distinction between catholic and protestant enemies.[51] From late 1642 'malignant' was being used increasingly often as a singular noun to label a specific person, but this was still relatively rare.[52] The string 'a malignant' occurs fewer than 50 times in total in the Journals from 1640 to 1646.

'Malignant' and 'delinquent' are both derived from participles of Latin verbs, stressing action rather than an underlying essence. The only enemy term which privileges feelings is 'ill-affected', and this is much less common. Although 'well-affected' is near the top of friendly words and is more common than 'ill-affected', it is only slightly ahead of 'malignant' and a long way behind 'delinquent'. Even when feelings were mentioned, they often tended to be linked to actions rather than represented as important in their own right. For example, the Kent petition asked the Commons 'to empower us with such a Proportion of Ammunition and Arms, to be magazined in these Parts, whereby we may be enabled to manifest our Affections and Obedience to the Command of King and Parliament'.[53] Without external help to provide arms, the petitioners would be unable to act, and their affection would be useless. While feelings seem to have been slightly more important for friends of Parliament, enemies were largely defined by what they had done. These definitions were related to specific actions taken against them, which will be examined in the next section.

Property

Parliament's enemies could be killed in combat. Irish prisoners were routinely murdered after surrendering, and on at least one occasion this treatment was extended to female camp followers, but during the First Civil War it was very rare for English protestants to be executed without trial.[54] It was not unusual for delinquents to be imprisoned, but the most common penalties for supporting the royal war effort involved loss of some or all property.

---

[50]   *CJ*, vol. 2, 746.
[51]   *CJ*, vol. 2, 813.
[52]   *CJ*, vol. 2, 802, 867; *CJ*, vol. 3, 284.
[53]   *CJ*, vol. 2, 746.
[54]   Donagan, *War in England*, 206–9.

Disarmament

The King had already started raising cavalry before Parliament passed the Propositions Ordinance. On 14 May 1642 he made a proclamation summoning horsemen to appear at York on 20 May, ostensibly to form a 'bodyguard'.[55] Although this was partly an attempt to call out the trained band cavalry, it invited any other people to attend even if they had no militia obligation. Parliament found out about this proclamation almost immediately, probably in letters received from their committee at York, and tried to stop it. On 16 May the Lords and Commons appointed a committee 'to meet presently, to consider of some Way to prevent the Meeting of the Horse at Yorke on Friday next'.[56] The following day Parliament ordained that it was illegal for the militia or any other people, unless they were 'bound thereto by special Service', to obey the royal summons or take up arms for the King.[57] A further order on 27 May required sheriffs, justices of the peace and other officers of towns and counties within 150 miles of York to stop all arms and ammunition going towards the city, and apprehend all persons going with them.[58] In practice, horses seem to have been treated as arms. On 3 June the Commons were informed that a war horse had been stopped by the Mayor of Northampton, 'in Pursuance of an Order of the Lords and Commons, for stopping of all Ammunition, or warlike Preparations going to Yorke'.[59] This action did not depend on any particular label or identity being imposed on the owner. The focus was very much on the horse and where it was going. In another case, the identity of the owner was crucial for deciding whether horses should be detained. The Mayor of St Albans stopped seven horses and some wagons in early June, but these were released when it was discovered that they belonged to the Prince of Wales.[60] At this point Parliament was still avoiding treating the King and his children as enemies or traitors. Soon after this, horses were explicitly included with arms and ammunition. The Lords made a general order to stop them from going to York on 11 June and ordered it to be printed on 15 June.[61] Over the next two weeks more horses were apprehended in Tottenham, Enfield, Northampton and Greenwich.[62] An order of the Commons on 4 July extended searches to include money and plate as well as horses, saddles, weapons

---

[55]   *HMC*, Hodgkin, 97.
[56]   *LJ*, vol. 5, 67; *CJ*, vol. 2, 573–4.
[57]   *CJ*, vol. 2, 577.
[58]   *CJ*, vol. 2, 590.
[59]   *CJ*, vol. 2, 604.
[60]   *CJ*, vol. 2, 610, 611; *LJ*, vol. 5, 113.
[61]   *LJ*, vol. 5, 126, 135.
[62]   *CJ*, vol. 2, 636, 637, 646.

and ammunition.[63] Cromwell's seizure of the Cambridge University plate on 10 August fits with this policy and was not unusually aggressive or early.[64] Sir William Bronckerd was given special permission to take his coach and saddle horses to York, 'provided they be not Horses for the great Saddle', meaning not suitable for cavalry.[65] The King's appeals for help were clearly receiving a positive response as horses and arms were sent in from many different places. In August the problem became more difficult to deal with as York was no longer the only centre of resistance. The mayor of Arundel was given power to stop suspect persons, horses and supplies from going to Portsmouth.[66]

At this stage it was still usual for horses or inanimate objects to be detained because of what they could be used for and where they were said to be going. Even when owners were named in the proceedings of Parliament, they were strangely distanced from their property and not even treated as having committed an act. It was only vaguely implied that they had done or would do anything wrong. One unusual effect of this reticence was to allow the horses more identity and agency than might have been expected. In these cases the journals often made the horses the subjects of the active verb 'going' or 'went' rather than saying that they were being taken or sent. The horse stopped in Northampton on 3 June was 'going to Yorke to Captain Nevill there'; on 22 June the Commons heard that 14 horses 'went through Totnam-high-crosse last Night towards Yorke'; and on 30 June there was information 'concerning Twelve Horses of the Lord Mowbraie's, at Greenwich, ready to go to York'.[67] An apparent reluctance to name individual men effectively led to horses being blamed. This could be explained by divisions within Parliament. In May 1642 puritan militants were probably already preparing to put Stephen Marshall's words into action by coming to help the Lord against the mighty, but at the same time moderate members were trying to avoid polarization and confrontation. Official orders claimed that Parliament was trying to prevent a civil war which was blamed entirely on the King. This situation may have created pressure to avoid accusing and censuring specific individuals. Dolan has found a similar paradox in laws against sending children overseas to receive a catholic education, since focusing on the responsibility of fathers would undermine their patriarchal prerogative to control and educate their own dependants.[68]

---

[63] *CJ*, vol. 2, 649.
[64] Clive Holmes, *The Eastern Association in the English Civil War* (Cambridge, 2007), p. 54.
[65] *CJ*, vol. 2, 657.
[66] *CJ*, vol. 2, 721.
[67] *CJ*, vol. 2, 604, 636, 646.
[68] Dolan, *Whores of Babylon*, 144–6.

The prince's horses were an exception to the general rule. The first report of the incident in the *Commons Journal* mentioned 'the Words spoken by the Men that conducted those Horses as they passed through Harrow of the Hill'. The words are not recorded, but it seems likely that they disparaged Parliament and that the men were mentioned only because of what they were alleged to have said. Once it was agreed that the horses belonged to the prince and should not be detained, they were transformed into passive objects again as the Commons ordered that 'Mr. Armer shall have a Note under Mr. Speaker's Hand, to carry these Horses of the Prince, which are now stayed at St. Albans, to Yorke'.[69]

Sir John Lucas was the first man to be classed as a delinquent by Parliament specifically because he had tried to take horses and arms to the King. Before Lucas could set out on 22 August, his house was attacked by a mob from Colchester, possibly with the collusion of the mayor. As John Walter discovered, this action fits with the pattern of mayors and other local officials stopping horses and arms from going to the King, and so the claims of the rioters to be acting for Parliament must be taken seriously.[70] In this way, people who were too poor to afford horses could still influence horse supply. On 23 August the Commons received a report of the incident from the mayor of Colchester and resolved that the horses, arms, ammunition, money and plate seized should be inventoried and then sent to London.[71] A week later Lucas appeared before the Commons in person, having been 'sent for up, as a Delinquent, for making Provisions of Horse and Arms to be sent to the King, for Maintenance of a War against the Parliament, and the whole Kingdom, contrary to the Orders and Declarations of both Houses', and 'confessed, That he had Twelve Horses ready, with which he intended to attend his Majesty, for the Guard of his Person'.[72] The clergyman Thomas Newcomen was sent for as a delinquent at the same time, 'for the like Offence', and both were imprisoned. A committee which included radical extremist Henry Marten was then ordered to prepare an impeachment of Lucas, but nothing seems to have come of it. On 30 September the Commons voted by 53 to 36 that Lucas should be released on bail provided that he stayed in London.[73] It is not certain whether the treatment of Lucas was a symptom of the ascendancy of the militants in Parliament or whether events in Colchester helped to increase polarization. After this it became more common for suppliers of horses to be labelled delinquents. On 10 September Sir George Devereux

---

[69]   *CJ*, vol. 2, 610, 611.

[70]   John Walter, *Understanding Popular Violence in the English Revolution: The Colchester Plunderers* (Cambridge, 1999), pp. 14, 140, 282, 287, 307.

[71]   *CJ*, vol. 2, 732.

[72]   *CJ*, vol. 2, 743.

[73]   *CJ*, vol. 2, 788–9.

'was called in to the Bar, as a Delinquent: Being demanded, whether he sent any Horses to Coventry, did confess he sent Two to the King, when the King was there', for which he was sent to prison.[74] Soon after this, general orders were issued to take horses and arms from enemies of Parliament. On 27 September the Lincoln committee was told:

> You are hereby authorized and required to disarm all Popish Recusants, all the aforenamed Persons that have levied War against the King and Parliament, and to take from them all Tents, Waggons, Horses for Service, great Saddles, and all other Warlike Furniture whatsoever; and from all such other dangerous and ill-affected Persons, as well Clergymen as others, as have sent Monies, Horses, Arms, Ammunition, or Victuals, to the said Rebels, towards the Maintenance of the said Force raised in the said County or City, or have sent any Money, Arms, Ammunition, or Horses, to assist the Delinquents and malignant Party now about the King, or to any other Place, to be employed against the Parliament; and also all such as have testified their Disaffection to the Commonwealth, and Malice against the Proceedings of Parliament, by subscribing that insolent, seditious, and most scandalous Petition sent unto the House of Commons by the Sheriff of that County, a true Copy of which Petition, and of the Names subscribed, you shall receive unto it, under the Hand of the Clerk of the House of Commons; as also all such as have put the Commission of Array in Execution, adjudged illegal by both Houses of Parliament.[75]

This went a long way beyond named individuals who had been summoned before Parliament as delinquents or traitors. The committee was authorized to disarm anyone whom they judged to have met the criteria set out in the order. These criteria were mostly based on specific actions, while affections were secondary at best and collective identities were only vaguely defined. The 'popish recusants' were the biggest exception. The catholic traitor was already a well-established stereotype and was used to justify treating all catholics as potentially dangerous without further explanation. The need to include further categories of people forced Parliament to admit that not all enemies were catholic. Apart from the named rebels and traitors, who included Lord Willoughby of Eresby and several Lincolnshire gentlemen, these people were given a much less definite identity. People who had supplied the King's forces were described as 'dangerous and ill-affected', but were not the same as 'the said rebels' or 'the Delinquents and malignant Party now about the King'. Although their ill affections were mentioned, the danger that they posed and the things which they had done were

---

[74] *CJ*, vol. 2, 760.
[75] *LJ*, vol. 5, 375.

just as prominent. The disaffection and malice of the petitioners was taken more seriously. Parliament may have taken signing the petition as evidence of hostile intentions which suggested more dangerous actions in the future, or it could be that making exaggerated claims about motives was a way of delegitimizing the petition and representing it as more threatening and extreme than it actually was. Ultimately, all the different kinds of people identified in the order were to be subjected to the same process of disarmament. Meanwhile, it was usual for horses to be taken from people who were summoned as delinquents for any reason. The Commons sent for three men on 22 October 1642 because they were alleged to have discouraged the Buckinghamshire trained bands from their duty. The sheriff and deputy lieutenants were ordered to apprehend them and seize their horses and arms.[76] Parliament also issued more general orders for finding and taking enemy horses. On 1 December Richard Wright, linen draper, was given a general warrant to search for money, plate and horses 'in the Houses of all Papists and Malignants whatsoever' in London and Westminster.[77] In March 1643 Sir Michael Livesey was authorized to seize horses and arms from 'Papists, and other Malignants' in Kent.[78]

On 14 October the boundary between friends and enemies shifted drastically when the Commons resolved that people who had not contributed to the Propositions should be secured and disarmed. The resolution was followed by an order of the Lords and Commons to arrest ten named individuals from London 'as it appears by the Report from the Committee, they have not contributed as they ought, to the Charge of the Commonwealth, in this Time of imminent Necessity'.[79] During the next two weeks, the deputy lieutenants and committees of Norfolk, Surrey and Derbyshire were specifically authorized to disarm non-contributors, and the order was made general for all counties on 1 November.[80] These orders were not necessarily put into effect. The Norfolk committee voted to disarm delinquents but did nothing for months.[81] Meanwhile, several named men from London, Norfolk, Surrey, Kent and Sussex were sent for as delinquents or ordered to be imprisoned for not contributing.[82] In the summer of 1642, when Propositions contributions were satisfactory, Parliament largely ignored uncommitted people who were not active for either side. Stephen Marshall had condemned 'neuters' in *Meroz Cursed* but this had little influence

---

[76]   *CJ*, vol. 2, 819.
[77]   *CJ*, vol. 2, 870.
[78]   *CJ*, vol. 3, 10.
[79]   *CJ*, vol. 2, 808.
[80]   *CJ*, vol. 2, 813, 826; *LJ*, vol. 5, 428.
[81]   Holmes, *Eastern Association*, 60.
[82]   *CJ*, vol. 2, 819–21, 824, 829, 830.

on parliamentary policy before the autumn.[83] It was only in October that Parliament suddenly started treating neuters as enemies and subjecting them to the same punishment as people who had acted for the King. A different identity was imposed on people who had not necessarily changed their actions or opinions. The new measures strongly echoed Marshall's 'certaine rule, for it is Christs rule, he that is not with me, is against me'.[84]

Parliament started to retreat from this extreme position in late November by imposing the twentieth part assessment on non-contributors (see Chapter 5). This was not a sudden change, but the start of a long and messy process which further complicated the question of allegiance. Initially, the assessment only applied in and near London. Like the Propositions, it was extended to the counties in a gradual and haphazard way. Outside London, non-contributors were still treated as enemies. General instructions sent to the Sussex committee on 7 December 1642 included the order that 'You shall take away the Arms and Horses of such as shall refuse to contribute Horse, Men, or Arms, upon the Propositions.'[85] Orders like this increasingly conflated non-contributors with enemies. On 31 January 1643 the Lords ordered officers in Norwich to take horses, arms and ammunition from people who were

> Popish Recusants; or have not lent or given any Money, Plate, or Horse, upon the Propositions for the Defence of the King and Parliament; or such Clergymen or others, as have publicly preached or spoken reviling, scandalous, and reproachful Words against both or either Houses of Parliament, or the Proceedings thereof.[86]

The shibboleth oath imposed on the Eastern Association reinforced the perception and treatment of neutrals as enemies. Refusing the oath or the contributions that went with it was another offence which could lead to disarmament. In January 1643 the deputy lieutenants of Essex were ordered to take horses, arms and ammunition from 'such Persons in the County of Essex, as have refused to contribute upon the Propositions, to assist the Parliament; or that have refused to associate themselves'.[87] Lord Grey of Warke issued a warrant to disarm papists, malignants, non-contributors and oath refusers in

---

[83]   Stephen Marshall, *Meroz cursed, or, A sermon preached to the honourable House of Commons, at their late solemn fast, Febr. 23, 1641 by Stephen Marshall* .. (London, 1642), TT E.133[19], pp. 22–4.

[84]   Ibid., 23.

[85]   *LJ*, vol. 5, 480.

[86]   *LJ*, vol. 5, 583.

[87]   *CJ*, vol. 2, 942. Similar orders were to be sent to Norfolk, Suffolk and Cambridgeshire.

Norfolk on 1 March 1643.[88] Even in London and Middlesex the line between friends and enemies was not clear. Despite the twentieth part assessment, the Commons ordered the disarmament of non-contributors in the City and suburbs on 14 January 1643.[89] The confusion was partly resolved later in the year by the consistent application of the new fifth and twentieth assessment on non-contributors and by harsher measures against active enemies.

Sequestration

As the Civil War escalated, Parliament moved from disarming people labelled as delinquents to confiscating their whole estates, including land and credit, in a process called sequestration. Firth and Rait's compilation *Acts and Ordinances of the Interregnum* gives a false impression that this started suddenly in early 1643.[90] In fact the system had a longer and more complex history, and was not entirely unprecedented. In English law, forfeiture of property was a well-established principle. The estates of convicted traitors were usually confiscated by the crown. The third Earl of Essex had lost his inheritance when his father was found guilty of treason.[91] Catholics were subjected to loss of property under the law of praemunire.[92]

Before the outbreak of the civil wars, the verb 'to sequester' was already used to describe the confiscation of property or offices, particularly clerical livings.[93] It was in this sense that the verb was most commonly used in the early proceedings of the Long Parliament, often because clergymen complained that they had been unfairly deprived of their livings by Archbishop Laud. For example, on 30 November 1640 the Commons dealt with the case of a Mr Wilson, who 'hath been sequestred Four Years from his Living, worth Sixty Pounds per annum; only for not reading the Book for Recreations on the Lord's Day'.[94] 'Sequester' could also mean temporarily putting property into the custody of a third party until a dispute was settled.[95] In May 1641 the Lords read a petition of George Warner and ordered that 'in the mean Time, the Ship mentioned in the said Petition shall be sequestered into the Hands of the Lord Admiral, until the

[88]   BL, Add. 22619, fol. 29.
[89]   *CJ*, vol. 2, 927.
[90]   *A & O*, vol. 1, 106.
[91]   Vernon F. Snow, *Essex the Rebel: the Life of Robert Devereux, the Third Earl of Essex 1591–1646* (Lincoln, NE, 1970), pp. 16–17.
[92]   Leys, *Catholics in England*, 16, 22, 59; *OED*, sv 'praemunire', n. 2b.
[93]   *OED*, sv 'sequester', 2, 3a.
[94]   *CJ*, vol. 2, 39.
[95]   *OED*, sv 'sequester', 3b.

Cause be heard'.[96] Another traditional legal definition was 'to divert the income of a benefice to the payment of debts due from the incumbent, or for the purpose of making good dilapidations; to hold the income of a benefice during a vacancy for the benefit of the next incumbent'.[97] The Long Parliament used this procedure to give dispossessed clergymen support before their livings were formally returned to them. Lambert Osbaston had been deprived of his living, fined and subjected to corporal punishment by the courts of Star Chamber and High Commission. On 2 April 1641 the Lords ordered that his livings should be returned to him and 'the Profits of them, already sequestered unto his Use, by Order of this House, shall be restored, and delivered forthwith into his Hands'. When reporting on this case, the Committee for Petitions explicitly stated that 'in Truth, the one Court nor the other had or hath Power to sentence any Subject of this Realm out of his Freehold and Inheritance'. [98] Within two years Parliament and its executive committees were routinely sentencing subjects out of their inheritance without going through any court.

Although sequestration became one of Parliament's most arbitrary acts, the system grew incrementally from established precedents. In 1642 there were moves to confiscate the estates of specific individuals who had been impeached for treason. Lord Capel was an obvious target since he was one of the richest men in England and one of the nine lords impeached in June 1642 for joining the King at York.[99] Since these lords refused to return to Westminster to answer the charges against them, they were sentenced in their absence on 20 July 1642 to be banned from the House of Lords, lose their parliamentary privilege and be committed to the Tower. This was a surprisingly mild punishment considering that they were explicitly accused of breaching an order of Parliament 'That the King, seduced by wicked Counsel, intends to make War against the Parliament, and that whosoever served or assisted him in that War was adjudged a Traitor.'[100] There was apparently no question of sentencing them to death, and confiscation of property was not brought up until much later. It was only in late September that the Lords decided that Capel's estate should be sequestered 'so the Rents may not be employed against the Parliament' and should instead be 'employed for the Service of the Commonwealth'. This action was justified by 'the Readiness of the Lord Capell, to assist the Marquis Herts with his Rents in the West' rather than

---

[96]   *LJ*, vol. 4, 255.

[97]   *OED*, sv 'sequester', 3a.

[98]   *LJ*, vol. 4, 205.

[99]   Ronald Hutton, 'Capel, Arthur, first Baron Capel of Hadham (1604–1649)', *ODNB*; *LJ*, vol. 5, 141.

[100]   *LJ*, vol. 5, 223.

the existing conviction for deserting Parliament.[101] Soon after this, the Commons impeached the Earl of Lindsey, his son Lord Willoughby and four knights for high treason and resolved that their estates should be sequestered.[102] Since this resolution never became an order, and there is no mention of the issue in the *Lords Journal*, it can be assumed that no action was taken. Lindsey had already been declared a public enemy and sent for as a delinquent in early June, but this did not have any immediate implications for his property.[103] In February 1643 the Commons ordered that Sir Ralph Hopton's real and personal estate should be sequestered because he had invaded Devon 'in a hostile and rebellious Manner'.[104]

When Parliament started to consider general sequestration of its enemies in England in September 1642, catholics were the first targets. The Commons ordered a committee to look into 'Sequestring the Rents and Revenues of all Papists' on 13 September, but very little seems to have been done.[105] The threat of losing estates soon spread beyond catholics. The instructions for the Lincoln committee on 27 September included provision for using delinquents' estates to compensate people who had been driven out of their homes by the King's forces.[106] On 14 October the Commons resolved that 'the Fines, Rents, and Profits, of Archbishops, Bishops, Deans, Deans and Chapters, and of such notorious Delinquents, who have taken up Arms against the Parliament, or have been active in the Commission of Array, shall be sequestered for the Use and Service of the Commonwealth'.[107] This resolution was passed immediately after the resolution to secure and disarm people who had not contributed to the Propositions, suggesting a coherent plan to redraw the boundaries of allegiance. Although non-contributors were treated harshly, they would still be clearly distinguished from active delinquents, who were to be treated even worse. But this plan fell apart because the actions against non-contributors were immediately put into effect while sequestration of delinquents was not, effectively erasing the boundary between the two groups. The Lords agreed to the principle of general sequestration on the following day, but both houses referred the matter to a committee to decide on the details of implementation.[108] Very little seems to have been done for several weeks, despite repeated orders for

---

[101] *LJ*, vol. 5, 367; *CJ*, vol. 2, 785.

[102] *CJ*, vol. 2, 766, 787.

[103] *LJ*, vol. 5, 102–3; *CJ*, vol. 2, 615.

[104] *CJ*, vol. 2, 973–4.

[105] *CJ*, vol. 2, 763–4.

[106] *LJ*, vol. 5, 375.

[107] *CJ*, vol. 2, 808.

[108] *LJ*, vol. 5, 402; *CJ*, vol. 2, 808.

committees to consider the matter and bring in an ordinance.[109] A letter from Lord Fairfax, received by the Commons on 16 December, provoked a resolution that 'the Armies and Forces raised against the Parliament are for the Rooting out of the Protestant Religion, and the Protestants out of England; and for the Advancement, and Bringing in, of Popery'. Both houses then agreed to an order that the Committee for Advance of Money should arrest 'all Papists that are of Estate, or dangerous' in London and the suburbs, and sequester their estates.[110]

The question of sequestering protestants was still unresolved. The issue was raised again in the Commons on 21 December with yet another request to bring in an order 'to enable the Committees and Assessors in the several Counties to seize the Rents and Profits of such Persons as are in the King's Army, or have contributed either Horse, Money, or Plate, to this unnatural War'.[111] The order was read the next day but referred back to a committee again.[112] Ungodly clergymen were an easier target than gentlemen. The Lords moved to sequester the livings of ministers who had joined the King so that they could be used to compensate Godly ministers who had been plundered by the King's forces, resulting in many orders for sequestration of specific parishes in early 1643.[113] Meanwhile, general sequestration of delinquents fell off the agenda until 2 February 1643, when Henry Marten and others were appointed to a committee 'to consider of the Sequestring and Seizing the Estates, real and personal, of all such Persons as have been, are, or shall be, in actual War or Arms against the Parliament'.[114] It was difficult to get agreement because attacking property rights was very controversial.[115] An ordinance was read in the Commons on 7 March and avoided being recommitted by only 51 votes to 42.[116] Sir Simonds D'Ewes described it as 'that most unjust and illegall Ordinance which had passed the howse in an afternoone when many were gone out and expected no busines of weight', and he 'spake very freely and shewed the injustice and illegalitie of it'.[117] The ordinance was sent up by the Commons on 15 March, but the Lords did nothing with it for some time.[118] It appears that a majority of peers assented only when they received news that the King was sequestering the estates of people

---

[109]   *CJ*, vol. 2, 813, 830–31, 852, 856, 876.
[110]   *CJ*, vol. 2, 891, 892; *LJ*, vol. 5, 496.
[111]   *CJ*, vol. 2, 898.
[112]   *CJ*, vol. 2, 899.
[113]   *LJ*, vol. 5, 510.
[114]   *CJ*, vol. 2, 953.
[115]   Holmes, *Why*, 88.
[116]   *CJ*, vol. 2, 993.
[117]   BL, Harleian 164, fol. 330r.
[118]   *CJ*, vol. 3, 1.

who supported Parliament.[119] The sequestration ordinance, passed on 27 March 1643, began by naming several bishops but went on to include in its definition of delinquents:

> all other person and persons, Ecclesiasticall or Temporall as have raised or shall raise Arms against the Parliament or have been, are or shall be in actuall warre against the same; or have voluntarily contributed, or shall voluntarily contribute not being under the power of any part of the Kings Army at the time of such contributing, any Money, Horse, Plate, Arms, Munition, or other Ayd or Assistance, for, or towards the maintenance of any forces raised against the Parliament, or for the opposing of any force or power raised by authority of both Houses of Parliament; or for the robbing spoyling plundering, or destroying of any of the Kings Subjects, who have willingly contributed or yeilded obedience to the Commands of both Houses of Parliament; and of all such as have joyned or shall joyn in any Oath, or Act of Association against the Parliament; or have imposed, or shall impose any Taxe or assessment upon His Majesties Subjects, for or towards the maintenance of any forces against the Parliament; or have, or shall use any force, or power to levy the same, shall be forthwith seized and sequestred into the hands of the Sequestrators, and Committees hereafter in this Ordinance named; and of such other persons as shall at any other time hereafter be appointed and nominated by both Houses of Parliament ...[120]

Sequestrators were appointed in every county to take the whole estates of anyone who met these criteria, and two thirds of the estates of 'all and every Papist', even if they had done nothing for the King. This delegated the identification of delinquents to county level, confirming a new definition which did not depend on being summoned before Parliament. The sequestration of an estate had repercussions for many people besides the owner because the state required rents and debts to be paid to the sequestrators. Therefore tenants and debtors were forced to choose sides. This could be much more contentious and traumatic than paying taxes to the state because obeying Parliament might mean betraying a friend, but it may also have provided a way to take revenge on an unpopular landlord. Classifying an individual as a delinquent affected their whole credit network. Captain William Pease was sued by his landlord John Castle, who had been sequestered for delinquency, for paying rent to the state.[121] The law of coverture further complicated the effects of sequestration. Before the outbreak

---

[119]   *LJ*, vol. 5, 669; *CJ*, vol. 3, 20–21.

[120]   *A & O*, vol. 1, 106–7. The ecclesiastical 'persons' could only have been men, since women were excluded from the clergy.

[121]   TNA: PRO, SP 24/69, part 3, Pease vs Castle; Ian Gentles, *The New Model Army in England, Ireland and Scotland, 1645–1653* (Oxford, 1992), p. 128.

of the civil war, Lodwicke Middleton borrowed £25 from Jane Thomas, who at that time was a spinster. In 1643 she married John Evans, who then took up arms for the King and was sequestered by Parliament. Ownership of the debt passed to John Evans by marriage and then to the state by sequestration.[122]

The criteria for sequestration were expanded in subsequent ordinances.[123] An additional ordinance in August 1643 added strict new measures to identify catholics, and extended the status of delinquent to:

> all such as voluntarily absenting themselves from the usual places of their abodes, or dwellings, Trade, Offices, or Imployments, and have gone, or shall go to any of the Kings Armies, or other Forces raised without consent of both Houses of Parliament, and have there continued, or shall there continue, and shall not within ten daies after Seizure or Sequestration of their several Goods or Estates, stay made of their Rents or by force of the said Ordinance (which said Sequestrators are hereby required to do) shew sufficient cause to be allowed by the Committee of the County, City, or Place, in which the said Seizure or Sequestration, or stay of Rents, is, or shall be made, of such their absence, going, and continuing in any of the said Armies or Forces: And all such as shall fraudulently imbezle, conceal, or convey away, all, or any part of their Goods, Money, or Estates, without valuable consideration, or not bona fide thereby preventing or avoiding the payment of any taxes or assessments laid upon them by any Ordinance of both Houses of Parliament, or any distress or seizure in case of non-payment thereof; or that after any such Tax or Assessment laid on them, convey themselves away, or refuse to be spoken with, whereby any Tax or Assessment laid upon them by Ordinance of both Houses of Parliament cannot be executed upon them or their Estates, according to the true meaning and purport thereof: Or that wittingly or willingly conceal or harbour any Goods or persons of Delinquents, within this or the said former Ordinance, or that have had any hand in the late horrid and desperate Conspiracy and Treason of Waller, Tompkins, Challinor, and their Confederates, whether they be already, or hereafter shall be Convicted to be privy or consenting thereunto (except such as being not yet convicted, shall discover and Confess all that they know thereof, within the time limited by both Houses of Parliament, to such Person or Persons as are or shall be appointed to take such discoveries and confessions) or that shall sue or molest any Person or Persons who shall have yielded obedience or conformity unto the Orders, Ordinances, or Commands of both Houses of Parliament, or have been, or shall be imployed by authority of both the said Houses, for, or by reason of any thing done, or to be done, in execution or performance thereof,

---

[122] TNA: PRO, SP 24/64, part 1, Middleton vs Evans.

[123] John Morrill, *Revolt in the Provinces: The People of England and the Tragedies of War, 1630–1648* (London, 1998), p. 92.

or that have willingly harboured any Popish Priests or Jesuits in their houses or dwellings since the 29 of November 1642. or that shall hereafter so harbour any ...[124]

Given such a wide range of qualifying actions, married women could easily have met the criteria for delinquency, but if they were under coverture with no separate estate then they could not be sequestered because they did not legally own any property.[125] This paradox had already made it difficult to punish catholic wives for recusancy. Although treating fines as debts or punishing husbands who did not make their wives conform were partially successful remedies, the paradox could not be fully resolved without undermining the law of coverture.[126] Erickson has pointed out that when a woman got married it was usual for her to suffer the same loss of property rights inflicted on male traitors and delinquents.[127] The August ordinance allowed part of sequestered estates to be kept for maintenance of wives and children, representing married women entirely as passive dependants and denying them any agency. For men, confiscation of their estates had symbolic as well as practical implications because removing their financial independence undermined their masculinity. Gentry honour was very closely connected with inherited land. Gentlemen were prepared to fight feuds over pieces of land which had little economic value in order to maintain their honour.[128] This was probably one of the reasons why gentlemen who supported Parliament were reluctant to sequester their neighbours and relatives.[129]

Sequestration was not a significant source of remounts for parliamentary armies. The existing powers to disarm delinquents already covered horses, so the confiscation of whole estates did not provide a new supply. Relatively few inventories of sequestered goods have survived, and they cover a disparate range of dates and places. This makes it difficult to judge the immediate impact of the March 1643 ordinance, but the surviving documents give the impression that horses fit for military use had already gone by the time the inventory was taken. In May 1643 the goods of Sir Philip Musgrave and Lady Wotton were valued at £308. This included cows, sheep, bees and deer in the park, but the only horses were two mares and four colts, valued at £11 together.[130] The colts

---

[124]   *A & O*, vol. 1, 254–5.

[125]   Amy Louise Erickson, *Women and Property in Early Modern England* (London, 1995), pp. 24–6, 100, 103–7.

[126]   Dolan, *Whores of Babylon*, 60–66, 68–9.

[127]   Erickson, *Women and Property*, 229.

[128]   Daniel C. Beaver, *Hunting and the Politics of Violence before the English Civil War* (Cambridge, 2008), pp. 37–8.

[129]   Holmes, *Why*, 88.

[130]   TNA: PRO, SP 28/217A, part 1, fols 106–7.

were probably too young for useful work, and the average value of less than £2 suggests that these were not good-quality horses. Thomas Andert of Lancashire had £124, 14s of personal estate taken in September 1643, including 25 cows and calves, 45 sheep and various carts and ploughs. His horses were listed as a colt, an old mare and a horse worth £6 together, and another horse jointly valued with a cow and a bull at £4, 6s, 8d.[131] Again these were low-value horses, some of which were too old or young. The inventory of Dr Samuell Hinton's property mentioned a stable, but there were no horses in it.[132] Goods of Sir Edward Sydenham valued in July 1643 included a coach and harness without any horses.[133] Hundreds of sheep were seized from Sir Thomas Cave in May 1645, but only five horses, with an average value of £3.[134] There were still eight horses left on the estate of Edmund Chamberlaine at Stratton Audley in 1646, but one was lame, one was old and another was blind. Their average value was just over £2.[135] Many other inventories show no trace of horses. Supplying horses to the King was one of many acts which could make a person into a delinquent, and horses were among the easiest possessions to move if the owner's property was under threat. For example, Cornet Thomas Gwyn alleged that 'Mr Richard Jones of Glastree in [th]e County of Radnor (a Delinqu[en]t) had convayed away a Horse to a freind, to p[re]serve him from sequestrac[i]on'.[136] For these reasons, it would not be surprising if there were no valuable horses left by the time an estate was sequestered. Any serviceable horses which had not been removed could have been seized under the old disarmament powers as soon as the owner was labelled a delinquent.

Compounding

Eventually, Parliament developed a new system for raising revenue from delinquents in which sequestration could be removed in return for a fine of a fraction of the value of the estate. The Goldsmiths Hall committee, which had been set up in September 1643 to raise money for the Scots army, first started compounding with delinquents in August 1644 and eventually developed into the Committee for Compounding. Like sequestration, the system expanded and took shape slowly. In August 1645, general rules were first set out specifying the proportion of the value of an estate which had to be paid in composition fines,

---

[131]   TNA: PRO, SP 28/217A, part 2, fol. 171r.
[132]   TNA: PRO, SP 28/217A, part 1, fol. 54v.
[133]   TNA: PRO, SP 28/217A, part 2, fol. 243.
[134]   TNA: PRO, SP 28/217A, part 2, fols 212v–213r.
[135]   TNA: PRO, SP 28/217A, part 2, fols 273–4.
[136]   TNA: PRO, SP 24/50, part 2, Gwyn vs Jones.

but this was changed several times, and there were different rates depending on the seriousness of delinquency and date of surrender. In June 1646 the Covenant and Negative Oath were made compulsory for compounders, but before this they had been optional, with the incentive of a lower fine for taking them.[137] The process began with the delinquent petitioning the committee with an admission of guilt and certifying the value of the estate.[138] Delinquents who were allowed to compound would inevitably have to pay a fine, but they could still contest the amount.

This system institutionalized changes of allegiance. In order to compound, people had to accept the identity of delinquent which had been imposed on them by the state and admit that they had acted against Parliament, but by paying their composition fines and taking the necessary oaths they were admitted to the well-affected and effectively stopped being delinquents. If they had previously chosen allegiance to the King they would have to give it up, since they were acting against him by compounding even if they did it with mental reservations. As Weil put it, compounding was 'a crossing of the boundary from disaffectedness into well-affectedness'. Despite this, Weil found surprisingly few conversion narratives in compounding petitions.[139] This observation is supported by cases relating to horses in the First Civil War. Some petitions presented changing sides as a positive action, hinting at a change of heart but making more of the practical effects of desertion. Henry Coker, of Maypowder in Dorset, confessed that he:

> served the kinge in this unhapie warr as a Col[one]l of Horse but above a yeare since beinge sensible of his Error, quitted his imploymente and wholy diserted that servis, w[hi]ch was an acceptable servis to the state his horse beinge in number above 400, not thirty of them Continewinge in arms a munth after ...[140]

Other petitioners distanced themselves from the King without claiming much affection for Parliament. William Lochard of Herefordshire admitted that:

> being unadvisedly misled did take upp Armes against the Parliam[en]t as an officer or Captaine of Horse, which yo[u]r petic[i]oner held but for some fewe monethes and p[er]ceaving his owne Error ever since for the space of three yeres and more hath

---

[137]   *CCC*, vol. 1, 5–24.

[138]   James Scott Wheeler, *The Making of a World Power: War and the Military Revolution in Seventeenth Century England* (Stroud, 1999), p. 107; Weil, 'Thinking About Allegiance', 185.

[139]   Weil, 'Thinking About Allegiance', 186–7.

[140]   TNA: PRO, SP 23/176, p. 395.

utterly forborne to meddle or be imployed in that kynde, and hath lived privately at
his own place of abode ...[141]

This presented his delinquency as a mistake which he soon regretted, and which
was supposed to be compensated for by deserting and then doing nothing for
years. Some officers explicitly claimed that they had laid down their commissions
because they objected to the presence of catholics in the King's army.[142]

It was very common for petitioners to allege that royal forces had compelled
them to act. As Weil pointed out, 'people obviously told the committee what
they thought it wanted to hear', and they had strong incentives to deny sincere
affection for the King's cause and plead unwillingness instead, not least because
the March 1643 sequestration ordinance applied to people who had supplied
the enemy only if they did it voluntarily while not under power of the King's
forces.[143] But we must also take seriously Morrill's argument that people who
did not willingly do anything could be classed as enemies because of what they
were forced to do or how they were perceived.[144] Therefore there is no way of
knowing if compounding narratives are true, and we cannot 'correct for bias'
by speculating about what compounders 'would have' done. As Weil suggested,
this does not have to be a problem. The committee could not know either: it
could get third-party evidence of actions but not of motives. John Harvey of
Somerset pleaded that he and three other men had only collected taxes for royal
forces 'against theire wills' under threat of imprisonment and torture.[145] Francis
Sherrington did not explicitly claim that he had been forced to provide a horse
and arms but subtly insinuated it by adding 'when the Earle of Darbie prevayled
in these parts'.[146] Robert Elcock, 'having had his habitac[i]on betweene the
twoe contrary garrisons of Nantwich and Beeston Castle & so under the power
of them both, & thereby inforced to some Contribuc[i]on on both sides & a
demeanour necessary for his p[re]servac[i]on', but apparently had no affection
for either.[147] He later served as a soldier at the siege of Chester, but even this fact
was not used as a display of affection for Parliament. Elcock's petition simply
stated what he had done and what was done to him, constructing the image of
a helpless victim alone in a hostile world. As well as denying his responsibility

---

[141]   TNA: PRO, SP 23/189, p. 70.
[142]   Newman, 'Roman Catholic Royalists: Papist Commanders Under Charles I and Charles
II, 1642–1660', 397.
[143]   Weil, 'Thinking About Allegiance', 185; A & O, vol. 1, 106.
[144]   Morrill, *Revolt in the Provinces*, 189.
[145]   TNA: PRO, SP 23/175, p. 99.
[146]   TNA: PRO, SP 23/194, p. 320.
[147]   TNA: PRO, SP 23/178, p. 848.

for alleged delinquency, he insinuated that Parliament had failed to protect him from the enemy garrison. It was not unusual for civilians to be taxed by two rival garrisons. Martyn Bennett has even found that some garrisons which were ostensibly on opposite sides colluded to avoid confrontation by arranging their tax collections for different days.[148] In this situation, the civilians effectively changed sides as often as twice a week.

We should not expect constancy to have been highly valued by a committee which managed, and raised money from, the process of changing sides. But as Weil found, at least a few compounders did try to present themselves as already or always well-affected, even if they had been forced to commit delinquent acts.[149] Timothy Turner pleaded that 'he hath bin ever well affected to the Parliam[en] t And was during the warres commonly famed in his countrey soe to be', but because he was surrounded by enemies 'he was by terror of them thrust out of his way w[hi]ch gave him occasion for the p[re]sent to adhere unto them for some tyme by maynteyning a horse & man armed for that service And is become a delinquent'.[150] This presented delinquency as a process of becoming rather than a state of being, and while it was motivated by emotion, this was fear rather than affection. He was apparently unable to list anything that he had done for Parliament and so brought in the actions of his family instead, mentioning that his son and one of his servants were killed fighting against the King and that he was related to the governor of Bridgnorth castle. The actions of servants could just as easily reflect badly on their master. Sir Thomas Bowyer of Sussex told the committee that he 'hath never sent any horse armes or money to [th]e King or any w[i]th [th]e King unless yt was when [th]e sheriffe at Chisester forces his servants to yt'.[151] Bowyer was unusual in stressing that he had come in 'out of his affection and reddiness to serve the p[ar]liament' rather than to gain the benefits of composition.

Even when constant affection was included in a petition, it was likely to be linked with actions. Mary Robinson, a Lincolnshire widow, wrote that she had 'given ample testimony of her good affecc[i]on to the Parliam[en]t, and hath bene willinge to serve the same w[i]th her estate from the begininge, by lendinge of money upon proposic[i]ons and contributinge according to the ordinance of the fift and Twentith p[ar]te and div[er]s other wayes'. Although she initially denied knowledge of any reason why she should be sequestered, she later confessed that she had provided her son with a horse and arms and sent

---

[148]   Martyn Bennett, 'Contribution and Assessment: Financial Exactions in the English Civil War, 1642–6', *War and Society*, 4/1 (1986): 8.
[149]   Weil, 'Thinking About Allegiance', 186–7.
[150]   TNA: PRO, SP 23/196, p. 254.
[151]   TNA: PRO, SP 23/70, p. 281.

him to join the royal army, 'beinge hartily sorry for this her offence'.[152] Women are relatively rare in compounding cases, probably because of the unequal distribution of property, but this case shows that widows who held property in their own right could act the same and be treated the same as men. John Bourne of Somerset began his petition with positive actions:

> being well affected to [th]e proceedings of [th]e Parliament did give unto Colonell Wroth the sum[m]e of 50li towards [th]e raysing of his regim[en]t of horse in [th]e said County and did likewise voluntarily furnish the County w[i]th two light horses men and armes and did all [th]e good offices hee could for [th]e preservac[i]on of [th]e well affected of [tha]t County', but 'being over awed by the potency of [th]e Enimy hee was constrayned to serve as a grand Jury man, but did never acte more then hee was by them inforced ...[153]

The claim to have been well-affected all along could not easily be tested. The committee received reports from county committees about what a person had done, but because they could be forced or insincere, actions were not a reliable guide to internal feelings. Sir Daniel De Ligne initially offered a brief petition, blandly stating that he 'never was in Armes ag[ains]t the Parlym[en]t but was sometymes in the kings Quarters w[hi]ch by reason of the power of [th]e Enemy then in those p[ar]ts hee could not avoid, For w[hi]ch cause and noe other yo[u]r petition[ers] Estate is sequestred'.[154] The Lincoln committee certified that De Ligne 'was as we then conceived a friend to the Parliament; w[hi]ch he manifested' by petitioning the King to return to Parliament and lending horses and money on the Propositions, but after this he had apparently changed sides, paying an allowance to his son in the King's army, living in enemy garrisons and contributing to their forces, and hiding from parliamentary forces.[155] Even after this betrayal, the committee apparently was not particularly hostile to turncoats and maintained that De Ligne had been sincere before his change of sides. The report acknowledged that the change had occurred with 'the Ennemy prevaileing in those p[ar]ts', meaning that his affections were still ambiguous. Was he forced to act this way as he claimed, did the change of military occupation allow him to reveal his true allegiance, or had his opinions changed? After being allowed to compound, De Ligne tried to get his fine reduced by submitting a very different petition to Parliament:

---

152 TNA: PRO, SP 23/184, pp. 916, 918.

153 TNA: PRO, SP 23/179, p. 613.

154 TNA: PRO, SP 23/184, p. 678.

155 TNA: PRO, SP 23/184, p. 687. One of the horses contributed is confirmed in TNA: PRO, SP 28/131, part 4, fol. 30v.

Sheweth That yo[u]r pet[itione]r being firmly principled in and abundantly satisfied
of the justnes of this cause, for w[hi]ch this honorable house so seasonably appeared,
did at first w[i]th others the Gentry of his Country petic[i]on the King at York for
his returne w[hi]ch proving fruitles he ingaged w[i]th them by his free and large
contribuc[i]on of Men Money Horses and Armes towardes their support and service,
never departing from his former groundes either in affec[i]on or Judgm[en]t.[156]

He continued to deny that he had voluntarily gone to the enemy and also stressed
that he had been sequestered by the King for contributing to Parliament, a fact
which is supported by a warrant dated 29 March 1643 ordering his rents to be
paid to royal officials.[157]

What is perhaps most surprising is that some petitioners who presented
themselves as unwilling victims of the King's forces did not try to claim that
they were well-affected to Parliament. John Pierce listed nothing more than a
balance sheet of actions (he had lived in the enemy's garrisons but then lent £55
on the Propositions), without saying anything at all about affections, motives or
compulsion.[158] While some people presented contributing horses or money on
the Propositions as evidence of affection, others did not, simply stating the fact
that they had done it. Sir Michael Wharton did not say why he had contributed
11 horses to Parliament, and only vaguely implied that it was voluntary by
pointing out that he did this before he was sequestered.[159] As Chapter 1
demonstrated, the date of a contribution has major implications for its possible
meanings, as pressure to subscribe increased at certain times. Although they
were made compulsory in October 1642, horse contributions were inadequate
by December, after which the system became largely irrelevant to military horse
supply and was supplemented or replaced by other methods. Despite this,
the Propositions had a fairly long afterlife. A trickle of horses continued until
at least July 1643, when the surviving accounts of the London commissaries
stop. The symbolic value of a contribution was partly related to how early it
had been given. John Harvey specified that he had 'at the beginninge of these
unnaturall warrs voluntarily contributed money and sent in a Musquiteer and
horse to assist the Parliam[en]t'.[160] There was not a simple opposition of valid
and invalid contributions based on an arbitrary cutoff date. Later contributions
could still count for something. Lindley Wren of Durham had served against
Parliament, but implied that this was unwilling because the Earl of Newcastle's

156   TNA: PRO, SP 23/80, p. 117.
157   TNA: PRO, SP 23/80, p. 118.
158   TNA: PRO, SP 23/180, p. 697.
159   TNA: PRO, SP 23/187, p. 310.
160   TNA: PRO, SP 23/175, p. 99.

forces 'threatned Ruine'. He changed sides in April 1643 and then 'willinglie gave 3 horses' to Parliament.[161] John Pierce mentioned lending £55 on the Propositions, but not until January 1645.[162]

Even not contributing enough to the Propositions could be spun into something positive. Joshua Nuttall 'haveing had an horse in service for the parliam[en]t and refusing to find another, being more then his estate wold beare hath been sequestred onely for voluntarily contributing to the forces raised against the parliam[en]t'.[163] William Thompson constructed a narrative of obedience to Parliament which was only interrupted by enemy force. He wrote that he

> was high Constable of the Hundred of Flaxwell, and executed the said office faithfully and truely for the service of the Parliam[en]t That he freely and voluntarily gave a horse upon the first Proposic[i]ons for the service of the Com[m]on wealth, paid his fifth and 20th p[ar]te & and was conformable to all Ordinances of Parliam[en]t untill about Mich[aelm]as last was Twelve moneth, at w[hi]ch tyme he was fetched out of his bedd and carryed Prisoner to Newarke by some of the Forces of that Garrison, and there he doth acknowledge that he inhabited and contributed money towards paym[en]t of the souldiers of that Garrison ...[164]

This stressed conformity and not affection. The value of contributing on the Propositions was partly undermined by the inclusion of the fifth and twentieth, which showed that his contribution was judged insufficient, but this still helped to give the impression of constant obedience.

It was not always in petitioners' interests to deny their actions. When garrisons or armies negotiated their surrender to parliamentary forces the concessions which they could gain included a guarantee of lower composition fines. This happened when Exeter surrendered to Sir Thomas Fairfax in April 1646.[165] Because Sebastian Isaac of Comb, Devon, claimed the benefit of the Exeter articles his fine was reduced from a sixth to a tenth of his estate, saving him £130.[166]

It was certainly no exaggeration for Weil to describe a compounding narrative as 'excruciatingly subtle', concluding that the petitioner's 'very lack of clarity was a strategy for keeping his options open'.[167] Many petitions can be read as carefully

[161]   TNA: PRO, SP 23/134, p. 325.
[162]   TNA: PRO, SP 23/180, p. 697.
[163]   TNA: PRO, SP 23/186, p. 327.
[164]   TNA: PRO, SP 23/206, p. 309.
[165]   Gentles, *New Model Army*, 84; Hopper, *Black Tom*, 181.
[166]   TNA: PRO, SP 23/184, pp. 554, 558, 560; *CCC*, vol. 2, 1332.
[167]   Weil, 'Thinking About Allegiance', 188.

constructed propaganda, designed to signify certain ideas and prime the committee to respond in certain ways while maintaining plausible deniability. The penitent, confused or evasive narratives offered to the Committee for Compounding contrast with the legends of Sir Francis Wortley drawing his sword or John Smith rescuing the standard at Edgehill, but are perhaps no less significant for the construction of allegiance.[168]

Conclusion

Even at their most arbitrary and widespread, measures for taking property from catholics and delinquents never provided enough resources to sustain the parliamentary war effort. Wheeler calculated that the central treasury received only around £112,000 from sequestration and compounding from 1643 to 1645, which was much less than tax revenues and not adequate to fund Parliament's armies.[169] Seizure of property also denied resources to the royal war effort, although the growing list of offences was likely to impose sequestration on many people who did not necessarily have any intention of helping the King. Funding the war depended on making the neutrals into friends rather than enemies. Sequestration played an important part in this process by defining collective identities and maintaining boundaries between groups. Defining people as delinquents was not just a means to get their property but also a way of setting them apart from the rest of society. Getting people behind Parliament required an Other against which the well-affected could be defined. Anti-popery already made a stereotypically foreign, effeminate and tyrannical scapegoat culturally available. The Long Parliament used this as much as possible, but also had to deal with the problem of protestant English enemies, leading to confused and unstable identities. The identity of 'papist' tended to be more essentialized than 'delinquent'. Popery was effectively treated as an underlying condition which could be discovered using oaths, but this was not quite a fixed essence or an authentic self. Discovering it depended on the relationship between conscience and external structures, and catholics often had the option of recanting to save themselves. Oaths were also used to discover protestant enemies, but with much less success because there were no points of religious or political doctrine which set all supporters of one side apart from all supporters of the other. Parliament's interpretation of the two bodies was probably rejected by anyone who supported

---

168 Andrew J. Hopper, 'The Wortley Park Poachers and the Outbreak of the English Civil War', *Northern History*, 44/2 (2007): 109; Peter Young, *Edgehill 1642: The Campaign and the Battle* (Kineton, 1967), pp. 284–5.

169 Wheeler, *World Power*, 108.

the King (whether they coherently argued against it or just did not understand it), but was not accepted by all MPs at Westminster.[170] Delinquents were defined by actions much more than by beliefs. By publishing these, definitions Parliament had to admit that it was not fighting solely against catholics. In practice, the boundaries were blurred because Parliament treated its protestant enemies like catholics and continued to use anti-popery for propaganda purposes. At the very least, protestant delinquents were insinuated to be helping a popish plot to eliminate the protestant religion. The identity of delinquent was also problematic because both qualifying offences and resulting punishments changed frequently, making it difficult to relate outward actions to an inner essence. Once imposed, delinquency was not a permanent state. Compounding was a formal process of making enemies into friends as well as raising money. Ultimately, anyone who refused to act as a supporter of Parliament was threatened with the loss of their estate. If the Watford petitioners and other early contributors to the Propositions were good examples, sequestered delinquents were horrible warnings.

---

[170] Rachel Foxley, 'Royalists and the New Model Army in 1647: Circumstance, Principle and Compromise', in Jason McElligott and David L. Smith (eds), *Royalists and Royalism During the English Civil Wars* (Cambridge, 2007), pp. 168–9. See Chapter 3 of the present book for Henry Marten's extremist disregard for the doctrine, and Chapter 5 for D'Ewes's moderate conservative opposition to taxation without royal assent.

Chapter 3

Seizure

The previous chapters have focused mostly on people who were active for the King or Parliament. As the war continued, horses were increasingly taken from anyone who had them. This tapped into the large number of horses owned by people who were not active for either side. The advantages of opening up a new source of supply were outweighed by the risk of antagonizing people who had not previously been actively opposed to Parliament. Arbitrary seizures also alienated many of Parliament's supporters. This may have been partly based on self-interest, but critics of the armies were also defending important principles of fairness, the rule of law and the security of individual property rights. These were the very things which Parliament claimed to be securing against a popish conspiracy. Sometimes requisitioning was authorized by ordinances of Parliament. These orders were controversial, leading to confrontations between and within the two houses. Often authority to seize horses came from generals rather than politicians, sometimes in defiance of the orders of Parliament. In practice, soldiers also took horses spontaneously in response to an immediate need without waiting for authorization. As well as conflict between military and civilians, there was competition between different armies for the same resources. The boundaries of allegiance became increasingly blurred.

Bard and Browne

On 15 November 1642 the House of Lords accepted an offer from the City of London to raise 1,000 cavalry and 3,000 dragoons. This force was

> to be under the Command of both the Houses of Parliament, or under the Command of the Earl of Essex the Lord General alone; and that, in their Proceedings, they shall not be countermanded, or called to an Account, by any but the Lord General the Earl of Essex, by the Advice of both Houses of Parliament [1]

---

[1] *LJ*, vol. 5, 446.

It appears that neither localism nor hostility to the Lord General were completely dominant at this time. Philip Skippon was recommended to command the force under Essex. Skippon's military experience was probably as significant as his strong links with London. Colonel John Urry, a Scots professional soldier from Essex's army, was to be second in command.[2] The soldiers were to be mounted on 'Horse seized, and to be seized ... by virtue of any Order or Ordinance of both or either House of Parliament'. Such an order passed the Lords later that day.[3] It authorized several named men, and any others appointed by them, to seize any horses which had not already been listed for the army within five miles of London. The order did not specify that horses were to be taken only from delinquents or non-contributors. Almost anyone was liable to have their horses requisitioned. The only exception was for members and assistants of either house of Parliament who were not delinquents. Repayment with interest would be promised to 'such Persons as shall be thought fit to receive Recompence', but the horses would not be returned to their owners unless five members of a parliamentary committee found cause. This was a major change in parliamentary policy on property rights. Parliament had already ordered the seizure of horses in the City and suburbs around the time of Edgehill, but the order stated that this was an emergency response to the expected approach of the King's army, and that the horses would be returned to their owners when the danger had passed.[4] Another order issued on 4 November empowered the deputy lieutenants of Bedfordshire to take horses only from 'such ill-affected Persons as they shall think fit', and even these people were to be promised repayment.[5] The order of 15 November had a much wider scope and did not guarantee repayment. It had first been proposed by the Commons on 10 November, when the King's army was approaching London, and was passed by the Lords two days after Turnham Green, by which time the royal army was retreating but still nearby.[6] The exception for members of either house was not in the first draft of the ordinance entered in the *Commons Journal* and was added later at the insistence of the Lords.[7] This compromise secured enough support for the order to pass both houses, but the implementation of the scheme proved very controversial. The unusually extreme terms of the order were perhaps a result of the atmosphere of imminent danger around the time of

---

[2]   Alan Turton, *Chief Strength of the Army: Cavalry in the Earl of Essex's Army* (Leigh-on-Sea, c. 1992), p. 66.

[3]   *LJ*, vol. 5, 447.

[4]   *LJ*, vol. 5, 416, 419, 420; *HMC*, 5th report, 55.

[5]   *CJ*, vol. 2, 834.

[6]   *CJ*, vol. 2, 843.

[7]   *CJ*, vol. 2, 851–2.

Turnham Green, but they remained in force after the crisis was over and caused many problems.

The commissaries empowered to take horses were named as Maximilian Bard, William Dodson, Nicholas Alvy, Robert Norwood, John Styles, William Booth, Thomas Mason, William Barton, Mr Williamson, Thomas Flanner, Thomas Browne, Richard Overton, George Day, John Hinde, Daniel Waldo, Walter Story and Mr Harsnett. Many of these men had previously signed radical petitions.[8] Styles and Booth were probably the horse dealers of the same name.[9] Their expertise would be useful in finding and valuing horses. It could also be suspected that they benefited by protecting their own stock from seizure. Styles was certainly active, since he was summoned to answer a complaint about horse seizure on 21 December.[10] In practice, the most prominent of the group appear to have been Bard and Browne. Maximilian Bard had been imprisoned by the Lords but the Commons successfully pressed for his release, 'because he is a Man so useful for this Employment, that they know not what to do without him'.[11] This suggests that there was already some hostility between Bard and the Lords. The commissaries were required to enter details of requisitioned horses in a book as the Propositions commissaries had done. The complete book has not survived, but there are several unidentified fragments of horse lists covering dates roughly consistent with the 15 November order.[12] These lists record a minimum of 700 horses.

The most definite records of the commissaries' activities are several complaints against them dealt with by Parliament. On 25 November 1642 the Commons ordered Browne to return two horses which he had taken from Sir Henry Cholmley and delivered to a Captain Boswell.[13] According to the powers granted by Parliament, the commissaries had the right to take Cholmley's horses even though he had lost another four horses at Edgehill, where he served as colonel of a foot regiment in Essex's army, but MPs apparently found this a reasonable cause to reverse Browne's decision. This incident raised an awkward point: the powers vested in Browne, Bard and the rest gave no special protection

---

[8]   Keith Lindley, *Popular Politics and Religion in Civil War London* (Brookfield VT, 1997), pp. 231, 432. The Richard Overton is not the future leveller.

[9]   Peter Edwards, *Dealing in Death: The Arms Trade and the British Civil Wars* (Stroud, 2000), p. 162.

[10]   *CJ*, vol. 2, 898.

[11]   *LJ*, vol. 5, 447.

[12]   TNA: PRO, SP 28/3A, part 2, fols 188–92; TNA: PRO, SP 28/5, fols 227–30, 256–7; TNA: PRO, SP 28/144, part 1, fols 40–54; TNA: PRO, SP 28/237, unfol.

[13]   *CJ*, vol. 2, 863. This was probably John Boswell, who was raising a cavalry troop by commission from the Earl of Warwick around this time: Turton, *Chief Strength*, 21.

to supporters who were not covered by parliamentary privilege, no matter how much or how early they had contributed to the war effort. Horse seizures risked antagonizing and impoverishing some of Parliament's most active supporters, and further discouraging people who had not contributed. There was also a danger of disrupting economic activity in and near London. The Commons reacted to this problem the same day by ordering the discharge of any horses that had not yet been sent to the army and which had been taken from 'Persons that have contributed in a considerable Proportion to the Parliament', and banning the seizure of horses carrying provisions.[14] This was not a permanent solution, because it did not prevent the taking of horses from Propositions contributors in the future. Concerns about seizure of horses from contributors were raised at a conference between the two houses on 1 December. John Glynne reported back to the Commons that 'several Complaints are made concerning the Seizing of Horses of Persons that have contributed to the Parliament: And desire that some Course may be taken to remove the Abuse: And that it might be considered what Number will serve the Turn.' The Commons ordered a committee to consider how many horses were needed for the army, but completely ignored the part about removing abuses.[15] On 5 December a Commons committee was appointed to investigate abuses in taking and disposing of horses, but their instructions were more concerned with theft of state horses by troopers than with protecting the rights of civilians.[16] Another order of 5 December extended the geographical scope of horse seizure at the same time as increasing protection for Propositions contributors. The county committees of Essex, Suffolk, Cambridgeshire, Hertfordshire, Bedfordshire, Huntingdon, Norfolk, Kent, Hampshire and Leicestershire were required to raise 2,000 troop horses and deliver them to Bard and Browne.[17] These horses were not to be taken from 'such Persons as have contributed upon the Propositions'. All carriers' horses and plough horses were also to be protected.

On 6 December the Commons considered the case of Mrs Highlord, from whom Browne and Bard had seized two coach horses when she came from Essex to London, 'though she hath contributed in a very liberal Proportion to the Parliament'.[18] The Commons insisted that it was 'a great Disservice done to the Parliament to seize the Horses of any Member of this House, or any other that have contributed in a liberal Manner to the Parliament'. The focus was very much on the actions of contributors, not their opinions. MPs seem to have

14   *CJ*, vol. 2, 863.
15   *CJ*, vol. 2, 871.
16   *CJ*, vol. 2, 876.
17   *LJ*, vol. 5, 478; *CJ*, vol. 2, 876.
18   *CJ*, vol. 2, 879.

been expecting disobedience, since 'if the said Mr. Browne, or Mr. Beard, or any other Person whom it may concern, shall refuse to deliver the said Horses, this House shall account it as a high Contempt committed against them'. This is very strong language for people who were supposed to be on the same side. It has to be suspected that the commissaries had already refused to return some horses. Changes in attendance, individual opinions, factional alignments and external circumstances could make the behaviour of the Commons very unstable. Many things must have changed since seizures were approved in mid-November. While the majority in the Commons on 6 December seemed strongly opposed to taking horses from contributors, it did not fundamentally change the terms of Bard and Browne's authority, only ordering that horses should be released if ordered by the Commons or the relevant committee and if the owners had contributed to the Propositions.

A further problem was that Bard and Browne did not even stick to the terms of the original order. The Lords had been careful to protect their own property by adding the exemption for members and assistants of either house. The order did not explicitly state that this was derived from parliamentary privilege, but it fits with the peers' attempts to secure their property and privileges in earlier parliaments.[19] On 14 December 1642 the Lords ordered the restoration of horses which had been taken from Dr Bennett, an assistant of the upper house.[20] On 16 December they ordered Thomas Browne to attend on the following day, but he does not appear to have turned up as he was summoned again on 19 December to appear the next day.[21] The 16 December summons also required Browne to account for taking horses from Lady Spencer, who was explicitly stated to be the wife of a peer. The position of women was ambiguous because they were not explicitly mentioned in the Lords' exception to the order. Coverture normally disadvantaged women, but in this case wives of MPs and peers could potentially gain an advantage by claiming that they were under coverture and therefore exempt from horse seizure. The exemption for members of either house was conditional on their 'not being Delinquents'.[22] Despite this, the Commons ordered the restoration of two coach horses which had been taken by unnamed commissaries from Rachael, Countess of Bath.[23] There could be no doubt about the delinquency of her husband, the Earl of Bath, who was imprisoned in the Tower at this time because he had attempted to execute the commission of array

[19] Vernon F. Snow, *Essex the Rebel: the Life of Robert Devereux, the Third Earl of Essex 1591–1646* (Lincoln, NE, 1970), pp. 104, 108, 169.
[20] *LJ*, vol. 5, 491.
[21] *LJ*, vol. 5, 494, 498.
[22] *LJ*, vol. 5, 447.
[23] *CJ*, vol. 2, 892.

in Devon.[24] This created a paradox because, according to the terms of the 15 November ordinance, there was no logical way that a woman could be protected by parliamentary privilege unless the property in her possession counted as owned by her husband by virtue of coverture, but the protection due to the earl should have been negated by his delinquency. The countess may have had a marriage settlement giving her separate estate, but in this case it is hard to see how her own property could have been covered by her husband's privilege. Rather than remaining passive victims, both women were able to use the privileges of their social rank and family connections to get redress. Hughes has suggested that wives of delinquents were well-placed to lobby Parliament for return of property because they were less likely than men to be seen as political agents and could manipulate the stereotype of feminine vulnerability.[25] By giving help, peers and MPs demonstrated their own masculine role as paternal protectors of people who were not directly represented in Parliament. Giving a few concessions to a few women may have been a way of reinforcing male privilege.

The growing controversies were not confined to the privileges of peers. On 26 December the Commons ordered that Bard and Browne should restore a horse taken from Sir Henry Heyman, who was an active member of the Commons and almost certainly not classed as a delinquent at this time.[26] This order explicitly mentioned parliamentary privilege. Although members of the Commons had not exempted themselves from the original order, they made use of the protection inserted by the Lords. Again, resistance seems to have been expected: the order threatened that the commissaries would 'answer their Contempt or Neglect herein'. Bard and Browne were in trouble with the Commons again in January 1643 for two horses which they had taken from Mr Dudley Palmer of Grey's Inn and delivered to Captain Edmund Harvey of the London militia.[27]

By January 1643 the Lords were questioning the rights of the commissaries to take any horses. The *Lords Journal* recorded on 2 January that 'Upon a Complaint, "That Horses are yet seized;" it is Ordered, That Enquiry shall be made by what Authority the Horses are now taken, the Order being re-called.'[28] It is not clear how the peers could have reached this conclusion, since there is no record in the proceedings of either house of the powers being revoked before

---

[24]   Caroline M. K. Bowden, 'Fane, Lady Rachael [married names Rachael Bourchier, countess of Bath; Rachael Cranfield, countess of Middlesex] (bap. 1613, d. 1680)', *ODNB*; Victor Stater, 'Bourchier, Henry, fifth earl of Bath (c.1587–1654)', *ODNB*.

[25]   Ann Hughes, *Gender and the English Revolution* (Abingdon, 2011), p. 46.

[26]   *CJ*, vol. 2, 903; Mary Frear Keeler, *The Long Parliament 1640–1641, a Biographical Study of its Members* (Philadelphia, 1954), p. 214.

[27]   *CJ*, vol. 2, 922, 941, 948.

[28]   *LJ*, vol. 5, 523.

this date. The situation became more serious on 4 January when the Lords heard that horses had been taken from some gentlemen bringing a petition from the county of Essex the previous night.[29] When Browne appeared before the house on the following day, he produced the 15 November order but denied that he had taken horses from the Essex gentlemen or from Lady Elizabeth Gurney.[30] The Lords then drew up an order to remove authority for horse seizing and conferred with the Commons on 6 January; John Pym brought the draft order to the Commons where it was referred to a committee, effectively delaying it for more than two weeks.[31]

Another conference was called on 23 January, by which time the balance of power in the Commons had changed. Whereas the previous attempt to stop horse seizing had been derailed by militant leader John Pym, this time it was anti-war MP Denzil Holles who reported back from the conference.[32] Control of the house could change hands very quickly. On the morning of 23 January Sir Robert Harley proposed carrying up a bill for abolishing bishops but Holles persuaded the Commons not to, ostensibly because the Lords might lay it aside if they were preoccupied with the conference.[33] While Holles was away at the conference, Harley carried the bill up to the Lords anyway.[34] On 26 January a resolution of the Commons concurred that the order of 15 November should be revoked, and the Lords ordained that Bard, Browne and the rest should not seize any more horses, otherwise 'they shall be proceeded against as Felons, according to the Laws of this Land'.[35] The question of supplying remounts for the army clearly had practical implications for the choice between continued war or negotiated peace, but the issues also intersected in other ways. The Essex gentlemen who had lost their horses were bringing a petition in favour of peace, and were dismissed by the Earl of Warwick as 'the slightest Part of the Country, and Men of no Religion or Credit'.[36] Militants were apparently dominant again in the Commons on 3 February, when they denied that the house had assented to the passing or printing of the ordinance of 26 January, thanked Browne and Bard for their efforts and granted indemnity to all of the commissaries.[37]

[29] *LJ*, vol. 5, 526.
[30] *LJ*, vol. 5, 530.
[31] *LJ*, vol. 5, 532; *CJ*, vol. 2, 917.
[32] *CJ*, vol. 2, 938–9.
[33] BL, Harleian 164, fol. 280.
[34] *CJ*, vol. 2, 938.
[35] *CJ*, vol. 2, 943; *LJ*, vol. 5, 571.
[36] *LJ*, vol. 5, 530; Clive Holmes, *The Eastern Association in the English Civil War* (Cambridge, 2007), p. 42.
[37] *CJ*, vol. 2, 953–4.

According to Lawrence Whitaker, the controversy was over the words 'they shall be proceeded against as Felons, according to the Laws of this Land', which were never approved by the Commons.[38]

It is not clear whether the City's planned force of cavalry and dragoons was ever completed. In practice, the horses taken by the commissaries were often used as remounts for existing units in Essex's army and the London militia.[39] This was necessary because of the decline of the Propositions. There is no record of the Earl of Essex's position in the controversies surrounding Bard and Browne. As commander of the army, he needed more horses for his troopers, but as a peer he had a vested interest in protecting his own privileges and property and preserving the established social order. Revoking the commissaries' powers did not solve the problems which their activities had raised. The conflicts continued for several months and became even more divisive.

Military Necessity

Armies always had the ability to take what they needed from civilians by force, regardless of an individual's perceived allegiance or place of residence. There was no point during the First Civil War when this could not happen. Horses were particularly vulnerable because they were in demand, valuable and easy to move compared to inanimate objects. If a horse died or went lame on the march, the quickest and easiest way to replace it was to requisition another from a nearby civilian. Horses could be taken in greater numbers, especially when there was no reliable alternative source of remounts. Quantifying horse seizures is problematic because of the limitations of surviving records. In most cases there are no warrants authorizing payment because payment was not offered. Sometimes tickets promising repayment were given instead, but where payment was not actually made these documents have mostly disappeared. When drawing up their accounts, officers had a strong incentive to minimize the number of horses which had passed through their hands so that they would not be charged for them. The parish accounts collected by the Committee for Taking Accounts of the Whole Kingdom and its local sub-committees are the best source for horse seizure.[40] In

---

[38]   BL, Add. 31116, fol. 23. Whitaker was MP for Okehampton, Devon.

[39]   *CJ*, vol. 2, 863, 941, 948; TNA: PRO, SP 28/5, fols 251–7.

[40]   TNA: PRO, SP 28/148–204; Donald H. Pennington, 'The Accounts of the Kingdom 1642–1649', in F.J. Fisher (ed.), *Essays in the Economic and Social History of Tudor and Stuart England* (Cambridge, 1961), pp. 182–203; Jason Peacey, 'Politics, Accounts and Propaganda in the Long Parliament', in Chris R. Kyle and Jason Peacey (eds), *Parliament at Work: Parliamentary Committees, Political Power, and Public Access in Early Modern England* (Woodbridge, 2002), pp. 59–78.

this case, the best is not particularly good. Coverage is variable and not complete for any county. Although Buckinghamshire has a particularly good survival rate, there is no trace of any account for around half of the parishes in the county.[41] Accounts of charges compiled for particular officers contain references to some parish accounts which must have existed but can no longer be found.[42] While most parts of Buckinghamshire have at least a few accounts, it appears that none were ever collected in Newport hundred. Where accounts do survive, there are still problems. Without any corroboration it is difficult to be certain how accurate the given details are, but the biggest problem is a lack of detail. Many entries do not give dates. Sometimes the incident is tied to a memorable event, such as the Earl of Essex's march to Gloucester, but more often the date is vague or completely absent. Attributing the seizure to a particular army is also difficult. Sometimes the army is explicitly stated and sometimes no clue is given, but more often entries give only the rank and surname of an officer. Some of these can be traced to one army or another but many are ambiguous because there are multiple officers with the same name, or because the same officer served in more than one army at different times. Despite these limitations, the parish accounts can at least give an impression of the impact of war on civilians and provide a few detailed examples.

Essex's Army

Draught horses   Until October 1642, the Propositions provided a good source of cavalry horses, but there was no system for supplying draught horses. The 80 horses delivered to Worcester in October 1642 are the only draught horses known to have been owned by the state before Edgehill.[43] These had probably been listed on the Propositions, as some of the horses in the cavalry list came with draught harness and there is no evidence that draught horses were purchased at this time. Some horses and wagons were hired to take supplies to the army, but their numbers were also relatively small. Essex's artillery train seems to have had serious problems during the Edgehill campaign which were almost certainly caused by a shortage of draught horses.[44] There was clearly no adequate system for providing draught horses. Most horses had to be impressed from the countryside during the army's march. A horse sent in by the constable of Bredwardine in

[41]   TNA: PRO, SP 28/39, part 5, fols 462–3, 543, 591–2; TNA: PRO, SP 28/41, part 5, fols 469–7; TNA: PRO, SP 28/43, part 7, fols 929–30; TNA: PRO, SP 28/148–51; TNA: PRO, SP 28/219, unfol.; TNA: PRO, SP 28/221, unfol.

[42]   TNA: PRO, SP 28/149, part 2, fols 200–210 and 222–32.

[43]   TNA: PRO, SP 28/262, part 4, fols 438–9.

[44]   Peter Young, *Edgehill 1642: The Campaign and the Battle* (Kineton, 1967), p. 100.

Worcestershire when Essex's army moved away from Worcester was subsequently lost at Edgehill.[45] At the same time, Samuel Ashworth of Kineton lost two wagon horses which were being used by Essex's foot regiment, and had another two horses plundered by deserters fleeing the battle. Meanwhile, Anne Mushen of Pillerton Priors, not far from the battlefield, lost a cart and five horses worth £30.[46] After the battle, two teams from Old Milverton spent nine days pulling the army's ammunition wagons from Warwick into Northamptonshire.[47] From November 1642 to January 1643 the artillery train took delivery of 524 draught horses which had almost certainly been listed on the Propositions.[48] These state-owned horses only covered about half of the artillery's requirements. An account compiled in 1644 shows that the artillery train had 558 state horses, around 179 horses hired on a long-term basis and up to 300 temporarily impressed.[49]

Although the impressment of draught horses was supposed to be temporary, it was inconvenient for their owners at best and at worst caused the permanent loss of horses. For the army the main advantage was that it was cheap – in 1644 drivers of impressed horses were only allowed 1s per day whereas hired horses were paid at a rate of 2s, 6d per horse per day[50] – but the practice made the supply of draught horses unpredictable and had great potential to antagonize civilians. Essex and his officers often issued warrants to the constables of hundreds or parishes near the army's quarters requiring them to bring in draught horses. One of these warrants, requiring carts and provisions from the hundred of Elthorne in Middlesex, was read in the Commons on 12 November 1642 and declared illegal, despite the urgent need to protect London from the approaching royal army.[51] Essex was asked to 'take some speedy Course to free the good Subjects from these and the like Oppressions'. Parliament's decision did not prevent the practice, which continued throughout the war. For example, on 7 August 1643 Anthony Fastolfe, commissary for Essex's artillery train, wrote to the high constables of the hundred of Elmbridge in Surrey, demanding 20 teams of horses with harness and drivers by virtue of Essex's warrant. These horses had to be delivered to Uxbridge by 12.00 pm the following day in order to draw carriages to Kingston, where they would be discharged. The constables were to arrest anyone who refused to serve, and were warned that if they failed they would answer at

---

[45]　TNA: PRO, SP 28/187, part 1, fol. 101.
[46]　TNA: PRO, SP 28/182, unfol.
[47]　TNA: PRO, SP 28/183, unfol.
[48]　TNA: PRO, SP 28/143, Account of Anthony Fastolfe, fol. 30.
[49]　TNA: PRO, SP 28/146, fol. 183.
[50]　TNA: PRO, SP 28/146, fol. 183.
[51]　*CJ*, vol. 2, 846.

their utmost peril.[52] Periods of service were supposed to be short, but sometimes the pressures of campaigning demanded longer service, and the operational needs of the army were put before the cost and inconvenience imposed on civilians. Four teams impressed from Padbury, Buckinghamshire, spent 17 days drawing artillery to Windsor, which the owners claimed had cost them £17.[53] Edmund Grove was promised that his horse would only have to go from Beconsfield to Aylesbury, but he never saw it again and was not compensated for the loss.[54] The burden was not evenly distributed because the army spent more time in some places than in others. Buckinghamshire parishes had to meet repeated demands. The people of Wing had 'remooved my lord generalls carrages at severall times to [th]e val[ue] of [£]30'.[55] The transport required for Essex's advance to Thame and retreat to Brickhill was impressed from several parishes including North Marston, Oving and Stoke Mandeville.[56]

Buckinghamshire was also the jumping off point for the expedition to relieve Gloucester in 1643, a very memorable event which has left many traces in the parish accounts. Because this was a long march into enemy territory, impressed horses had to stay with the army for a considerable time. Roger Nash's horses and cart spent 31 days in the artillery train, for which he claimed to have lost £10, 6s, 8d.[57] A horse from Stoke Mandeville was gone for eight weeks.[58] Thomas Aris of Water Stratford had to travel 40 miles to retrieve one of the horses which he had sent on the same expedition, while the other never returned.[59] Many other civilians lost their draught horses on the march to and from Gloucester and at the first battle of Newbury. The inhabitants of Wing stated that 'wee lost 8 horses & harnis when my lord generall went to releive gloster and carters wages to [th] e val[ue] of [£]34'.[60] Battles always brought the risk of death or capture by the enemy. Prince Rupert's cavalry probably did not discriminate between the state's horses and those owned by civilians. Seven horses from Chalfont St Giles had been captured in the raid on Chinnor in June 1643.[61] Even ostensibly friendly troops could be a threat to the wagoners and their horses since the artillery train

---

[52] TNA: PRO, SP 28/244, unfol.
[53] TNA: PRO, SP 28/150, part 1, fol. 108v.
[54] TNA: PRO, SP 28/149, part 4, fol. 630v.
[55] TNA: PRO, SP 28/148, part 2, fol. 366r.
[56] TNA: PRO, SP 28/150, part 2, fol. 166; TNA: PRO, SP 28/151, unfol.; TNA: PRO, SP 28/221, unfol.
[57] TNA: PRO, SP 28/151, unfol.
[58] TNA: PRO, SP 28/150, part 2, fol. 266r.
[59] TNA: PRO, SP 28/43, part 7, fol. 930r.
[60] TNA: PRO, SP 28/148, part 2, fol. 366r.
[61] TNA: PRO, SP 28/149, part 4, fol. 586v.

was in competition with the rest of the army. Some of the horses lost by civilians on the Gloucester expedition were explicitly stated to have been taken by Essex's cavalry. William Hill of Ellesborough claimed that a horse which he lost on the way to Gloucester 'was taken away by troopers in [th]e Earle of Essex armie'.[62] Two horses borrowed from Ivinghoe were 'taken from the Carter comaunded by Cap[tain] Saltkills Quartermaster Swede'.[63] The army went even further afield in 1644, but still caused problems in Buckinghamshire. The inhabitants of Cippenham 'say That they lost with the Earle of Essex in Cornwall one Cart, fower paier of harnesse and 2 horses'.[64]

Cavalry horses   Essex's cavalry had started taking horses from civilians in the summer of 1642, despite having a good supply of horses and money from the Propositions. On 30 August soldiers under Sir Samuel Luke took a gelding worth £12 from John Brekett.[65] Direct requisitioning of remounts by soldiers seems to have increased as other sources of supply declined. Cavalry officers from Essex's army took up several horses from Mitcham, Sutton and Morden in Surrey in January and February 1643.[66] At least some of the owners received tickets signed by the officers in question, giving estimates of the value of the horses. Some parishes in Hertfordshire also recorded losses of horses in early 1643. John Berners, a gentleman of Tharfield, lost a horse worth £10 on 28 March.[67]

The men who took these horses had not explicitly been granted any specific powers by Parliament. Most entries in accounts do not specify by what authority the horses had been taken, and some explicitly state that they did not know. Soldiers sometimes offered vague justifications based on necessity. Richard Walton of Ipslie in Warwickshire was only able to say that his grey gelding had been taken by some soldiers under Essex to be employed in the service of the state.[68] Around Michaelmas 1643 horses were taken from Joan Lee and Jane Fenden, both widows of Effingham in Surrey, on pretence that the soldiers needed horses for the service.[69] If horses needed to be replaced on the march they could be taken from nearby civilians. John East had a horse worth £2, 10s 'taken

---

[62]   TNA: PRO, SP 28/150, part 2, fol. 244v.

[63]   TNA: PRO, SP 28/219, unfol. This was almost certainly Christian Swede, quartermaster of William Salkeld's troop in Dalbier's regiment: Turton, *Chief Strength*, 59.

[64]   TNA: PRO, SP 28/150, part 2, fol. 251r.

[65]   TNA: PRO, SP 28/144, part 1, fol. 15.

[66]   TNA: PRO, SP 28/178, unfol.; TNA: PRO, SP 28/179, unfol.

[67]   TNA: PRO, SP 28/155, unfol.

[68]   TNA: PRO, SP 28/38, part 3, fol. 202.

[69]   TNA: PRO, SP 28/178, unfol.

by an Ensigne of foot in the Earle of Essex his march'.[70] Places where soldiers were quartered suffered heavily. John Watkins of Amersham lost a horse worth £8 by soldiers of Essex's army when it quartered there. Thomas Dew also lived in Amersham but 'lost a horse taken from him uppon the high waie by Collo[nel] Dalbiers men'.[71] Ultimately, soldiers were able to take horses by force, even if they had no higher authority. The accounts of Mitcham specify that Captain John Farmer took a horse by violence from Edmund Walter.[72]

In some cases it is clear that Essex had issued a warrant authorizing his men to requisition horses. In February 1644 Lieutenant Matthews, who claimed the authority of a warrant from Essex, broke into the stable of Mr William Green in East Barnet, Hertfordshire, and took a stallion claimed to be worth £25.[73] This authority did not guarantee a peaceful transfer of the horse, since Matthews was specified to have used force. Captain Lionel Copley's accounts admitted that in June 1643 he seized four horses in Marlow, Buckinghamshire, by virtue of Essex's warrant, from 'such as were reputed malign[an]ts'.[74] In many cases there is no evidence that officers made any accusations of delinquency before taking horses by warrant. Claims to have Essex's warrant were not usually challenged when complaints were heard in Parliament, but there was still scope to dispute whether the warrants should have been issued.

Some of the biggest controversies over horse seizure were caused by a commission to raise a cavalry regiment which Essex granted to Henry Marten in the spring of 1643. The original commission is not known to survive, so it is impossible to be certain of its exact date or terms, but it was mentioned when Marten's activities were discussed in Parliament. Whitaker's diary stated that the commission allowed 'taking of any Horses, [tha]t were like to be Employed ag[ains]t [th]e Parl[iamen]t'.[75] The existence of this commission is very surprising considering the hostility between the two men. Marten had already questioned Essex's competence in December 1642, and in 1643 he was one of a group of radical MPs who were trying to take power away from Essex by creating a new army under Sir William Waller.[76] Essex was sometimes pressured into commissioning his political enemies, such as when he was forced to grant a

---

[70]   TNA: PRO, SP 28/37, part 1, fol. 132v.

[71]   TNA: PRO, SP 28/149, part 4, fol. 563r.

[72]   TNA: PRO, SP 28/245, unfol.

[73]   TNA: PRO, SP 28/155, unfol.

[74]   TNA: PRO, SP 28/147, part 2, fol. 299v.

[75]   BL, Add. 31116, fols 47v–48r.

[76]   Ian Gentles, *The English Revolution and the Wars in the Three Kingdoms, 1638–1652* (London, 2007), p. 159; Sarah Barber, *A Revolutionary Rogue: Henry Marten and the English Republic* (Stroud, 2000), p. 7.

new commission to Waller later in the year, but in this case there is surprisingly little evidence of his attitude.[77] The Lord General's army had earlier benefited from the horses taken by Bard and Browne, and its officers continued to cause trouble by taking horses from civilians. Essex's desperate need for cavalry may have overridden all other considerations. His behaviour in cases of horse seizure does not fit easily with the traditional view that he was aligned with the peace group. If Essex did not agree with the radical aims of men like Marten, he could still take advantage of their policies to increase the power of his own army.

On 15 April the Lords sent for a man called De Luke, who was probably a quartermaster in Marten's regiment, because he had taken horses from the Earl of Kinnoull.[78] Because he was a member of the Scottish peerage, the earl was not covered by privilege of the English Parliament but the Lords still acted to protect his property. Marten's men went on to attack the English peerage more directly, in the same manner as Bard and Browne. The Lords received a petition from Rachael, Countess of Bath, on 26 June, complaining that soldiers had broken into her house and taken four horses from the stable.[79] The countess related that she showed the men an order of Parliament which allowed her to keep four coach horses and protected them from seizure, but when she asked them for their warrant they showed their pistols. She also alleged that although two of the horses were in the service of Parliament, she had seen the other two drawing a hackney coach. According to the petition, the soldiers had said they were under Sir Arthur Hesilrige, but the Lords found that they were actually from Marten's regiment. The next day Captain Pile appeared before the house and said that he took the horses by Marten's warrant.[80] It was then found that Marten had already given orders to restore the horses and that Pile had refused, so the captain was ordered to be kept in custody until he complied. Marten's officers were also in trouble with the Commons, which took exception to the seizure of horses from Lancelot Lake on 3 July. The captain responsible was sent for as a delinquent, not only for taking the horses, but also because he 'affronted and abused' John Glynne, who was MP for Westminster, recorder of London and a deputy lieutenant for Middlesex.[81] It is perhaps significant that Glynne was also a supporter of the Earl of Essex and opposed Marten's scheme for a general rising under Waller's command. Glynne had previously been a teller for the yea when the Commons voted to bail Sir John

---

[77]   Snow, *Essex*, 376–7, 379.

[78]   *LJ*, vol. 6, 3.

[79]   *HMC*, 5th report, 92; *LJ*, vol. 6, 107.

[80]   *LJ*, vol. 6, 111. This could be Seymour Pile or Pyle, who was commissioned on 10 April 1643 and later served as a captain of horse in Essex's army: Turton, *Chief Strength*, 55.

[81]   *CJ*, vol. 3, 152; Keith Lindley, 'Glynne, Sir John (1603–1666)', *ODNB*.

Lucas in September 1642, whereas Marten had been appointed to a committee to prepare an impeachment (see Chapter 2).

Despite the hostility between Essex and Marten, both men antagonized the Lords by requisitioning horses. An ordinance passed on 10 May 1643 began 'The Lords and Commons now assembled in Parliament, being informed of the great Abuses in the several Counties of this Kingdom, by the Taking of Horses for the Service of the Parliament'. It went on to regulate horse seizure by insisting that army officers should not take any horses without the permission and supervision of two deputy lieutenants or county committee members, who were authorized to arrest any officers who disobeyed.[82] A further ordinance on 29 May modified this system, requiring the county committees to provide horses when the Lord General requested them. Essex was still allowed to issue warrants to his officers for seizing horses, but only if the counties had failed to fulfil his requests.[83] In practice, requisitioning by soldiers continued long after it had officially been restricted. The parish account of Dinton in Buckinghamshire stated that two horses were taken from Mr Chew 'by the Earle of Essex his Troopers in their March to Gloucester' in August 1643. Roger Nash lost a horse worth £4 to Sir William Balfour's troop in March 1645.[84]

The new ordinance failed to secure an adequate supply of remounts for the army. Essex wrote to the speaker of the Commons on 22 June complaining about the 'insufferable inconvenience & mischeife I too evidently see groweinge upon the Armye by meanes of the restraint of taking horses'. He demanded the return of his powers to issue warrants because the committees of Bedfordshire, Hertfordshire and Huntingdon had failed to send the horses which he had requested weeks before, warning that his army would be unable to fight without a constant supply of remounts.[85] There is no evidence that Essex's soldiers had ever stopped seizing horses, but the claim that the army was not getting enough remounts from the counties was probably true. The mayor and aldermen of Colchester organized subscriptions for Essex's army on 26 June, but were only promised six horses.[86] At this time the Lord General was in a vulnerable position, having advanced to Thame, a few miles east of Oxford, in early June.[87] His army

---

[82]   *A & O*, vol. 1, 155–6.

[83]   *A & O*, vol. 1, 162–3.

[84]   TNA: PRO, SP 28/151, unfol.

[85]   Bodleian Library, Tanner 62, fol. 126.

[86]   ERO, D/Y 2/2, pp. 221–32. More people agreed to provide muskets or small amounts of money but many subscribed nothing. It is not certain whether the subscriptions were actually brought in.

[87]   Malcolm Wanklyn and Frank Jones, *A Military History of the English Civil War* (Harlow, 2005), p. 90.

was getting weaker and was unable to advance any further. In the early hours of 18 June Prince Rupert raided the quarters of some of Essex's cavalry at Chinnor, but another group of parliamentary cavalry, led by John Hampden, caught the prince's force at Chalgrove before it could escape. The ensuing skirmish has often been mistaken for a decisive defeat because Hampden was mortally wounded there.[88] Although Rupert's raiding party got away and Essex's cavalry suffered casualties, this would have been fairly inconsequential if Hampden had not been hit. The weakness of Essex's army at this time was caused more by logistical problems than by defeat in battle. The cavalry could not easily be kept up to strength because there was clearly no adequate system for supplying horses. Rupert apparently had enough cavalry to stop Essex from operating freely, but seems to have been unable or unwilling to seek a truly decisive battle. Essex's infantry and artillery were prevented from advancing on Oxford, but were not destroyed.

Cromwell and the Eastern Association

Cromwell began the war as captain of a horse troop in Essex's army. In early 1643 he left to take up a commission as colonel of a horse regiment in the Eastern Association, taking his troop with him.[89] The ordinance of Parliament of 20 December 1642 named Lord Grey of Warke to command the association, and he received a further commission from the Lord General in February 1643.[90] This was one of several associations formed around this time. It was not obvious or inevitable that it would succeed and the others would fail.[91] In January 1643 the deputy lieutenants of Essex were

> required by this House, to seize on the Arms, Ammunition, and serviceable Horses of such Persons in the County of Essex, as have refused to contribute upon the Propositions, to assist the Parliament; or that have refused to associate themselves with the rest of the Gentlemen of that County, that have entered into an Association with Four other Counties.[92]

Anyone who refused to take the oath of association was treated as an enemy, adding yet another dimension to the construction of allegiance. Similar orders

---

[88]   Gentles, *English Revolution*, 172; Michael Braddick, *God's Fury, England's Fire: A New History of the English Civil Wars* (London, 2008), pp. 287–8.

[89]   Turton, *Chief Strength*, 27; Ian Gentles, *Oliver Cromwell: God's Warrior and the English Revolution* (Basingstoke, 2011), p. 24.

[90]   *A & O*, vol. 1, 51–2; Holmes, *Eastern Association*, 69.

[91]   Holmes, *Eastern Association*, 62, 68.

[92]   *CJ*, vol. 2, 942.

were issued to other county committees, but Essex was the only one that made significant efforts to impose the oath.[93]

Because of opposition from county committees, it took a long time for the association planned in December 1642 to come into existence. It was not until February 1643, when Lord Grey arrived with his commission, that all of the constituent counties agreed to implement the ordinance. The central committee at Cambridge did not begin to meet until April. While Lord Grey and the Cambridge committee were nominally in command of the association, county committees were effectively autonomous because they retained control of raising and spending money.[94] At this time there were very few local forces in existence other than the militia. The contributions required by the oath were probably inadequate, as even when people subscribed they did not always bring in what they promised. Lord Grey set quotas for these subscriptions backed up by threats of disarmament, but even then many wealthy people avoided paying.[95] The most militant supporters of Parliament had already put a large amount of resources into the Propositions in 1642. Most of these resources had gone to Essex's army, although some were later returned when units such as Cromwell's troop were detached from the field army. Contributions of Proposition money in the association recovered briefly in early 1643 and were often kept for local defence, with or without permission.[96]

Cromwell raised several new troops to form his regiment in the spring of 1643.[97] Many of their horses were seized in Northamptonshire. Peter Baker specified that Captain Ayres had taken a grey horse from him in April 1643. Ayres and other captains under Cromwell took more horses from Oundle and Barnwell on unspecified dates.[98] Cromwell and some of his subordinates were granted powers to requisition horses by ordinance of Parliament.[99] William Hull of Barnwell had a horse worth £6 taken by Captain Disbrowe, but did not know by what authority.[100] Other inhabitants lost horses to Captain Ayres and were equally unsure of his authority. Meanwhile, Captain Edward Whalley took a horse valued at £10 from Henry Henson, leaving a ticket signed by Cromwell

---

[93] Holmes, *Eastern Association*, 65–6.

[94] Ibid., 69, 85.

[95] Ibid., 76–9.

[96] Ibid., 80–81.

[97] C.H. Firth, 'Raising the Ironsides', *Transactions of the Royal Historical Society*, 13 (1899): 25; Holmes, *Eastern Association*, 78.

[98] TNA: PRO, SP 28/172, unfol.; TNA: PRO, SP 28/173, unfol.

[99] *A & O*, vol. 1, 138.

[100] TNA: PRO, SP 28/171, part 3, fol. 274. John Disbrowe was later promoted to major, so this incident probably happened in 1643.

himself.[101] Whalley was commissioned as a captain in Cromwell's regiment on 18 February 1643 and promoted to major on 15 May, which helps to date this incident reasonably precisely.[102]

Cromwell's regiment expanded further as the year went on, and in 1644 consisted of 14 troops.[103] In July 1643 Sir Thomas Martyn's troop was transferred to Cromwell's regiment and put under the command of Captain Lawrence.[104] Martyn had seized many horses in Cambridgeshire to bring his troop up to a full strength of 80, as well as delivering horses to other troops in Cromwell's regiment. Oliver Cromwell junior received eight horses taken from Thomas Tempest of Whaddon, Thomas White of Connington and a Mr Gardiner. Martyn noted in his account that he had delivered John Ingrey's horse 'to Colonel Cromwell with his owne hands'.[105] The raising of Captain Swallow's troop was partly funded by a subscription of £240 from young men and women of Norwich, and so was labelled 'the virgins troop'. Cromwell wrote to them saying that he would provide the horses.[106] It is very unlikely that Cromwell owned enough horses to mount a troop, or had enough money to buy them out of his own pocket. He had already contributed £1,100 to the Parliament in the previous year, and had only found this sum by selling his property. He probably had little capital left by 1643. Therefore it is more likely that he provided these horses by persuading other people to donate them or by taking them by force. Thirteen men in Wisbech had their fifth and twentieth assessments reduced by the value of horses which they had delivered to Swallow.[107] This troop seems to have been completed by August 1643 and was part of Cromwell's regiment by 1644.[108]

Captain Margery came into conflict with the local gentry of Suffolk while requisitioning horses for his new troop. Cromwell wrote to the Suffolk committee on 29 August, asking them to help Margery to seize horses from malignants.[109] This must have led to some controversy, since Cromwell wrote

---

[101]   TNA: PRO, SP 28/171, part 3, fols 274–5.

[102]   TNA: PRO, SP 28/253A, fol. 42.

[103]   Firth, 'Raising the Ironsides', 25; Godfrey Davies, 'The Army of the Eastern Association', *English Historical Review*, 46/181 (1931): 90.

[104]   TNA: PRO, SP 28/196, part 3, fols 395–8.

[105]   TNA: PRO, SP 28/43, part 7, fol. 921; TNA: PRO, SP 28/196, part 3, fol. 395; TNA: PRO, SP 28/128, part 3, fol. 5.

[106]   Firth, 'Raising the Ironsides', 31–2.

[107]   TNA: PRO, SP 28/152, fol. 166.

[108]   Firth, 'Raising the Ironsides', 32.

[109]   W.C. Abbott, *Writings and Speeches of Oliver Cromwell* (Cambridge, MA, 1937), vol. 1, p. 256.

back the following month to answer the committee's complaints.[110] Cromwell made much of the distinction between public and private interests, arguing that 'I am sorry you should discountenance those who (not to make benefit to themselves, but to serve their country) are willing to venture their lives, and to purchase to themselves the displeasure of bad men, that they may do a public benefit'. This provocative statement insinuated that the committee, as well as the owners of the horses, were public enemies. The main issue was whether the horses had been taken from friends or enemies of Parliament. Cromwell claimed that he did not presume to 'justify all Captain Margery's actions, but his own conscience knows whether he hath taken the horses of any but malignants', apparently making the internal feelings of the officer more important than those of the suspect. In fact, Cromwell avoided the problem of internal allegiance, acknowledging that identification of malignants depended on perceptions and arbitrary criteria: 'I know not the measure that every one takes of malignants. I think it is not fit Captain Margery should be the judge; but if he, in this taking of horses, hath observed the parliament character of a malignant ...'. And of course this 'parliament character' was defined primarily by external actions, even if some, such as refusing the association oath, could be inferred to be driven by conscience.

Colonel Long in Essex

The increasing shortage of horses in early 1643 had effects a long way from the quarters of Essex's army. In March the Lord General sent Walter Long, MP for Ludgershall, Wiltshire, who also held the rank of colonel, into the county of Essex to collect horses and money. Long's presence was very controversial and he was withdrawn from the county in early June. Clive Holmes wrote an article which interpreted this incident in terms of binary oppositions between local and central, and between military and civilian.[111] In fact, the situation was much more complicated than this. From his arrival, Long was in competition with other officers belonging to the Eastern Association. Two parliamentary armies were trying to use the same resources, adding another dimension to the struggle over property rights and authority. Peter Joslyn, a yeoman of Rayne, was arrested by Long on 27 March and examined in the presence of local officials at Maldon, including the bailiff John Stevens and Henry Barrington, an alderman of Colchester. Joslyn admitted to having taken several horses and produced written authorization signed by Joseph Mann, a gentleman of Braintree who

---

[110]   Ibid., vol. 1, 261.

[111]   Clive Holmes, 'The Affair of Colonel Long: Relations between Parliament, the Lord General and the County of Essex in 1643', *Transactions of the Essex Archaeological Society*, 3rd series, 2 (1970): 211.

held the rank of quartermaster.[112] When he appeared to defend himself, Mann claimed to have been commissioned to take horses by both Lord Grey of Warke, commander of the Eastern Association, and the Earl of Warwick, lord-lieutenant of Essex, but could only produce a warrant from Grey dated 4 March. This warrant empowered Joseph Mann senior, William Mann junior and Ezekiell Hull to take all arms and ammunition from 'all papists malignants & other p[er] sons whatsoever that have or shall refuse to appear at Musters or to subscribe according to the p[ro]positions of both howses of Parliament or to enter into [th]e Associac[i]on', but did not explicitly give them power to make deputies.[113] Joseph Mann claimed that he needed to deputize Joslyn because sickness and other duties prevented him from carrying out Lord Grey's orders. Mann was able to produce a list of 33 horses which he had seized himself earlier in the month. Ten of these had been delivered to the Eastern Association forces, and the other 23 had been handed over to Colonel Long by order of Sir Richard Everard, one of the county's deputy lieutenants.[114]

The surviving documents relating to the examination of Joslyn and Mann suggest that the issue of horse seizure had not caused serious problems until the arrest of Joslyn on 27 March. Joseph Mann and Walter Long appear to have cooperated with Sir Richard Everard and each other. But on 17 April, Long wrote to the speaker of the Commons to defend himself from accusations of wrongdoing made by some unnamed people from Essex who had gone to London to complain about him.[115] The charges, which he described as 'slanders', appear to have been that he had taken horses from well-affected people and demanded money for the return of horses. Long admitted that such abuses had taken place, but blamed them on Joseph Mann and a Colonel Cook, who was supposed to be a commander of a foot regiment from Cambridge. In this letter, Long went to great lengths to secure his honour and reputation, stressing that 'I am now ymployd amongst Strangers whereof I am not soe well knowne and where it may bee such slaunders may receive some beleife.' He also claimed that he had cooperated fully with the county committee, 'w[i]thout whose advice and consent I have not don anie thing since my coming into Essex'.

The letter then gave an account of the examination of Joslyn and Mann. According to this narrative, Long and the committee men with whom he was working had received complaints about horse seizure, and responded by arresting Joslyn. Joseph Mann then came without being summoned and admitted that he had no commission from Warwick, 'But wee conceive hee used the Earle of

112   BL, Egerton 2646, fol. 188.
113   BL, Egerton 2651, fol. 138.
114   BL, Egerton 2651, fol. 139.
115   Bodleian Library, Tanner 62, fols 35–6.

Warwicks name to make theis pressures of his to bee borne w[i]th all, for my Lord of Warwicks sake w[hi]ch is much honored and beloved in this County.' This seems to be an accurate assessment. Warwick's reputation and influence in the county were important advantages for Parliament, but there was always a risk of his name being misused.[116] Long, Mann and Joslyn were all trying to claim legitimacy by any means possible. While Long had a commission from the Lord General, he was an outsider who had no credit or reputation in Essex. Mann and Joslyn were local men operating close to their homes, and Mann at least was authorized by a legitimate warrant from Lord Grey, head of the association of which Essex was a member. But this was apparently not enough. At least one of Mann and Joslyn knowingly lied about having a commission from the Earl of Warwick. This attempt to give a vague impression of legitimacy undermined itself when they were examined under oath and admitted that there was no such document. In his letter to the speaker, Long further attempted to undermine the legitimacy of his rivals by questioning whether the warrant from Lord Grey was genuine. Perhaps this was pushing the argument too far, but it raises important questions about written authority. Responding to another incident in August, Sir Thomas Barrington wrote 'when horses are suffered to be taken, w[i]thout the Deputy Lieuten[an]ts, who are able to Judge, whether the Authoritie be as is p[re]tended ... the Country is very much unsatisfied.'[117] The authority supposedly contained in documents relied on authority from outside the text. Ultimately a general's warrant was just a piece of paper. The authority it granted in theory could not be put into practice without the cooperation of the county elite, even if the document was genuine and did not contravene any ordinances of Parliament. The officers involved in the dispute in March all claimed to have cooperated with and been supported by the deputy lieutenants. Joslyn deposed that he had released a horse on the orders of Sir Richard Everard. While he admitted taking money to release other horses, he claimed that he had intended to pay this to Everard.[118] Mann and Joslyn were kept imprisoned, apparently with the approval of Stevens and Henry Barrington.

There was clearly some personal animosity between Long and the local elite, but it is difficult to say how far this was a cause and how far a consequence of their disputes over jurisdiction and property. In the end Parliament ordered Long out of Essex and gave the county committee the undisputed right to assess non-contributors. This was not a victory for the people who had lost their

---

[116] Holmes, *Eastern Association*, 37–9.
[117] Bodleian Library, Tanner 62, fol. 285r; Holmes, 'Colonel Long', 214.
[118] BL, Egerton 2646, fol. 188.

horses. Rather than being returned to their owners, or even kept for local forces, 100 horses taken by Long were to be sent up to London for the use of the state.[119]

Redress of Grievances

Taking Accounts

In 1644 Parliament set up the Committee for Taking Accounts of the Whole Kingdom, which was to audit accounts and certify arrears of pay.[120] Subcommittees were set up at county level to audit local forces and to take accounts of losses from every parish. These committees created or examined many of the surviving financial records of the parliamentary war effort. Despite the apparently mundane nature of these records, the central committee was not neutral. It was dominated by members of the Presbyterian faction, who used the process of taking accounts and certifying arrears to reward their friends and punish their enemies.[121] The committee also had a vested interest in reducing the amount of arrears due to officers and soldiers in order to save money. These arrears amounted to around £3 million by 1647, and paying this sum remained a major problem for years.[122] Officers' arrears were reduced by the value of any horses and equipment which they could not properly account for, and for anything which they had taken from civilians without paying. Therefore county subcommittees were particularly interested in parish accounts of losses. Drawing up these accounts gave civilians an opportunity to list their grievances against parliamentary forces, but ultimately they would not be repaid for their losses.

Parish accounts listed many instances of horse seizure, ranging from official requisitioning authorized by a general's warrant to unauthorized theft and extortion. The questions asked by the committees necessarily influenced the answers that were given. People constructed different kinds of narratives for different committees.[123] The parish accounts rarely made claims about allegiance, whether for or against Parliament. Like many compounding petitions, they listed things that had happened, focusing mostly on the economic impact of the war on local communities. In this context the financial value of a horse was the most

---

[119]   *CJ*, vol. 3, 180.

[120]   *A & O*, vol. 1, 387–91.

[121]   Peacey, 'Politics, Accounts and Propaganda', passim.

[122]   Ian Gentles, *The New Model Army in England, Ireland and Scotland, 1645–1653* (Oxford, 1992), pp. 49–52.

[123]   Rachel Weil, 'Thinking About Allegiance in the English Civil War', *History Workshop Journal*, 61/1 (2006): 189.

important fact and was very rarely omitted. This was usually an estimate of the likely market price, since actual prices were not negotiated when a horse was taken by force without payment. Thomas Marston junior of Bushey in Hertfordshire reckoned that he might have had £13 for the horse taken by 20 troopers under Major Samuel Boza on the road to Hemel Hempstead in August 1643.[124]

William Green of East Barnet claimed that the stallion which he had lost to Lieutenant Matthews in February 1644 was well worth £25. Doctor John Montfort of Tewin estimated that seven horses taken by Middleton's Regiment in February 1643 were worth at least £70.[125] In a few cases it was possible to make stronger and more specific claims about the value of a horse. Richard Walton of Ipslie in Warwickshire had recently bought a grey gelding for £6 when he lost if to Essex's soldiers.[126] Sometimes tickets were left promising return of the horses or repayment of their value, but in this case the value was often set by parliamentary officials, who were not impartial. William Salkeld's troop took two horses from Edward North senior of Tewin with the permission of local committee member Humphrey Packer, who valued them at £16. Two bay horses taken from John Capar in July 1643 were valued by his neighbours at £30.[127] Edward Whalley left a ticket with Henry Henson of Barnwell, Northamptonshire, for a horse valued at £10 by the officers of his troop.[128]

As well as the market value of the horses, parish accounts sometimes recorded the knock-on effects of the loss of the horse. Thomas Marston junior added that his horse was a great loss to him because his team was his only source of income.[129] Thomas Lane of Boveney in Buckinghamshire claimed £38 for 'Cart service, Horses & other goods & restraint from worke when the Earle of Essex his Army lay in these parts'.[130] Loss of horses could prevent farmers from ploughing, and horses were even taken while they were ploughing. At Drayton Beauchamp, Richard Martin 'had one horse worth 8l cutt out of his harnes att plowe upon noe necessitie' by a trooper from Vermuyden's regiment in Manchester's army.[131] In Cheddington, '3 horses were taken from William Fountaine, as they were at plow' by Richard Norton's regiment under Waller. The inhabitants of Maids

124   TNA: PRO, SP 28/155, unfol.
125   TNA: PRO, SP 28/155, unfol.
126   TNA: PRO, SP 28/38 part 3, fol. 202.
127   TNA: PRO, SP 28/155, unfol.
128   TNA: PRO, SP 28/171, part 3, fol. 275.
129   TNA: PRO, SP 28/155, unfol.
130   TNA: PRO, SP 28/149, part 4, fol. 575r.
131   TNA: PRO, SP 28/150, part 2, fol. 115v.

Moreton complained that five horses and two drivers had had been impressed for six weeks during harvest time, costing them £18.[132]

Persuasion

It was not unusual for horses to be transferred from civilians to the military by the simple application of force or the threat of force, but sometimes the process involved negotiation and did not automatically lead to the owners losing their horses. There are many cases of soldiers releasing horses in return for cash. In many cases this practice was represented as a deliberate attempt to extort money. On 15 May 1644, Major William Urry's troop quartered with Christopher Shrimpton in Bradenham, Buckinghamshire, and 'they tooke away my horse & made me pay for him 10[s]'.[133] This account assigned all of the agency to the soldiers and made the civilian a passive victim. In some other cases the horse owner was represented as much more active. John Winch of Little Missenden noted that 'Captaine Tyrrells men tooke from him one horse w[hi]ch cost to redeeme and in Charges goeinge after him thirty shillings'.[134] Rather than demanding money immediately, the soldiers had taken the horse away and only agreed to release it later. This kind of bargain was still not entirely fair for civilians, but they clearly made some effort to achieve it. Mrs Marie Sanders of Flamstead, Hertfordshire, regained her horses from Captain Salkeld 'with much ado' but claimed that she had lost £7 for the expenses of recovering them, loss of work at harvest time and spoiling of the horses.[135] The people who entered these details in their accounts were not ashamed to admit collusion, perhaps implying that they were blameless because the soldiers should not have taken their horses in the first place. They did not claim any affection for the parliamentary cause and had effectively hindered it by removing horses from the army. Demanding money for the return of horses was one of the abuses which often featured in arguments against horse seizure, but the surviving Buckinghamshire parish accounts show that it only happened in a small minority of cases. Of 598 horses claimed to have been taken by soldiers, only 32 (5.4 per cent) were released.

Courts and Indemnity

The parliamentary war administration did not have a monopoly on power in the areas which were nominally under its control. Revolution and civil war did

---

132   TNA: PRO, SP 28/151, unfol.
133   TNA: PRO, SP 28/150, part 1, fol. 96r.
134   TNA: PRO, SP 28/151, unfol.
135   TNA: PRO, SP 28/155, unfol.

not completely undermine the judicial system. In at least some areas courts continued to sit and enforce the traditional law. The courts offered an alternative way of redressing grievances against Parliament's arbitrary government and unauthorized acts by individual soldiers. An order of the Commons on 9 December 1642 required the justices of the peace at Newgate to release John Polgreene because he was 'a Person employed by this House in the Taking up of Horses belonging to Papists &c'.[136] On 18 May 1643 the Commons heard that John Pennyfather, John Kinge and Samuel Leadebetter, who had Essex's warrant to seize horses for the army, had been indicted at the Old Bailey for horse theft.[137] This case emphasized the conflict between military necessity and property rights. Even seizures which were authorized by Parliament and carried out according to specified procedure were still against traditional English law. The house ordered that proceedings should be stopped immediately and referred the case to the Committee for Examinations. Parliament increasingly tried to suppress the law courts during the First Civil War.[138] While this was another example of arbitrary government, it was a necessary part of the war effort.

The end of the First Civil War and the reopening of more courts increased the threat of soldiers being prosecuted for requisitioning horses. Indemnity from prosecution was one of the main political demands of the New Model Army.[139] On 21 May 1647 Parliament met this demand by passing an ordinance granting indemnity for acts committed by the authority of Parliament during the war.[140] The ordinance banned prosecution for these acts and set up the Indemnity Committee, giving it the power to hear witnesses, stop legal proceedings in the courts, award damages and imprison anyone who continued to prosecute a case against its orders. A soldier or official who was being prosecuted in court for acts committed on behalf of Parliament during the war could submit a petition to the Indemnity Committee describing the problem and asking for redress. If the Committee decided to take up the case, it would examine the evidence and decide whether the petitioner's actions were covered by the Indemnity Ordinance. If the Committee considered the petitioner's actions legitimate it could stop court proceedings and award damages, but in many cases it agreed with the courts

---

[136] *CJ*, vol. 2, 881.

[137] *CJ*, vol. 3, 91–2.

[138] John Morrill, *Revolt in the Provinces: The People of England and the Tragedies of War, 1630–1648* (London, 1998), p. 93; *A & O*, vol. 1, 191–2.

[139] Ann Hughes, 'Parliamentary Tyranny? Indemnity Proceedings and the Impact of the Civil War: a Case Study from Warwickshire', *Midland History*, 11 (1986): 52; Gentles, *New Model Army*, 121.

[140] *A & O*, vol. 1, 936–8.

that the petitioners were not covered by indemnity and dismissed the petition.[141] Indemnity proceedings created the paradox that the defendant in the court case became the plaintiff in the indemnity case and vice versa. From here on I will use these terms to refer to roles in the indemnity case, not the court case.

The total number of indemnity cases is uncertain. There are 58 boxes of surviving petitions and case papers, which Hughes estimated to cover around 2,000 cases, but including other cases mentioned in the Indemnity Committee's order books and allowing for loss of records, Shedd put the total at between 4,000 and 5,000.[142] Gentles found 1,116 which met his criteria for military cases, but many other cases concerned disputes between civilians over sequestered rents and debts.[143] Cases involving seizure of horses made up 30 per cent of Gentles's military cases, and Shedd estimated that these were about 10 per cent of all cases.[144] I have examined a sample of 269 horse seizure cases. My definition includes any disputes over the ownership of horses in which at least one party claimed that the horse had been possessed or used by soldiers or officials in the service of Parliament, except for horses distrained for non-payment of taxes. It also includes actions for assault or trespass which were alleged to have been committed during the taking of a horse.[145] Some of these cases do not relate to the First Civil War and some are of uncertain date. Table 3.1 shows the number of cases in which the horses were taken before or after 1 January 1648, an arbitrary but convenient cutoff point. Most petitions explicitly give the number of horses involved, but in 12 cases an unspecified number of horses is mentioned. The vast majority of cases contested the ownership of only one horse, and the average is 1.2 per case where known. Sometimes there was more than one case over the same horse, and so these horses have only been counted once.[146] It seems very unlikely that the number of horses disputed in indemnity cases for which petitions survive can be more than 500, and even allowing for lost records the total is probably lower than 1,000. The surviving cases come from all over

---

[141]   Hughes, 'Parliamentary Tyranny?', 59, 65; John A. Shedd, 'Legalism over Revolution: The Parliamentary Committee for Indemnity and Property Confiscation Disputes, 1647–1655', *Historical Journal*, 43/4 (2000): 1097–8, 1103–4.

[142]   Hughes, 'Parliamentary Tyranny?', 58; Shedd, 'Legalism over Revolution', 1095. The petitions are in TNA: PRO, SP 24/30–87.

[143]   Gentles, *New Model Army*, 130; Shedd, 'Legalism over Revolution', 1097, 1103–4.

[144]   Gentles, *New Model Army*, 130; Shedd, 'Legalism over Revolution', 1096.

[145]   The sample is not complete but probably includes at least 80 per cent of cases which meet my criteria. Using different criteria, Gentles found 341 military horse cases. Hughes found at least five Warwickshire horse cases that I missed. Gentles, *New Model Army*, 130; Hughes, 'Parliamentary Tyranny?', 59, 62, 65–6, 68–9.

[146]   For example, TNA: PRO, SP 24/37, part 1, Burton vs Bradshawe and TNA: PRO, SP 24/57, part 1, Ireland vs Gladman are about the same horse.

England in all three civil wars. As Hughes found, members of local forces were more likely to be prosecuted because they were easier to identify, but horse cases include at least a few examples from every major English field army.[147] Compared to all of the horses procured by parliamentary armies, the numbers involved in indemnity cases are very small. The figures given by Gentles and Shedd cannot be used to support the view that horses were unusually scarce in England in the 1640s.[148] Shedd suggested that 'such was the state of emergency that by 1649 a pass granted directly from parliament was needed to transport horses out of the country', but this had actually been standard practice since before the civil wars; licences were frequently granted even in the 1640s and 1650s, and were no longer required after 1657.[149] Although very large numbers of horses were requisitioned by parliamentary soldiers, it was exceptional for this to lead to an indemnity case.

Table 3.1   Indemnity cases involving horse seizure

Date of seizure	Cases	Horses
Unknown	53	59
Before 1 January 1648	161	215
After 1 January 1648	55	66
Total	269	340

Note: Total number of horses is estimated because 12 cases did not state the number of horses involved.

Sources: TNA: PRO, SP 24/30–87.

The sample used in the rest of this section will exclude cases where the horses were taken after 1 January 1648, giving a total of 214 cases involving around 274 horses. The majority of the cases were military in the narrowest sense. At least one of the petitioners was a present or former officer or soldier in 66 per cent of

147   Hughes, 'Parliamentary Tyranny?', 57.
148   Gentles, *New Model Army*, 130; Shedd, 'Legalism over Revolution', 1096.
149   Peter Edwards, 'The Supply of Horses to the Parliamentarian and Royalist Armies in the English Civil War', *Historical Research*, 68/159 (1995): 55, 57.

cases. Civilian officials (mostly constables) were petitioners in 13 per cent, and the remaining 22 per cent were civilians who held no office. An unusual feature of horse cases is that plaintiffs had often been prosecuted simply for possessing a disputed horse without any contention that they had taken it. While petitioners in 59 per cent of cases included at least one person who admitted to having been directly involved in the taking of the horse, 34 per cent of petitions were from someone who had only acquired the horse later. Horses could change hands many times, and because they were all recognizable individuals they could be identified by their previous owners long after they had been taken. This led to some very complicated cases. Parliamentary trooper Benjamin Coggan was allowed to keep his horse when he was disbanded and sold it to John Huddy of Crewkerne, Somerset, who sold it on to John Arding, who was then sued for the horse by William Polden, who claimed to be its original owner.[150] Sometimes a buyer who was accused of receiving a stolen horse reacted by suing the seller, even if this person had not originally taken the horse and could not have known that its ownership was disputed. George Symonds, Thomas Baugh and John Roberts, all civilians, jointly submitted a petition to the Indemnity Committee claiming that Symonds had bought a horse from Captain Bartholomew Helby and sold it on to Baugh who then sold it on to Roberts, who was then challenged by John Arram, who claimed to be the lawful owner. This 'caused yo[u]r Pet[itioner]s to sue one another to their great losse & vexac[i]on' as each sought redress from the man who had sold him the horse before they decided to join forces and appeal for indemnity because the horse had once been in Parliament's service.[151]

Whether the petitioners were soldiers or civilians, it was always important to establish that the horse had been used by parliamentary forces. Horse cases strongly confirm Hughes's observation that 'notions of the State and the public interest are ever-present'.[152] A very large majority of petitions (85 per cent) explicitly stated that the horse had been in actual service. The exceptions were mostly claimed to be prize goods taken directly from enemy soldiers, which became the rightful property of the soldiers who took them according to the established laws of war, even if courts sometimes found that this did not agree with English common law.[153] State service appears to have been far more important than other considerations to most petitioners. Only a minority of petitions (43 per cent) claimed that the horses had been taken by any specific authority, such as an ordinance of Parliament or orders from a superior officer.

---

[150] TNA: PRO, SP 24/31, part 3, Arden vs Polden; TNA: PRO, SP 24/41, part 3, Coggan vs Rascor.

[151] TNA: PRO, SP 24/75, part 3, Symonds vs Arram.

[152] Hughes, 'Parliamentary Tyranny?', 67.

[153] Gentles, *New Model Army*, 130.

Necessity for the state's service was cited as the only justification in 9 per cent of petitions, and 24 per cent claimed that the horses were lawful prizes, but the other 24 per cent offered no justification at all. In some cases these were civilians at the end of a long chain who did not necessarily know the circumstances in which the horse had been taken, but others were soldiers who had taken the horse themselves. Isaacke Malyn, a trooper in Francis Thornhagh's Nottinghamshire regiment, simply wrote that he had been sued in the Court of Common Pleas, 'for the takeinge of one Mare, w[hi]ch he imployed in the Parliaments service'.[154]

If the petitioner claimed no specific authority for taking a horse, the defendant could still be denounced as a delinquent or malignant, but only 27 per cent of petitions in horse cases used this strategy. Another 17 per cent made more personal accusations about the defendants, usually that the lawsuit was malicious or unreasonable, and that they should have known that the actions were covered by the Indemnity Ordinance. What is most surprising is that 57 per cent of petitions cast no aspersions at all on their opponents. This is partly because the changes of ownership which caused complex chains of suits and countersuits between innocent civilians also moved the dispute further away from the issue of King versus Parliament. Even in military cases, there was not always much need to denounce defendants. Soldiers and officials often had authority from Parliament or superior officers to take horses from almost anyone, regardless of allegiance. In the case of prize goods, neither party needed to dispute that the horse's original owner was an innocent victim of plundering cavaliers. The issue at stake was the conflict between military law and common law over how the taking of a horse by royal soldiers and then by parliamentary soldiers affected ownership. Petitioners were much more likely to make an issue of their own allegiance, but there were still a surprising number of exceptions: 21 per cent, coinciding almost entirely with the civilian petitioners, said nothing about supporting Parliament. Only 10 per cent used words which expressed any affection for Parliament, and these were often adverbs attached to actions. For example, Captain Walter Cowley wrote that he had 'constantly & faithfully served [th]e Parl[iamen]t'.[155] Most petitioners (69 per cent) mentioned only their actions and not affections. Horse cases are a notable exception to the general rule that indemnity proceedings encouraged petitioners to present themselves as well-affected and disparage opponents.[156] Indemnity petitions about horses made external allegiance more important than internal allegiance, and the allegiance of horses more important than the allegiance of people.

---

[154] TNA: PRO, SP 24/62, part 3, Malyn vs Bennett.

[155] TNA: PRO, SP 24/42, part 2, Cowley vs Lord.

[156] Hughes, 'Parliamentary Tyranny?', 67–9.

Friends of the People?

Parliament   Civilians who had lost their horses could complain directly to Parliament. This course of action was not equally open to all. There were only 92 cases in which either house objected to the taking of a horse from a specific individual, nearly all of them in 1642 and 1643. This is a very small number compared to the losses entered in parish accounts and can only account for a tiny fraction of the horses used by Parliament's armies. Some of these people were relatively humble. On 2 November 1642 the Commons discharged the horses of Richard Shank, a carrier from Dorchester.[157] The horses of some unnamed carriers were also released on 24 October.[158] These examples are quite unusual. The cases dealt with by Parliament are very heavily biased towards the upper end of society, even allowing for the fact that horse ownership was relatively exclusive. Tradesmen were more likely to be heard if they provided goods or services for Parliament. Joseph Alexander was given special protection by the Lords on November 1642 because he was employed to train cavalry horses for the army.[159] Mr Richard Baker, a collier of Chislehurst, gained similar immunity in May 1643 because he regularly supplied the house with charcoal.[160] Neither of these cases mentioned the men's affections. Businessmen gained extra benefits from their relationship with Parliament, even if they were motivated solely by profit.

Both houses seem to have been primarily concerned with protecting the privileges of their own members. At least a third of the complaints involved parliamentary privilege. The Lords were most aggressive in this respect. There were 15 cases involving horses taken from peers or their servants, and ten involving the wives or widows of peers. Browne and Bard were not the only ones to breach privilege in this way. On 15 February 1643 the Lords received an urgent message that 'some Persons are breaking open the Countess of Devonshire's Stable, for the Taking away of her Horses' and sent the trained bands to intervene. The perpetrator was a man called Gregson, who had already been sent for earlier that day for taking horses from an apothecary employed by the Earl of Leicester.[161] These horses appear to have been delivered to Sir William Waller, who was asked to return them. Gregson was called into the Lords the following day and claimed that he had broken into the stable while searching for two horses which were rumoured to have come from Oxford, but he found that they were not inside

---

157   *CJ*, vol. 2, 831.
158   *CJ*, vol. 2, 820.
159   *LJ*, vol. 5, 455.
160   *HMC*, 5th report, 87; *CJ*, vol. 3, 93; *LJ*, vol. 6, 34.
161   *LJ*, vol. 5, 606.

and so left without taking any horses.[162] He was released with a warning not to search any more stables. On 14 July 1643 Thomas Man, a tailor, was sent for by the Lords to answer for taking a horse from the Countess of Castlehaven, 'being a Breach of the Privilege of Parliament'.[163] Two coach horses belonging to Lady Elizabeth Gerrard, widow of Lord Gerrard, were taken from her stable in Long Acre in December 1642. In her petition to the Lords she described this as 'against [th]e priviledge of parliament, and an injury done her, she beinge a Barronesse of this kingdome'.[164] The peers agreed and ordered the restoration of the horses.[165] The Commons also protected their own: four cases explicitly stated that an MP's horses had been taken.

The Lords and Commons came into conflict over the horses of a Mr Carew or Cary, who had been apprehended in Marylebone Park on suspicion of being a spy from Oxford. Captain Player, who had taken possession of the horses when some soldiers brought them in to the court of guard at Tyburn on 14 April 1643, refused to obey an order of the Lords to restore them because he was acting on the orders of the Committee for Examinations. The Commons backed him against the Lords. The committee confirmed that they had ordered the detention of Carew's horses because he was 'a Man ill-affected to the Parliament, who used to come often from the King's Army hither, as a Spy' and that he had come from Oxford 'in a private Way'. The speaker told Player that 'he should keep and detain the Horses, till this House take further Order: And did, by the Command of the House, give him Thanks for his Obedience and Respect to their Commands; and will protect him in them; and take some further Course for his further Satisfaction.' Player provocatively repeated this to the Lords when they examined him again on 21 April and was dismissed without punishment. At this point the Lords did not accuse the Commons of breach of privilege, but there was clearly hostility between the two houses.[166] According to Whitaker, Carew was a servant of the House of Lords, and Sir Simonds D'Ewes specified that he had a pass from the upper house allowing him to go to and from Oxford, both implying that the Lords classed Player's actions as a breach of their privilege. The majority in the Commons certainly considered summoning

---

[162] *LJ*, vol. 5, 608.

[163] *LJ*, vol. 6, 131. It is not known whether he was related to the Joseph and William Mann involved in the case of Colonel Long in Essex.

[164] PA, HL/PO/JO/10/1/138, House of Lords Main Papers, 20 December 1642, Petition of Dame Elizabeth Gerrard.

[165] *LJ*, vol. 5, 504.

[166] *HMC*, 5th report, 81; *CJ*, vol. 3, 48; *LJ*, vol. 5, 719; *LJ*, vol. 6, 1, 3, 7.

Player as a delinquent to be a breach of their own privilege, but took no further action because the Lords let the captain go.[167]

Only a minority of cases mentioned allegiance to Parliament. On 19 June 1643 the Commons ordered Colonel Mainwaring to restore a horse to Lady Lucy Faunt, 'of whose good Affections to the Parliament the House is very well satisfied'.[168] This was very unusual because there was no mention of how they had been satisfied of her affections. In all other cases which mentioned affection to Parliament, this was specifically tied to contributing to the Propositions. A horse taken from John Browne of Kent in April 1643 was to be released not only because the owner was well-affected but because the horse had already been listed for service of Parliament.[169] The same was true of a horse taken from William Brocas in June 1643.[170] On 1 June 1643 the Commons ordered the arrest of Lieutenant Isaac Buke, who had taken horses from 'Mr. Smyth of Highgate, and others, who have contributed to the Parliament'.[171] Sir Thomas Hampson baronet was to get his pacing mare back in July 1643 because he 'expressed his Affection in a liberal Manner to the Parliament, and hath sent in Horses to the Lord General'.[172]

The Lords occasionally protected delinquents, even if they were not covered by parliamentary privilege. Thomas Coningsby, high sheriff of Hertfordshire had been arrested by Cromwell in January 1643 for publishing royal proclamations and trying to arrest people who fought for Parliament.[173] On 13 March he was called to the bar of the Lords and reprehended for speaking words against Parliament, but immediately afterwards the house considered his petition for the return of two coach horses which had been taken from his wife when she came to visit him.[174] They had been taken by Gregson, 'by power of some warrant as hee pretended', but Coningsby argued that this was against the January ordinance disempowering Bard and Browne.[175] The Lords ordered that Gregson should restore the horses unless he could show a warrant from the Earl of Essex.

---

[167]   BL, Add. 31116, fol. 44r; BL, Harleian 164, fol. 371.

[168]   *CJ*, vol. 3, 134.

[169]   *CJ*, vol. 3, 49.

[170]   *CJ*, vol. 3, 142.

[171]   *CJ*, vol. 3, 110–11.

[172]   *LJ*, vol. 6, 117.

[173]   Holmes, *Eastern Association*, 54.

[174]   *LJ*, vol. 5, 646.

[175]   PA, HL/PO/JO/10/1/145, House of Lords Main Papers, 13 March 1643, Petition of Thomas Coningsbie.

By May, both houses had turned against Essex's warrants, passing the ordinances to restrict seizure and devolve finding horses to the county committees.[176]

County committees   People who did not have easy access to Parliament could still appeal to their local committee or deputy lieutenants for help if their horses were taken by soldiers. This was a viable source of redress because county authorities were often in conflict with field army officers, even though they were ostensibly on the same side. Civilians could sometimes take advantage of these divisions to get their horses back, but in order to do this they usually had to present themselves as well-affected. In June 1643 John Dingley and Matthew Brend, members of the Surrey committee, wrote to Henry Marten asking for the return of three horses taken from Edmund Berkford, 'knowing of him to be an honist man for his fidellity and trust & one whom we doe imploy in the parliments service and doth both for his person and his purse what lyth in his power to doe for the parliment'.[177] The emphasis was very much on what Berkford had done, his fidelity apparently being derived from his actions. This appeal was successful as Marten ordered Captain Richard Stephens to release the horses.[178] Similarly, Harbottle Grimston wrote to his fellow MP Sir Thomas Barrington in July 1643, requesting the return of a horse taken from Richard Tayler, who had been very forward in the service of Parliament.[179] Complainants did not necessarily have to be already well-affected. The possibility of redressing grievances could be used to encourage compliance. The Stafford committee sometimes made the return of horses conditional on payment of the weekly assessment.[180] County committees were certainly not committed to protecting all local civilians regardless of allegiance. People identified as malignants were more likely to be targeted than protected. In December 1643 the Stafford committee ordered a local officer to take William Latkin's horses and other livestock because he had sent men and horses to the Earl of Newcastle.[181]

By treating people differently according to allegiance, county committees reinforced boundaries between the well-affected and ill-affected. But these identities were not just there waiting to be discovered. The parliamentary authorities helped to create them. County committees had the power to classify

[176]   *A & O*, vol. 1, 155–6, 162–3.

[177]   TNA: PRO, SP 28/7, fol. 485.

[178]   TNA: PRO, SP 28/7, fol. 483.

[179]   BL, Egerton 2647, fol. 22.

[180]   Donald H. Pennington and Ivan Roots (eds), *The Committee at Stafford 1643–1645: The Order Book of the Staffordshire Committee*, Staffordshire Record Society, 4th Series, vol. 1 (1957), pp. 16, 49.

[181]   Ibid., 18.

people and impose allegiance on them. Their disputes with outsiders can be interpreted partly as attempts to protect this power. As Holmes made clear, the conflict between Colonel Long and the Essex elite was primarily about jurisdiction.[182] This included the right to police the boundaries of allegiance. Since the status of 'well-affected' depended on external actions and reputation, local officials were in the best position to assign and record it. The ordinance of Parliament of 10 May 1643 justified regulating horse seizure because 'the Officers assigned for that Purpose can neither judge of the Affections nor Abilities of the People, not knowing what they have contributed, nor in what Proportion, to the Propositions'.[183] Long and the Essex MPs took very different views of the affections of Essex people. Long wrote that the county

> in the generall is full of affecc[i]on to the Parliam[en]t, but many of the gentrey soe opposite to the p[ro]ceedings thereof, that I am confident, if I weare not heere the ordinance for the weekly assesment would bee opposed, and little suply of anie kinde would bee had for the Army, the well affected being wearie still to Contribute to the wants thereof, when as the ill affected looke on w[i]th dirision upon them, but I hope when they have contributed in such manner as the others have done, w[hi]ch I hope I shall gett them to doe, they will bee all then well affected.[184]

But Essex MPs reportedly justified revoking Long's power because 'if hee should be permitted to go on in [tha]t rigorous Course w[hi]ch he had begun there, it would so much discontent [tha]t County, that we should wholly lose it, & be able to raise no more mony there'.[185] Both sides in the dispute presented allegiance as something that could be changed by external pressure, but whereas Long claimed to be improving the situation, the Essex gentlemen argued that he was making it worse. These contradictory narratives were both written in terms that were likely to appeal to Parliament. Each man insinuated that the other was hindering the war effort. Colonel Long was one of the most extreme cases of friction between field army officers and local elites. Some other officers sent by the Lord General did not provoke such hostility. Lionel Copley mounted his new troop on 72 horses which had been seized by, or with the cooperation of, the local authorities in Norwich in early 1643. The Norwich committee did not take exception to Copley until much later, when he fraudulently claimed to have paid for the horses out of his own pocket.[186]

---

182   Holmes, 'Colonel Long', 211–12.
183   *A & O*, vol. 1, 155.
184   Bodleian Library, Tanner 62, fol. 35.
185   BL, Add. 31116, fol. 54v.
186   TNA: PRO, SP 28/258, part 2, fol. 157.

The ordinances restricting horse seizure in May 1643 reinforced the power of county committees, but did not necessarily protect civilian property rights even when they were properly implemented. A lieutenant under Captain Hale was able to produce authority from the Hertfordshire committee when he broke into a stable on the night of 12 July 1643 and took two horses valued at £30.[187] The Essex gentry were not always as united as they were against Colonel Long. In May 1643 Sir Richard Everard arrested some of Henry Marten's officers who had taken a horse and used 'many insolent and threatning speeches'.[188] When Sir Thomas Barrington was informed, he agreed that 'their Menaceinge to bringe force uppon the people, theire rayleinge, and takeinge of horses w[i]thout any Distinction of p[er]sons I conceive very punishable', but did nothing except recommending that Everard take the problem to Westminster.[189] This may have been because Marten was a powerful figure who could expect strong support in the Commons. There were clearly limits on the power of the county gentry. When they were able to take action it was not necessarily motivated by a benign concern for the well-being of the county community. By opposing outsiders, county committees asserted their own rights to dominate the county.

Enemies of the People?

Intersections and conflicts between allegiance and social rank caused increasing problems in 1643. Wives of delinquent peers had already been given protection from Bard and Browne, but the House of Lords went further by defending delinquent peers themselves.

The Earl of Carlisle   The allegiance of James Hay, second Earl of Carlisle, was confused and contested. On 10 August the Lords received information that he intended to execute the commission of array in Essex and so sent for him as a delinquent.[190] He was not apprehended until 30 August, when Cromwell caught him in Cambridge before he could execute the commission there.[191] Carlisle was sent down to London, where the Lords committed him to the Tower.[192] On 19 September he was called to the bar of the house to answer charges that he had tried to execute the commission of array and raise a troop of horse for

187   TNA: PRO, SP 28/155, unfol.
188   BL, Egerton 2646, fol. 225.
189   BL, Egerton 2646, fol. 227.
190   John Walter, *Understanding Popular Violence in the English Revolution: The Colchester Plunderers* (Cambridge, 1999), p. 134; *LJ*, vol. 5, 280.
191   Holmes, *Eastern Association*, 55.
192   *LJ*, vol. 5, 334, 338.

the King. He denied these accusations, and when asked whether he thought the commission was illegal gave the evasive answer, 'Seeing both Houses of Parliament had voted the same to be illegal, he would not dissent from that Opinion'. This did not get the peers any closer to finding out what Carlisle thought, but they were satisfied enough that they immediately transferred him from the Tower to house arrest, and then restored him to his seat in the House of Lords on 24 December.[193] Even leaving aside the issue of what the earl 'really' thought, his status was very ambiguous. From 10 August to 19 September he was clearly defined as a delinquent, but he then spent three months in a liminal state of disgrace after conforming to Parliament and was readmitted to the ranks of the well-affected peers in December.

Carlisle was treated leniently by the Lords, but he suffered repeated attacks from common people. On 21 September he was given permission to go to his house at Waltham Abbey in Essex because country people were threatening to pull it down.[194] He reported back on 24 September that he had apprehended some of the people who had attacked his house and park and killed his deer. The Lords agreed to his request 'that the Officers of the Regiment of Colonel Essex may be commanded to keep good Order'.[195] This frustratingly ambiguous phrase could mean that regular infantry were needed to prevent further disorder, or that the soldiers themselves had taken part in the riot. It was not unusual for parliamentary soldiers to aid or initiate spontaneous violence against perceived enemies of Parliament and the protestant religion. Recruits billeted in Chelmsford had already helped local sectaries to intimidate a Laudian minister.[196] Another reason to suspect Charles Essex's regiment of involvement in disorder is that their pay was running short in late September.[197] Wharton's letters mentioned soldiers of Holles's regiment taking spontaneous action against catholics and malignants, engaging in iconoclasm, killing deer for food and mutinying to demand more pay.[198] If the soldiers did riot against the Earl of Carlisle there were many possible motives.

---

[193]   *LJ*, vol. 5, 362, 514.

[194]   *LJ*, vol. 5, 366.

[195]   *LJ*, vol. 5, 373.

[196]   William Hunt, *The Puritan Moment: The Coming of Revolution in an English County* (Cambridge, MA, 1983), pp. 299–300.

[197]   The period for which they had been paid in advance ended on 24 September. The Committee of Safety issued a warrant for one month's pay for the whole regiment on 27 September, and the money was paid on 4 October. I am grateful to Tom Crawshaw for this information.

[198]   Nehemiah Wharton, *Letters of a Subaltern in the Earl of Essex's Army*, Henry Ellis (ed.) (London, 1854), pp. 4–10, 12–15.

The attack on the earl's property was followed by an attack on his person. The Lords received information on 8 December, 'That the Earls of Suffolke and Carlile were taken out of their Coaches in London Yesterday, and knocked down by a Constable, and afterward carried to The Compter in London.'[199] Although the peers took exception to this treatment, the constable may technically have been in the right, since there is no official order in the *Lords Journal* releasing the earl from house arrest or summoning him to attend Parliament. Waltham Abbey was apparently targeted again, as on 4 January 1643 the Lords heard from Carlisle that 'divers Persons have in riotous Manner assaulted his House, and came and killed his Deer', and responded by sending for several Essex yeomen and tradesmen.[200] The motives for these attacks are obscure, but on the surface they fit the pattern of popular attacks on perceived enemies of the commonwealth, particularly in Essex.[201] Ordinary people may have played a crucial role in preventing Carlisle from executing the commission of array in Essex, since the Lords were told that he would have done it 'if he had not found that the Country would have opposed him'.[202] His nomination by the King to command the county was likely to be very unpopular because it usurped the position of the much-loved Earl of Warwick.[203] The assaults on the earl's house and deer were in some ways similar to the actions against the Earl of Middlesex's property in Gloucestershire in October 1642. Dan Beaver suggested that while the dispute was mostly over hunting and woodcutting rights, Middlesex's house at Forthampton was also targeted because it was decorated with stonework from Tewkesbury Abbey and so was perceived as a relic of popery.[204] Similarly, Carlisle's house at Waltham was built on the site of a medieval abbey and probably incorporated part of the ruins.[205] Carlisle's arrest and the repeated attacks on him suggest that he was popularly perceived as a delinquent even after this official status had been removed from him. The timing of the attacks of Waltham Abbey is very suggestive, since the first happened just after the Lords had released the earl from the Tower, and the second was not long after he had been restored to his seat in Parliament. The actions of the crowd may have been political messages directed at the House of Lords as much as personal attacks on Carlisle's honour and property. This cannot be proved, but the possibility complicates the idea of

---

[199]   *LJ*, vol. 5, 481.

[200]   *LJ*, vol. 5, 526.

[201]   Walter, *Understanding Popular Violence*, 31–68.

[202]   Ibid., 134; *LJ*, vol. 5, 280.

[203]   Holmes, *Eastern Association*, 38–9.

[204]   Daniel C. Beaver, *Hunting and the Politics of Violence before the English Civil War* (Cambridge, 2008), pp. 125, 140–41, 144–5, 149.

[205]   *VCH Essex*, vol. 5, 151–62.

'popular parliamentarianism'. Although the Colchester mob had got out of hand and alarmed even the puritan elite, they could still claim to be enforcing orders of Parliament to prevent horses and arms from being taken to the King. But the mobs at Waltham may have been disputing official classifications of allegiance as much as enforcing them.

Although Carlisle's loyalties were still suspect, his peers were perhaps more likely to see him as a relatively harmless victim of the many-headed monster, as unruly common people were often described by the elite. These different perceptions collided in a dispute over horses. On 4 March Carlisle informed the Lords that some troopers had broken into his stables at Newmarket and taken away some of his horses, which he described as a breach of privilege of Parliament.[206] The officer responsible was sent for as a delinquent, but apparently did not turn up and was summoned again on 9 March. Carlisle identified him as Lieutenant Whaly, under Captain Nelson, but when he finally appeared before the house on 21 March his identity was recorded as Captain Waly.[207] This man may or may not have been Cromwell's cousin Edward Whalley, later regicide and major-general.[208] According to a later certificate of account, Edward Whalley was commissioned as captain in Cromwell's regiment on 18 February 1643 and promoted to major on 15 May.[209] In 1642 he was listed as cornet under John Fiennes in Essex's army, but his career between these dates is unclear.[210] Nothing is known about Captain Nelson. In his defence, Waly claimed that:

> Coming to Newmarket, he was told, by a Constable, that the Earl of Carlile was a Malignant, and that he had Horses there: Upon this, he seized the Horses of the Earl of Carlile, which he acknowledged he was too hasty in, and craved their Lordships Pardon for the same, and professed his good Affections to the Parliament.[211]

Questions of allegiance were central to this case. Waly presented himself as loyal to Parliament. He justified his actions by showing that he had taken advice from a local official and that he believed Carlisle was an enemy, but at the same time admitted to being mistaken. By the time of this incident the earl had been forgiven for his earlier offences and was no longer officially classed a delinquent,

---

[206] *LJ*, vol. 5, 636.
[207] *LJ*, vol. 5, 643, 656.
[208] Christopher Durston, 'Whalley, Edward, appointed Lord Whalley under the protectorate (d. 1674/5)', *ODNB*. Firth, 'Raising the Ironsides', 43–4 and Holmes, *Eastern Association*, 81 both stated that it was Edward Whalley, without discussing the complications.
[209] TNA: PRO, SP 28/253A, fol. 42.
[210] Turton, *Chief Strength*, 42.
[211] *LJ*, vol. 5, 657.

but his public reputation could not be changed so easily. It cannot be assumed that taking his horses was genuinely a mistake. The case also shows that at this time the term 'delinquent' was still ambiguous. It was almost certainly applied to Waly in the traditional sense of someone who had breached privilege. There was apparently no suspicion that he had supported the King, since 'in regard of his good Service done to the Parliament, and upon the Mediation of the Earl of Carlile, this House is willing to pass by what he hath hastily done'.[212] Whether Waly's contrition was sincere or just a public transcript, it reiterated the earl's official change of status.

Carlisle had further trouble in July when Colonel Mitton took some of his horses by order of the Committee of Examinations. This committee countermanded an order of the Lords to release the horses, which it claimed had been 'carried to Waltham, to the Terror of the Country'. John Pym reported from a conference of both houses that the Lords 'conceive this to be a great Breach of their Privileges; and desire that Course may be taken that this Breach may be repaired, and their Privileges preserved', but the Commons simply referred the matter back to the Committee of Examinations.[213] There may also have been conflict within the House of Lords. When Mitton was examined by the house, he claimed that he had taken the horses by virtue of a warrant from the Lord General as well as one from the Committee of Examinations. The terms of these warrants are unknown because copies do not survive. Essex's army was desperate for horses at this time, which would be sufficient motivation for the warrant. At the very least, the Lord General was putting military necessity before the interests of his peers.

The basic issue in both of these cases was parliamentary privilege. Carlisle was not classed as a delinquent at the times when his horses were taken and so he qualified for full protection, as was standard practice. At the same time, the earl's temporary delinquency and continuing unpopularity added extra layers of meaning to the controversy. Protecting his property acquired greater symbolic significance when it had so often been attacked by mobs. Even before he received the Commission of Array, he had been troubled by riots. As chief keeper of Newlodge Walk in Waltham Forest, Carlisle was responsible for protecting the King's deer from poachers, a task which became increasingly difficult as order broke down. In April 1642 an armed mob killed deer in the forest and questioned Carlisle's authority.[214] Conflicts over the royal forests did not fit easily into the high politics of 1642 and sometimes challenged the authority of both sides.

[212] Ibid.
[213] *CJ*, vol. 3, 155–6; *LJ*, vol. 6, 119–20.
[214] Beaver, *Hunting*, 55–7.

The Waltham Forest rioters claimed that 'there was no law settled at this time', effectively denying the legitimacy of Parliament's 1641 forest statute as well as the royal prerogative.[215] In Windsor forest, some poachers told a constable who tried to arrest them that 'they cared neither for king nor parliament, neither would obey his warrant', before shooting his horse and escaping.[216] This was a different kind of neutrality from the equivocation and non-aggression pacts of the greater gentry, and from the obscure inactivity of the silent majority of the middling sort. Disputes over forest law were different, but not entirely separate, from the personal attacks on the Earl of Carlisle. Sometimes forest conflicts connected with the civil war in unexpected ways. Horses were seized from a keeper of Waltham Forest because two poachers denounced him as an enemy of Parliament.[217] Even if this was just opportunism, they had to adopt a position of well-affectedness and contribute to polarization.

Meanwhile, the Earl of Carlisle had more trouble with mobs. In May 1643 he told the Lords that he had the right to take tolls on the River Lea, but that 'of late some Bargemen have, in a riotous Manner, broken open the Lock, and refuse to pay the said Toll'.[218] On the surface this looks like an economic grievance, but it must have added to the impression that order was breaking down and that peers in general, and Carlisle in particular, were under threat. Furthermore, the question of the earl's allegiance had not been settled. He had evidently deserted to the King by 28 October 1643, when his wife, Margaret, petitioned Parliament to complain that she had been denied her jointure at Waltham Abbey because the estate was under sequestration.[219] The earl was still absent from the Lords without permission on 22 January 1644, but changed sides yet again, taking the Covenant on 6 May.[220] In August he petitioned the Committee for Compounding, admitting that he had a commission from the King to raise a horse regiment but claiming that he had never actually raised it and had 'discov[er]ed his dislike of the Kings p[ro]ceedings' before returning to Parliament.[221] Although he had been a delinquent twice he apparently did very little, and this may have influenced his lenient treatment in both cases. Even so, his fluctuating allegiance was potentially an embarrassment to the peers who had protected him. Carlisle's story emphasizes the external and mutable aspects of allegiance. Classing him as a 'side-changer' would not be helpful because his

---

[215]   Ibid., 55, 87.
[216]   Ibid., 122–3.
[217]   Holmes, *Eastern Association*, 81.
[218]   *LJ*, vol. 6, 47.
[219]   *LJ*, vol. 6, 282.
[220]   *LJ*, vol. 6, 387–8, 542.
[221]   TNA: PRO, SP 23/127, p. 585.

allegiance partly depended on perceptions and reputation. The way that he was classified by other people and organizations was at least as important as what he chose to do.

Lord Conway Another conflict broke out between the Lords and Commons over the horses of Viscount Conway in June 1643. Conway was a loyal follower of the Earl of Northumberland, and Parliament had given him command of a foot regiment raised for service in Ireland, but in June 1643 he was imprisoned on suspicion of involvement in Edmund Waller's plot to betray London.[222] Shortly after Conway's arrest, Captain Herriot Washborne of the London militia seized some of his horses. On 14 June the Lords ordered Washborne to restore the horses and to appear before a group of eight peers to explain himself.[223] They were headed by Conway's ally, Northumberland, and also included the earls of Holland and Bedford, who had been advocating negotiated peace and who defected to Oxford not long afterwards. This suggests that there was an element of factional politics in the dispute. Washborne appeared before the Commons rather than the Lords, testifying that he had a warrant from the Lord General as well as authority from two unnamed deputy lieutenants of Middlesex who were also MPs and sequestrators.[224] Therefore he had acted correctly according to the May ordinance regulating horse seizures, but the Lords insisted that 'this House approves not of the Manner of taking the Horses'.[225] The warrant placed Essex on the militant side again, in opposition to the peace faction and the majority of his peers. The two houses seem to have reached a compromise based on the principle of innocent until proven guilty, agreeing that Conway's horses and other goods should be placed in the custody of Sir Robert Harley until the accusations of complicity in Waller's plot had been investigated further.[226] Harley seems to have been an acceptable choice on both sides since he was aligned with the puritan militants and was also Conway's brother-in-law.[227] The discovery of the plot disturbed assumptions about allegiance and provoked a new shibboleth, the Vow and Covenant. Where the Protestation had been too vague and moderate to draw a clear line between friends and enemies, the new vow was too extreme even for some supporters of Parliament, since it did not include any commitment

---

[222] John Adamson, *The Noble Revolt: The Overthrow of Charles I* (London, 2007), p. 498; James Knowles, 'Conway, Edward, second Viscount Conway and second Viscount Killultagh (bap. 1594, d. 1655)', *ODNB*.

[223] *LJ*, vol. 6, 95.

[224] *CJ*, vol. 3, 131.

[225] *LJ*, vol. 6, 98.

[226] *CJ*, vol. 3, 131; *LJ*, vol. 6, 98.

[227] Knowles, 'Conway, Edward'.

to defend the King's person or prerogatives.[228] It was hard to find anything which united all of Parliament's supporters and divided them from all of the King's supporters. On 28 July the Lords ordered that Conway should be released and his horses restored because he had not been charged.[229] Soon after this he fled to Oxford. Conway was considered for a prestigious command in the King's forces, but after it was awarded to another candidate he deserted the court and compounded with Parliament.[230]

Henry Marten against the Monarchy   Henry Marten caused some of the same problems as other officers commissioned to seize horses, but went much further and brought about even more serious confrontations between the Lords and the Commons. On 2 May 1643 the Lords were informed that someone had broken into the royal mews and taken two young horses belonging to the King.[231] The house immediately ordered that the horses should be returned and that the people who took them should be called in to show their authority. A deputy of the gentleman usher was sent to deliver these orders. He reported back that the horses had been taken to a stable in Smithfield by Quartermaster De Luke in Marten's regiment, who refused to release them without orders from his colonel. Marten told the deputy that he had given De Luke specific orders to take the horses and that he would not return them, sending a letter back to the Lords stating his intention to raise the matter in the Commons rather than obey the orders of the Lords. They 'conceived this to be a great Contempt to the Honour of this House' and took 'this Carriage of Mr. Marten's as a great Disrespect to their Lordships and the Authority of this House', calling for a conference with the Commons and resolving to 'send to the Lord General, to acquaint him with Mr. Marten's Actions, and of the Abuse of his Power in this Particular, and desire him to re-call his Commission given to him, lest, by the Power he hath, further Inconveniences may ensue'.[232] The majority in the Commons was equally belligerent, taking Marten's side against the upper house. They resolved that he 'did well, in not delivering these Two Horses, till he had made this House acquainted therewith', that he should keep the horses until the Commons gave him further orders and that 'the Lord General be desired not to

---

[228]   Edward Vallance, *Revolutionary England and the National Covenant: State Oaths, Protestantism and the Political Nation, 1553–1682* (Woodbridge, 2005), p. 56.

[229]   *LJ*, vol. 6, 153.

[230]   Knowles, 'Conway, Edward'; Ann Hughes, 'The King, the Parliament and the Localities during the English Civil War', *Journal of British Studies*, 24/2 (1985): 252; Ronald Hutton, *The Royalist War Effort, 1642–1646* (London, 1984), pp. 118–19; *LJ*, vol. 6, 518.

[231]   *LJ*, vol. 6, 26.

[232]   *LJ*, vol. 6, 28.

do any thing in the Business concerning Mr. Marten, till he hear further from this House'.[233] Hexter and Barber suggested that Pym tried to protect the Lords from Marten's attacks, but if that was the case he must have lost control of the Commons on this day.[234]

While this confrontation was similar to previous controversies over breach of privilege, there was an even bigger constitutional issue at stake. Parliament did not class Charles I as a delinquent or malignant at this time, and did not hold him personally responsible for the civil wars until 1648. Since the Propositions Ordinance in June 1642, Parliament had justified taking up arms by claiming that the King had been seduced by wicked counsel. By assuming executive power, peers and MPs effectively treated Charles as if he had abdicated or become incapacitated.[235] The fundamental basis of English armed resistance to Charles was the theory of the king's two bodies: Parliament could exercise the powers of the crown independently of Charles's person. This meant that taking horses from the King himself was not as straightforward as taking them from his supporters. The majority in the Lords treated the horses in the mews as Charles's personal property by protecting them from requisitioning. Horses had particularly important symbolic value for this issue. Henry Parker had used the example of horses to illustrate the difference between the King's personal property and the property of his subjects held in trust.[236] Henry Marten did not make this distinction. He was reported to have said that 'he sees no Reason but the King's Horses as well as His Ships may be taken, for the Service of the Kingdom'.[237] By treating Charles's own horses the same as the ships of the Royal Navy, which had been taken over by Parliament in the previous year, Marten was attacking the doctrine of the two bodies. This had disturbingly radical implications, although D'Ewes did not pick up this point, perhaps because he consistently opposed the war and so had no attachment to any justifications for it.[238] Marten's alleged words, which he apparently did not deny, and which provoked no official censure when they were repeated to the Commons, suggested a personal vendetta against Charles I, and perhaps a struggle against

---

[233] *CJ*, vol. 3, 68–9.

[234] Barber, *Revolutionary Rogue*, 10; J.H. Hexter, *The Reign of King Pym* (Cambridge, MA, 1941), p. 60.

[235] Morrill, *Revolt in the Provinces*, 64–5, 297; Peter Lake, 'Anti-Popery: The Structure of a Prejudice', in Richard Cust and Ann Hughes (eds), *The English Civil War* (London, 1997), p. 194.

[236] Christopher Brooks, 'Professions, Ideology and the Middling Sort in the Late Sixteenth and Early Seventeenth Centuries', in Jonathan Barry and Christopher Brooks (eds), *The Middling Sort of People: Culture, Society and Politics in England, 1550–1800* (Basingstoke, 1994), p. 138.

[237] *LJ*, vol. 6, 28.

[238] BL, Harleian 164, fol. 383r.

the institution of monarchy itself. This was made clearer on 16 August, when Marten spoke in support of John Saltmarsh, arguing that killing the King and his family could be justified for the public good. This went too far even for the militant leader Pym, who perhaps deliberately overreacted as part of a scheme to get Marten out of the way.[239] While it cannot definitely be proved that Pym set Marten up, it was certainly in his interest to remove troublemakers. Marten's horse requisitioning has not been examined in detail by his biographers but provides an extra possible motive for plots against him. By targeting peers and the royal mews, he exacerbated tensions between the Lords and the Commons. Although his regiment was not completed, it gave him a certain amount of military power in London, directly threatening the peers. Whatever the motives might have been, the result was that Marten lost his seat in the Commons and was imprisoned in the Tower.

Essex's attitude is unknown, and his actions, or lack of them, are highly ambiguous. On 3 May the Lords had asked him to revoke Marten's commission, but the Commons asked him not to. According to D'Ewes, it was the 'fierie spirits' in the Commons who were responsible, and that

> they would send to the saied Earle of Essex Lord Generall to continue his saied commission: & it seames the same Earle was moore pliable to satisfie them then to satisfie the Howse of Peeres; for the saied Martins commission was not called in but hee raised his Regiment of horse by vertue of the same, w[i]th much violence & injurie to many: w[hi]ch hee well might for the Lords perceiving w[hi]ch way the saied Earle of Essex inclined, never at all sent unto him to call in the saied commission ... [240]

This view cannot simply be dismissed as bias, since Marten's activities clearly did continue for several months. But if Essex was hoping for reinforcements, he would have been disappointed. The commission was probably issued in April, but Marten had still not completed his regiment at the time of his ejection and imprisonment in August. On 12 July the Commons ordered that the existing troops should be sent to Essex's army, but this clearly did not happen since the Militia Committee was ordered to secure their horses and arms on 16 August.[241] At least two of the troops raised by Marten eventually went into active service. Seymour Pyle and his troop were part of Essex's army by December 1643. Richard Stephens, another of Marten's captains, joined the Lord General in

239   Barber, *Revolutionary Rogue*, 9–10.
240   BL, Harleian 164, fol. 383r.
241   *CJ*, vol. 3, 164, 206.

September and mustered 55 troopers on 14 October.[242] The political problems caused by the regiment were out of all proportion to its military effectiveness.

Conclusion

Arbitrary seizure of horses did not do anyone much good. When Sir Thomas Barrington wrote to Parliament to complain about soldiers taking horses in Essex and Hertfordshire in August 1643, he pointed out that if farmers lost all their horses they would not be able to support themselves or pay taxes, and that the county committee's war administration was being disrupted because horses had even been taken from deputy lieutenants.[243] If the emphasis on the implications for the war effort was a necessary strategy for appealing to Parliament, Barrington's arguments were still logically correct. Without horses, farmers could not plough or sow their fields and therefore could not make any money to pay rent or taxes.[244] He also warned that 'it will not in my opinion be possible, to p[re]serve the good affection of this County unlesse the wisdome of the P[ar]liam[en]t be pleased, to aply some remidy', hinting that allegiance was not only changeable but conditional.[245] The field armies did not necessarily do well out of the practice either. Soldiers and officers were sometimes prepared to accept bribes to release horses. While these were expensive for the owners, they only covered a fraction of the value of a horse, and so would not have been an effective way to pay for remounts even if the soldiers did not pocket the money. When cavalry officers and units were busy requisitioning horses they could not be doing anything else. It would have been inconvenient enough when cavalry had to interrupt their operations to find a remount or two, but some officers were sent away from the combat zone for weeks or months at a time. Colonel Long and his men arrived in Essex in March and were not recalled until June.[246] While Essex's army was busy relieving Gloucester in August, the remnants of Waller's cavalry were preoccupied with taking up horses in Hertfordshire (see Chapter 4). This was probably necessary in part because there were more horses available in areas which had not been constantly fought over by armies of both sides, but these areas were also an important source of other resources. By damaging the economy and antagonizing both taxpayers and local officials, horse takers probably helped to undermine the flow of tax revenues into central treasuries.

242 TNA: PRO, SP 28/7, fol. 483; Turton, *Chief Strength*, 55, 64.
243 BL, Egerton 2647, fol. 201; Bodleian Library, Tanner 62, fol. 285.
244 Hughes, 'Parliamentary Tyranny?', 50.
245 Bodleian Library, Tanner 62, fol. 285.
246 Holmes, 'Colonel Long', 211–12.

Finally, horse seizure provoked and exacerbated conflicts between different parts of the parliamentary war machine. In the first half of 1643 political divisions increased and the flow of resources declined.

The problem of horse seizure was reduced when alternative sources of supply were made available (see Chapters 4 and 5), but it never completely went away. Even the New Model Army took horses directly from civilians on a few occasions, although this was quite rare. Two inhabitants of Northamptonshire claimed to have lost horses to the New Model around the time of Naseby.[247] Another two horses were taken from Marsh Gibbon in Buckinghamshire 'by some of the souldiers of S[i]r Thomas Farrefax his Army as they went from Borestall to Naseby'.[248] In 1643 Essex and Waller continued to authorize large-scale seizures in defiance of Parliament and the county committees because they had no alternative. The overall impact of horse seizure is hard to quantify, but figures derived from the Buckinghamshire parish accounts at least give an impression. The surviving accounts cover 38 per cent of the parishes and boroughs in the county. In total they explicitly claimed 566 horses permanently taken by soldiers, 32 released for bribes and 81 lost during cart service, as well as some unspecified numbers. Based on this sample it can be conjectured that the whole county lost around 1,500 horses to arbitrary seizure by parliamentary forces during the First Civil War, on top of those lent on the Propositions or requisitioned in a more orderly fashion. While these losses were very heavy for civilians, the gains for armies were trivial. Local garrisons and the field armies of Essex, Waller and Manchester are all well represented in the accounts, which cover most of the First Civil War. On average, each force could only have taken a few hundred horses from Buckinghamshire in the whole period, a number barely adequate to cover typical losses for a couple of months. It has to be concluded that taking horses by force was hardly worth the trouble.

---

[247]   TNA: PRO, SP 28/172, unfol.
[248]   TNA: PRO, SP 28/151, unfol.

Chapter 4

Quotas

Crisis

Parliament faced a major crisis in the summer of 1643. Several field armies were competing with each other and with various local forces and garrisons for resources which were in short supply. There is no evidence of Parliament having an actual resource advantage at this time. The flow of resources to individual armies had almost certainly declined since 1642. Tactical and operational failures only made the situation worse. The army of the Fairfaxes in Yorkshire was relatively small and particularly short of cavalry. Lord Fairfax had adopted a Fabian strategy in order to cancel the numerical advantage of Newcastle's northern army. On 30 June the army of the Fairfaxes fought Newcastle at Adwalton Moor and was almost completely destroyed. The remnants of Sir Thomas Fairfax's cavalry escaped and eventually linked up with Cromwell in Lincolnshire, while Lord Fairfax took command of Hull, but the West Riding was lost.[1] Meanwhile, Essex's army was very weak (see Chapter 3). On 4 July the Lord General retreated from Thame, setting up his headquarters at Great Brickhill by 9 July.[2] This only made him less able to prevent reinforcements from Oxford going into the west. On 13 July a combined force of cavalry from the Oxford and western armies effectively wiped out Waller's army at Roundway Down near Devizes.[3] Again some cavalry escaped, but Waller was out of action for some time and Essex was unable to fill the gap. This gave the royal forces a window of opportunity to overrun large parts of the west before Parliament could raise any new forces to stop them. Nathaniel Fiennes surrendered Bristol on 26 July, significantly changing the balance of power.[4] With the Fairfaxes out

---

[1] Andrew J. Hopper, *'Black Tom': Sir Thomas Fairfax and the English Revolution* (Manchester, 2007), pp. 42–6, 211.

[2] Vernon F. Snow, *Essex the Rebel: the Life of Robert Devereux, the Third Earl of Essex 1591–1646* (Lincoln, NE, 1970), p. 371; LJ, vol. 6, 127.

[3] Malcolm Wanklyn and Frank Jones, *A Military History of the English Civil War* (Harlow, 2005), p. 105; Ian Gentles, *The English Revolution and the Wars in the Three Kingdoms, 1638–1652* (London, 2007), pp. 176–8.

[4] Wanklyn and Jones, *Military History*, 109.

of the way, Newcastle could move south. He took Gainsborough on 4 August and overran Lincolnshire, forcing Lord Willoughby to fall back to Boston.[5]

Defeat in battles and inadequate supply of resources fed into each other, bringing Parliament very close to losing the war. Small, poorly supplied armies had less freedom to operate and were more likely to be defeated in battles, although the chaos of the battlefield could still produce unexpected results. Adwalton Moor was much closer than the disparity of numbers would suggest, and Waller's defeat by a relatively small number of cavalry at Roundway Down could not easily have been predicted.[6] The loss of an army in a battle only made the resource situation worse because the losses had to be replaced. Parliament faced even more problems because of factional divisions. Some of these divisions were already apparent in late 1642 and they contributed to increasing failure in mid-1643. With the peace group attempting to open negotiations, conservative peers obsessing over their own privileges and property, and extremists such as Henry Marten antagonizing moderates, it became increasingly difficult to pass and implement orders to extract resources. Rivalry between Essex and Waller added a further complication to the competition for resources, as each had the support of powerful factions in Parliament.

The Flying Army

Negotiation

Throughout June and into the middle of July, the Lords and Commons were pushing in opposite directions on the issue of horse supply. The confrontations over specific cases examined in Chapter 3 were only part of the problem. Both houses tried to pass general ordinances concerning horse seizure, but while the majority in the Lords tried to ban it, the majority in the Commons encouraged it. On 3 June 1643 the Commons passed an ordinance 'for listing and exercising all the Horses in the City of London, the Suburbs and Twelve Miles Compass', but when the bill was sent up to the Lords, it was rejected.[7] A week later, the Lords ordered the King's counsel to draw up a bill, 'That no Horses shall be taken by any Person, in the Cities of London and Westm. and within Twenty Miles of London' without the permission of both houses.[8] When this ordinance was read in the House of Lords on 12 June, the limit had been increased to

---

5   Clive Holmes, *The Eastern Association in the English Civil War* (Cambridge, 2007), pp. 92–4.
6   Hopper, *Black Tom*, 45; Gentles, *English Revolution*, 178.
7   *CJ*, vol. 3, 113; *LJ*, vol. 6, 79; BL, Add. 31116, fol. 55r.
8   *LJ*, vol. 6, 88.

30 miles. At the same time, the peers drafted a letter to Essex informing him of the new ordinance and asking him to stop issuing commissions to seize horses.[9] The Commons read the ordinance on the same day but clearly had no intention of passing it, since they referred it to a committee and then sent a message to the Lords asking them to pass the previous ordinance to list all horses within 12 miles of London.[10] The lower house continued to press for this, even requesting Essex to grant commissions for listing horses according to the ordinance without waiting for the Lords to approve it.[11] A petition came in to the Commons from the government of the City of London on 22 June, requesting that the ordinance be passed.[12] From this it appears that the listed horses were to be 'kept in a Constant readynesse to bee made use of upon all emergent occasions' and that their owners should 'quietly enjoye the same' until they were needed to secure Parliament, the City and the suburbs, 'All which are in greate Jeapordy and Continuall Dainger through want of such a Considerable strength of Horse as might bee raysed thereby'.[13] In a conference between both houses on 27 June, the Lords 'agreed that the Thing should be done, but not in that Way as the Ordinance is now drawn up'.[14] A committee of peers considered the ordinance sent up from the Commons and made some alterations, to which the upper house assented.[15] But when the amended version was sent back down to the Commons on 3 July it was referred to a committee, which implies that the changes were not acceptable.[16] Because the journals do not contain any drafts of the ordinance in any of its forms, it is difficult to say what the points of contention were or what alterations were made.

The failure of the two houses to reach agreement did not help Essex's army, which was still suffering from a severe shortage of horses. The Lords received two letters from the Lord General on 11 July. The first, dated 5 July, demanded 500 horses to be sent to him immediately and the regular supply of 200 remounts per month. The second, sent from Great Brickhill on 9 July, reported the army's retreat and emphasized the operational problems caused by not having an adequate cavalry screen:

---

[9]   *LJ*, vol. 6, 90.

[10] *CJ*, vol. 3, 127.

[11] *LJ*, vol. 6, 100, 103; *CJ*, vol. 3, 137.

[12] *CJ*, vol. 3, 140.

[13] PA, HL/PO/JO/10/1/152, House of Lords Main Papers, 22 June 1643, Petition of the Lord Mayor, aldermen and common council of the City of London.

[14] *LJ*, vol. 6, 112.

[15] *LJ*, vol. 6, 114.

[16] *CJ*, vol. 3, 152.

> The Enemy being so strong in Horse, and this Army being neither recruited with
> Horses, nor Arms, nor Saddles, it is impossible to keep the Counties from being
> plundered, nor to fight with them, but where and when they list; we being forced,
> when we march, to move with the whole Army, which can be but slow Marches ...

Essex ended the letter by suggesting that the war should be settled through peace
negotiations or a prearranged trial by battle.[17] The Lords asked the Commons to
agree to send out any spare cavalry units in London in response to the first letter,
but voted against peace propositions until the King withdrew his proclamation
that the Parliament was illegitimate. Henry Marten's regiment should have been
eligible, but clearly did not go (see Chapter 3). The following day the Commons
tried to go ahead with the scheme for listing horses within 12 miles of London
despite the opposition of the Lords, ordering a commission from the Lord
General to be sent to the Militia Committee, who were authorized to print it.[18]
The Commons then started to look at alternative methods of raising horses. On
15 July they decided to seek voluntary subscriptions of men, horses, ammunition
and money with 'the publick Faith for Repayment'.[19] The order, which was
formally drawn up and passed on 17 July, invited contributions for Essex, Waller
and Lord Fairfax.[20] The intentions behind this move are not clear. It may have
been a well-meaning but naive attempt to revive the Propositions, which were
almost completely defunct by this time. Or it may have been a ploy to create the
impression of doing something for Essex and Waller while the main effort was
being diverted to another army. The treasurer of the southern division of Essex
collected £210 for Lord Fairfax and £48 for Waller, probably in response to this
order, but these sums are insignificant compared to nearly £4,000 advanced on
the Propositions in 1642.[21]

When John Dillingham's newsbook *The Parliament Scout* reported Essex's
letter and Parliament's response, it also called for 'a flying Army that might have
forst them to fight'.[22] It was not unusual for politicians to use the press to prepare the
way for new policies.[23] This looks like another example of this practice. Dillingham
was probably given privileged information by someone inside Parliament, since

---

[17]   *LJ*, vol. 6, 127.

[18]   *CJ*, vol. 3, 164.

[19]   *CJ*, vol. 3, 167.

[20]   *CJ*, vol. 3, 171.

[21]   TNA: PRO, SP 28/153, part 6, Account book of John Fenning.

[22]   Holmes, *Eastern Association*, 93; *The Parliament Scout*, 3, 6–13 July 1643, TT E.60[8],
p. 18.

[23]   Jason Peacey, *Politicians and Pamphleteers: Propaganda During the English Civil Wars
and Interregnum* (Aldershot, 2004), pp. 248–9.

his report matches the *Lords Journal* very closely.[24] The only discrepancy is Dillingham's claim that Parliament had agreed to send 500 cavalry to the army, whereas the actual response was to find an unspecified number from troops that were in London but not needed for its defence. The source of the leak may have been the Earl of Manchester, who was present as speaker of the Lords when Essex's letters were read. Later in the year, Dillingham actively promoted Manchester's political campaign to supersede Lord Willoughby of Parham as commander of Lincolnshire.[25] In the following year the Oxford newsbook *Mercurius Aulicus* alleged that *The Parliament Scout* 'puts himselfe unto the trouble of a large Apologie for the Earle of Manchester, whose pensioner he seemes to be'.[26] This is not conclusive evidence that Manchester and Dillingham colluded over the plans for a flying army, but it is suggestive considering what happened next.

On 18 July the Commons resolved to impose a quota of horses on several counties.[27] Rather than being used to recruit the existing armies, these horses would be put into a new independent cavalry force of four divisions, commanded by the Earls of Bolingbroke, Manchester and Pembroke, and Lord Howard of Escrick. Lawrence Whitaker's diary recorded this proposal in detail, explicitly describing it as 'a Flying Army'. According to Whitaker, the resolution was a direct response to news of Waller's defeat at Roundway Down, which had reached some MPs on 17 July.[28] An ordinance putting the plan into effect was passed by the Commons and sent up to the Lords on 22 July.[29] The Lords generally agreed with the ordinance, but made some amendments: as usual they exempted the horses of peers and their assistants; the Isle of Wight's obligation was removed; and the Earl of Manchester was recommended as sole commander because the other three peers nominated by the Commons wished to be excused.[30] The Ordinance was published in its final form on 25 July.[31] Each county was required to raise a specified number of horses, shown in Table 4.1 below. Newly raised units were to be augmented by militia cavalry and other existing local forces. Responsibility for raising these forces was devolved to the deputy lieutenants and county committees, who were to 'use all good and lawfull wayes and meanes

---

[24]   See ibid., 222–4 for other examples of leaks.

[25]   Clive Holmes, 'Colonel King and Lincolnshire Politics, 1642–1646', *Historical Journal*, 16/3 (1973): 455.

[26]   Peacey, *Politicians and Pamphleteers*, 187; *Mercurius Aulicus*, 23, 8 June 1644, TT E.52[7], p. 1009.

[27]   *CJ*, vol. 3, 171–2.

[28]   BL, Add. 31116, fols 63v–64r.

[29]   *CJ*, vol. 3, 177.

[30]   *CJ*, vol. 3, 179; *LJ*, vol. 6, 145.

[31]   *A & O*, vol. 1, 215–19.

Table 4.1   County horse quotas, 1643

County	Horses
Bedfordshire	200
Berkshire	200
Buckinghamshire	200
Cambridgeshire	200
Essex	500
Hampshire	500
Hertfordshire	300
Huntingdon	100
Kent	600
London and Middlesex	1,500
Norfolk	600
Northamptonshire	400
Suffolk	500
Surrey	300
Sussex	400
Total	6,500

Source: A & O, vol. 1, 215–16.

for the effecting of this service, as in their wisdome, judgement and discretion shall be thought most conducing to the advancing thereof', and were authorized to seize horses from 'any person' within their counties.[32] Assessments were also to be made to provide a month's pay for the riders of the horses, but the exact method was left to the discretion of the county authorities. At this stage, the plan seems to have been to create an independent army which could operate anywhere. While the eastern counties were included in the quotas, and some

---

[32]   *A & O*, vol. 1, 217.

officers already serving in Lord Grey's army, including Cromwell, were named as subordinates to Manchester, this was not initially a plan to reinforce the Eastern Association. The allocation of counties to the four divisions cut across the association and would have split it up if the original plan had been implemented. The ordinance offered a way of avoiding existing disputes by reducing arbitrary seizures, giving a bigger role to county committees and giving command to a new man who was not closely associated with Essex or Waller.[33] Its quick passage through both houses with relatively few amendments suggests that it was an acceptable compromise.

The idea of horse quotas was not entirely new. Lord Grey had suggested minimum contributions for the Eastern Association earlier in the year, and the Surrey committee had set quotas of dragoon horses on each parish in mid-May.[34] In 1642 the Committee of Safety had demanded 1,000 dragoons from the county of Essex.[35] The idea can perhaps be traced back even further to militia obligations, but the scheme put forward in July 1643 was much more ambitious. The demand for 6,500 cavalry from 15 counties was unprecedented. In 1637 the entire English militia had mustered 5,239 cavalry in 40 counties.[36] Henry VIII invaded France in 1544 with an army of between 35,000 and 50,000, but England had to provide only 3,684 cavalry.[37] There is no evidence in the ordinance of Parliament or in the financial records of its implementation that Propositions contributors were excused or treated more leniently. This was a new obligation which applied to every property owner. Nor was there any attempt to link contributions to any oath or vow, despite the imposition of the Vow and Covenant in June 1643.[38] The preamble appealed to self-interest as much as public interest: 'Not doubting but all good people will readily and willingly contribute their best Assistance, unto a work so necessary, for the good of the Kingdome, and their owne preservation.' The emphasis was mostly on the threat which royal cavalry posed to the safety and property of the people, while the similar threat posed by parliamentary cavalry was erased. The rhetoric of anti-popery was still present in the labelling of royal forces as 'that Popish Army which is pretended to be raised by the Kings Authority', but Parliament no longer explicitly claimed to be defending religion. The mood seems very

---

[33] Holmes, *Eastern Association*, 109–14.
[34] Ibid., 76–9; TNA: PRO, SP 28/35, part 3, fols 365–6.
[35] ERO D/Y 2/9, p. 71.
[36] TNA: PRO, SP 16/381/66, fols 143–4.
[37] Mark Charles Fissel, *English Warfare, 1511–1642* (London, 2001), p. 14.
[38] Edward Vallance, *Revolutionary England and the National Covenant: State Oaths, Protestantism and the Political Nation, 1553–1682* (Woodbridge, 2005), pp. 56–7.

different from the Propositions Ordinance of June 1642. This was an attempt to tap the resources of neuters through a mixture of persuasion and compulsion.

Implementation

Once Parliament had passed the ordinance, it had to be implemented at a local level. The county committees were given responsibility for fulfilling the quotas by whatever means they saw fit. In practice the methods varied.

The Essex committee had one of the hardest tasks because a further ordinance of Parliament gave the county an extra quota of dragoons on 12 August 1643. This ordinance required an assessment of £13,500 to pay for the 1,000 dragoons and 500 cavalry.[39] The assessment was divided between the hundreds of the county, ranging from £195, 17s for Clavering to £926, 1s for Barstable.[40] Rather than waiting for the assessments to come in, the committee started raising the horses very quickly. Militia obligations were used to demand horses from some individuals, but Sir Henry Mildmay protested that he would have been willing to send in his horse if it had not already been taken away by Colonel Long.[41] The troop which Nathaniel Rich had been raising in the county was put towards the quota. In order to complete his troop, Rich was authorized by the county committee to take 40 horses from civilians.[42] Unlike Colonel Long's activities earlier in the year, this seems to have been relatively uncontroversial, following the best practice set down in the ordinance of 10 May 1643. The troop's quartermaster, Ezekiell Hall, took a horse from John Stubbing of Helions Bumpstead on 31 July, leaving a certificate which recorded that the horse was taken by warrant of the deputy lieutenants of the county and valued by two neighbours at £11.[43] A note added to the certificate in December 1644 stated that the promised repayment had not been made. A similar certificate, for a horse worth £11, was issued to Henry Walker, a yeoman of Orsett, on 3 August, and ordered to be paid by the county treasurer on 23 August. On 16 September John Peacock of Ardleigh received £8 for a horse taken by warrant of the county committee. The committee's order authorizing payment mentioned that Peacock had 'paied all assesments And conformed himselfe to all our orders of parliament'.[44] Allegiance had an important bearing on whether the horse owners

---

[39]   *A & O*, vol. 1, 245–6.
[40]   TNA: PRO, SP 28/227, unfol.
[41]   BL, Egerton 2647, fols 123, 251.
[42]   TNA: PRO, SP 28/300, part 1, fol. 232.
[43]   TNA: PRO, SP 28/227, unfol. This is probably the same Ezekiell Hall or Hull involved in the Colonel Long case.
[44]   TNA: PRO, SP 28/227, unfol.

would get paid, but in this case it was judged entirely in terms of external actions. The committee does not seem to have cared how enthusiastic people were as long as they were obedient. Henry Walker had not contributed anything to the Propositions, but the fact that he had paid his fifth and twentieth was apparently enough.[45] Rich took another four horses valued at £45 from William Comyns, who received his money on 10 September.[46] It was January 1645 when Nathaniel Andrew of Radwinter finally got paid for a horse taken by Robert Johnson, a trooper under Rich, on 31 July 1643.[47] More horses were requisitioned in Essex for other units. Henry Barrington of Colchester took up 24 horses valued at £172 on 4 August, and delivered them to Romford. The committee paid this money, along with £6 for incidental charges, on 7 August, and £233, 10s to Thomas Westwood of Farnham on 4 August for another 24 horses which he had delivered to Romford.[48]

This kind of compulsory purchase was not the only method used to fulfil the Essex quota. The county committee also bought some horses from the London horse dealer John Styles. Major Sparrow was sent to London to find horses. He sent a letter back to the county committee on 31 July, carried by Styles himself, informing them that he had contracted for 40 horses and could procure another 100 by the following Saturday, but that the dealer required £100 in advance and had come along with the letter to collect it.[49] The committee issued a warrant for this money on 4 August, specifying that it was in part payment for 60 horses which were to be delivered the following day, and the money was actually paid on 7 August.[50] The accounts of the southern division record that Styles was given a payment of £100 out of the fifth and twentieth assessment.[51] Another warrant from the county committee, dated 6 September, authorized payment of £400 to Styles for the 60 horses and £5 for the charges of keeping them, stating that he had formerly received £200. This money was paid in three instalments: £60 on 19 September, £160 on 23 September and the remaining £185 on 9 March 1644.[52]

The committees of Hertfordshire and Middlesex divided their quotas between hundreds and parishes in a similar way to tax assessments. Many Hertfordshire parishes paid in kind with horses and arms rather than collecting money. It appears that parish constables were responsible for setting rates on

45   TNA: PRO, SP 28/153, part 6, Account book of John Fenning.
46   TNA: PRO, SP 28/227, unfol.
47   TNA: PRO, SP 28/300, part 1, fol. 232.
48   TNA: PRO, SP 28/227, unfol.
49   BL, Egerton 2647, fol. 84.
50   TNA: PRO, SP 28/227, unfol.
51   TNA: PRO, SP 28/153, part 6, Account book of John Fenning.
52   TNA: PRO, SP 28/227, unfol.

individuals in their parish. The constables of Sacombe and Baldock both returned accounts of the money they had raised towards the 300 horses set on Hertfordshire.[53] The parish of Thundridge delivered a horse worth £15, 5s, 6d to Sir John Norwich, the officer in charge of the cavalry to be raised in Hertfordshire.[54] In some cases, the charges of horses would be split between more than one parish, perhaps because one parish was not capable of providing an entire horse on its own. The parishes of Yardley and Hinxworth joined together to provide two geldings with arms and furniture and £7 towards a month's pay for Sir John Norwich's regiment in September 1643. The total cost was £37, 11s, of which the parishioners of Hinxworth contributed only £4, 8s, 3d.[55] Some individuals in Middlesex parishes were required to bring in horses in kind. In Tottenham, Sir John Cooke and Sir Robert Barkham were each assessed for a whole horse worth £16.[56] In most cases money was paid in to the collectors, who used it to buy horses and arms and give a month's pay to the riders. It usually cost around £20 to provide a horse, with equipment and pay. Of the £32, 12s collected in Chelsea, £13, 3s was spent on two horses, £2, 8s on saddles, £7, 16s on helmets, swords, pistols and holsters, and £12 for a month's pay for the riders.[57] In Hendon, six horses were bought from local men for prices ranging from £5, 10s to £10.[58]

Complications

The projected flying army was originally to be separate from, and even opposed to, the Eastern Association. Pym's attempt to make an alliance with the Scots had already weakened the association by leaving it without a leader. Lord Grey of Warke was nominated to the embassy to Scotland on 22 June but refused to go, and by 18 July had been sent to the Tower for contempt.[59] The Earl of Manchester was appointed to command the association on 8 August, and the following day Parliament made it clear that the whole of the flying army would still be available to him.[60] Because of the quotas imposed by the ordinance, several counties outside the association were still obliged to provide horses for Manchester's army. Meanwhile, Waller needed to replace losses suffered

53 TNA: PRO, SP 28/21, part 2, fol. 258.
54 TNA: PRO, SP 28/10, fol. 46.
55 TNA: PRO, SP 28/197, unfol.
56 TNA: PRO, SP 28/167, unfol.
57 TNA: PRO, SP 28/166, unfol.
58 TNA: PRO, SP 28/165, part 4, fol. 421.
59 Holmes, *Eastern Association*, 87; *LJ*, vol. 6, 104, 134.
60 Holmes, *Eastern Association*, 94–5.

at Roundway Down, and Essex's army continued to suffer from a shortage of horses. On 20 July Essex's council of war sent a letter from Great Brickhill, warning that disease, desertion and severe shortages of money, clothing, horses and arms 'will be the Destruction and Overthrow of this Army, if speedy Course be not taken to supply these Wants'.[61] When the Lords received this letter on 22 July, both houses were preoccupied with the flying army ordinance. The Commons resolved to provide money to fulfil Essex's request for 500 horses and a further 200 per month, but this resolution never became an order and nothing further was done.[62] Another letter from the Lord General was read in the Lords on 31 July, stating that the strength of his cavalry had fallen from 3,000 to 2,500 through loss of horses, inadequate supplies of remounts and men deserting to join the new army. He now demanded 800 horses immediately and a monthly supply of 200, among other things.[63] Further resolutions were made to satisfy these demands, although the 800 horses were dropped, but just as little seems to have happened as before.

Waller was able to get more support in Parliament, leading to a series of contradictory orders as rival factions competed for control of the new cavalry units. The Committee of Safety wrote to the Essex committee on 28 July ordering them to loan four troops of cavalry, including Rich's, and 1,000 dragoons to help the London forces under Waller, promising that they would be returned later.[64] It is not certain whether this was actually done, as not long afterwards the Essex horse and dragoons were reported to be on their way to Cambridge. Further attempts were made to reallocate the 1,500 horses of the London and Middlesex quota to Waller. On 12 August 1643 the London Militia Committee issued a warrant to Captain Charles Gheste and others to take up 1,000 of these horses within the City and suburbs and send them to Waller, specifying that the owners were to be repaid out of the assessment for Manchester's army.[65] The Commons ordered on 1 September 1643 that the troops raised in Middlesex should also be put under Waller's command.[66] According to Walter Yonge's diary, this move was proposed by Waller's ally, Sir Arthur Hesilrige.[67] The order was not necessarily put into practice, since John Alford, named in the order as

---

[61] *LJ*, vol. 6, 144.
[62] *CJ*, vol. 3, 180.
[63] *LJ*, vol. 6, 160.
[64] BL, Egerton 2647, fol. 80.
[65] *CSPD 1641–3*, 476.
[66] *CJ*, vol. 3, 224.
[67] BL, Add. 18778, fol. 28r. Yonge was MP for Honiton, Devon.

commander of the Middlesex troop, continued to serve under Manchester.[68] On 12 September the Commons decided that Waller should command all the horse raised in the counties south of the Thames.[69] Later in the year, Parliament made some similar orders diverting part of the quotas to Essex's army. The Commons recommended on 3 October that the Lord General should command the horse raised in Hertfordshire, even though this county was within the Eastern Association, and that notice of this should be given to Manchester.[70] On 28 November the Lords assented to a request from the Commons that the troops raised in Middlesex not already with Manchester's army should be sent to the Lord General, which implies that the previous order to put them under Waller had not been put into effect.[71]

Another complication was addressed on 24 August when Parliament passed on ordinance clarifying the obligations of landlords and tenants.[72] This acknowledged that the original ordinance had not made any provision for extracting money from tenants, and that many landlords who were assessed were absent or had too little personal estate to cover the sums demanded if they were distrained. According to the new order, tenants were required to pay a share of the assessment and deduct it from their rent, being liable to distraint themselves if they failed. Parliament's oversight probably delayed the collection of horses and money in the counties.

Results

The success of the quota system varied from county to county. Essex appears to have been the most successful. Sir Thomas Barrington claimed that the county committee had reached its full quota of 1,500 by 23 August, and that 500 were already at Cambridge, with the other 1,000 on their way.[73] The county's surviving financial records do not account for the whole quota, but clearly show that the committee had been very active in implementing the ordinance soon after it was passed. The Essex committee bought 442 saddles from John Gower and William Pease, and took delivery of at least 369 pairs of pistols.[74] In total, 942 dragoon

---

68   Godfrey Davies, 'The Army of the Eastern Association', *English Historical Review*, 46/181 (1931): 89.

69   *CJ*, vol. 3, 238.

70   *CJ*, vol. 3, 262.

71   *LJ*, vol. 6, 315.

72   *A & O*, vol. 1, 261–2.

73   Bodleian Library, Tanner 62, fol. 285.

74   TNA: PRO, SP 28/227, unfol. The number of pistols could be as high as 469 but the records are partly for deliveries and partly for payments, and do not always specify the unit which

horses were received, although 61 were sold as unfit or surplus to requirements, and others were issued to cavalry troops or used as draught horses.[75] The mayor and aldermen of Colchester sent in 38 of the 50 horses charged on the town but the remaining 12 were still outstanding in March 1644.[76] In the southern division, Lady Handford of Woodford and Mr Overman of Stratford both paid large fines for not sending in their horses.[77]

Collections in Hertfordshire were disrupted by soldiers sent to requisition horses for Essex and Waller. The remnants of Waller's cavalry which had escaped from Roundway Down returned from Bristol and quartered in London and Middlesex from late July into September.[78] In order to replace their losses they repeatedly raided the ostensibly friendly territory of Hertfordshire for horses. The parish account of Sandon stated very precisely that Major Battersby under Sir William Waller had taken two horses on 23 August 1643. Battersby had already taken a horse from Raphe Fordham of Tharfield on 9 August. Inhabitants of Sacombe recorded losses on unspecified dates to Major Battersby, captains John Bennett, Butler and Moore, and Quartermaster Cooke, all identified as Waller's men.[79] Some of these identifications are corroborated by the army's own records. Waller authorized quartering bills for captains called John Bennett and Nicholas Moore around this time.[80] In November there was a Quartermaster Cooke in Robert Harley's troop in Waller's own horse regiment.[81] Battersby, Moore and Cooke were all alleged to have taken bribes of 5s each to release the horses they had taken in Sacombe. The losses noted by John Capar of Sandon emphasize that this behaviour did not help the county committee to meet its quota for the flying army. On 1 August Captain Sanderson took nine of his cart horses valued at £100 and a week later Major Battersby took two coach horses worth £40, both officers showing authority from Waller. After losing 11 horses, Capar was then charged with £17 for a horse for Manchester, presumably being unable to send a horse in kind. Around the same time, Essex's officers were also active in the county. It was around this time that Major Samuel Boza's troop took

---

received them, which leads to a risk of double counting.

[75]   TNA: PRO, SP 28/153, part 5, Account book of Edward Birkhead, pp. 29, 39–40; BL, Egerton 2647, fols 227, 249. John Styles, the Smithfield horse dealer, bought up 40 of the surplus animals.

[76]   BL, Stowe 189, fol. 15.

[77]   TNA: PRO, SP 28/153, part 6, Account book of John Fenning.

[78]   TNA: PRO, SP 28/10, fols 40, 74, 77, 82, 84–6, 105, 107, 109–12, 302–5.

[79]   TNA: PRO, SP 28/155, unfol.

[80]   TNA: PRO, SP 28/10, fols 74, 105, 107, 109–10.

[81]   TNA: PRO, SP 28/11, fol. 24.

Thomas Marston's horse on the road between Bushey and Hemel Hempstead.[82] Sir Thomas Barrington complained that army officers were disrupting the economy and the war effort by taking horses in Hertfordshire and Essex.[83] On 13 September the Commons acknowledged that the Hertfordshire committee had already raised some of the required horses but reminded them to bring in the rest and send them all to Manchester.[84]

The authorities in Middlesex put the ordinance into effect within a few weeks, but soon encountered significant resistance. On 14 August the Lords sent for several Middlesex gentlemen as delinquents because they refused to send in their horses.[85] Many other individuals were slow to pay the assessment. The horses which were brought in quickly probably all went to Manchester's army, while in practice the order transferring the remainder to Essex only gave the right to collect outstanding arrears. The parish of South Mimms was required to pay £130 for six horses, according to an assessment made on 11 August 1643. By 22 August the parishioners had delivered three horses worth £45 along with £18, 6s cash to John Alford of Manchester's army, but £15 for the fourth horse was not paid until 17 November. The remaining two horses were only delivered to Sir Robert Pye, a colonel of horse under Essex, in May 1644.[86] Alford received all of the horses and money raised in Harrow in 1643.[87] Thomas Young refused to pay his share of one of the four horses sent in from Tottenham, and another two horses required from the parish failed to appear at all.[88] Little Stanmore was assessed at £41, 6s for two horses on 15 August, and the collectors received nearly half of this sum within three days. John Nicholl initially refused to pay his assessment of 6s, 8d, and the remaining £21, owed by Lancelott Lake esquire, was not paid until 6 March 1644.[89] Only six out of the nine horses assessed on Hendon could be sent in because £65, 17s, 4d remained outstanding.[90] Ealing was assessed at £58, 17s, 1d for three horses, but the collectors recorded over £13

---

[82]   TNA: PRO, SP 28/155, unfol.

[83]   BL, Egerton 2647, fol. 201; Bodleian Library, Tanner 62, fol. 285.

[84]   *CJ*, vol. 3, 238–9.

[85]   *LJ*, vol. 6, 180. The men were Sir Thomas Allen of Finchley, Michaell Grigg esquire of Hadley, Carew Rauley esquire of Sunbury, George Pitt esquire of Harrow, Sir Nicholas Raynton of Enfield, Henry Wroth esquire of Enfield, George Longe esquire of Clerkenwell, Humphrey Wilde esquire and Sir John Wild. Pitt and Raleigh were released on 18 August: *LJ*, vol. 6, 186.

[86]   TNA: PRO, SP 28/165, part 4, fol. 400.

[87]   TNA: PRO, SP28/168, unfol.

[88]   TNA: PRO, SP 28/167, unfol.

[89]   TNA: PRO, SP 28/163, unfol. This could be the same Lancelot Lake whose horse was taken by Henry Marten.

[90]   TNA: PRO, SP 28/165, part 4, fols 418, 421.

for defaulters.[91] On 1 September the Commons granted the deputy lieutenants of Middlesex the power to imprison defaulters, but it is not certain if this power was ever used.[92]

The situation was even worse in some counties. The Commons sent an order to the Surrey committee on 7 August, reminding them to 'raise such Horses as they are required, either in Specie, or by levying Monies, after the Rate of Ten Pounds a Horse', implying that they had not reacted as quickly as the Essex committee.[93] Apparently they had still done nothing by 13 September, when a further order insisted that they should 'forthwith, at their Peril, put the Ordinance for raising a Body of Horse, in Execution in that County; and raise the Horse, assessed upon them by the said Ordinance, with all Speed and Diligence'.[94] The same order was sent to Kent, whose committee had to deal with a major rebellion in July and probably could not spare any time or resources for Manchester's army.[95] The Surrey committee finally issued warrants for raising the quotas to the high constables of the hundreds of Elmbridge and Kingston on 5 October 1643, requiring the horses to be brought to Kingston on 10 October. The high constables of Elmbridge wrote back on 9 October to say that many people had complained about their assessments or refused to pay.[96] Counties were clearly failing to meet their required quotas. On 18 October, nearly three months after the original ordinance was passed, the Commons ordered that

> the Gentlemen of the several and respective Counties, assessed to bring in a Body of
> Horse, by the late Ordinance, do meet this Afternoon, and examine and see where
> the Obstruction is that the Horses are not brought in accordingly; and report where
> the Default is: And where the Default shall appear, Horses shall be raised in double
> Proportion: And my Lord General shall be desired to send Horse to raise them
> accordingly.[97]

Towards the end of 1643 the quotas dropped off the agenda, and Parliament turned its attention to other forces.

---

[91] TNA: PRO, SP 28/163, unfol.
[92] *CJ*, vol. 3, 224.
[93] *CJ*, vol. 3, 197–8.
[94] *CJ*, vol. 3, 238.
[95] *CJ*, vol. 3, 174.
[96] TNA: PRO, SP 28/244, unfol.
[97] *CJ*, vol. 3, 279.

The Turning of the Tide?

In the summer of 1643 the King came very close to winning the war. While the defeats of the northern and western armies and the weakness of Essex's army and the Eastern Association presented opportunities, they also left royal generals with strategic dilemmas. Parliament still had major garrisons which could not easily be ignored because they were in a position to interfere with resource gathering and communications. Gloucester controlled the River Severn and stood between South Wales and Oxford.[98] Hull dominated the East Riding of Yorkshire, and its garrison could easily raid Lincolnshire across the Humber estuary. Plymouth, Exeter, Barnstaple and Dartmouth denied control of Devon and threatened Cornwall.[99] If Essex's army was destroyed and the Eastern Association was prevented from recruiting a new army, then these garrisons would have no hope of relief and would fall sooner or later. But seeking a decisive battle was always risky because the outcome of battles could not be predicted. If the King was unlucky and Essex destroyed one or more of his field armies he would be in an impossible situation, having to deal with a parliamentary field army and the remaining garrisons without adequate forces. Parliament's weakness and shortage of resources probably made the destruction of Essex's army and invasion of the Eastern Association appear much less urgent than they seem with hindsight. Contemporaries could not easily have predicted that Parliament's forces would get stronger. The King and his commanders probably calculated that the capture of Gloucester would be easy and that Essex's army was already too weak to intervene.[100] Essex's cavalry had been unable to protect the army from Rupert's raids in June, resulting in the retreat to Great Brickhill. It would probably have been reasonable to assume that they would be similarly unable to screen the army on a march into enemy territory, making a relief operation extremely risky or impossible. For these reasons, concentrating on Gloucester, Hull and Plymouth cannot simply be dismissed as a mistake.

Expectations were confounded by what actually happened in August and September. Parliamentary militants chose to risk losing their last field army rather than risk losing one of their most important garrisons. With his army reinforced by units from the London militia and other local forces, Essex disproved the stereotype that he was sluggish and incompetent by launching a fast and aggressive march towards Gloucester. Royal cavalry under Wilmot and Rupert failed to stop the advancing army and the siege was raised.[101] After

---

98   Gentles, *English Revolution*, 187; Wanklyn and Jones, *Military History*, 114.
99   Wanklyn and Jones, *Military History*, 110–11.
100   Ibid., 114.
101   Ibid., 115–18; Holmes, *Eastern Association*, 105; Gentles, *English Revolution*, 189.

resupplying the garrison, Essex outmanoeuvred the King's army and got a head start for home. Rupert did not catch up with him until 18 September at Aldbourne Chase, where Essex's cavalry screen mostly succeeded in protecting the infantry and artillery as they marched away.[102] The royal army then blocked Essex's line of retreat, but failed to win the first battle of Newbury on 20 September and then withdrew to Oxford.[103] The King apparently authorized this retreat partly because his infantry were running short of gunpowder and were not certain to hold out until more supplies could be brought from Oxford.[104] This does not prove that Parliament had a resource advantage, but it does show that the influence of battles and logistics on each other could have important consequences. In the north, Newcastle failed to capture Hull and began to lose control of Lincolnshire. Sir Thomas Fairfax's cavalry had escaped across the Humber to link up with Cromwell. Reinforced by some of Manchester's new flying army units they defeated a royal force at Winceby on 11 October, clearing the way for Manchester to recapture Lincoln on 20 October. This left the royal garrison at Newark isolated and unable to exploit the resources of Lincolnshire.[105] Parliament had survived the crisis.

It is not obvious that this was the turning point of the war. The reversal of fortune in the Gloucester campaign shows that military operations were very unpredictable, and that material advantages did not automatically translate into success. It was not even inevitable that Parliament would gain a resource advantage. In 1643 its members and administrators were still experimenting with methods of extracting resources and had not yet developed a sustainable system which could increase the chances of winning a long war. The flying army levies had helped to change the balance of forces in Lincolnshire, and the diversion of resources had not prevented Essex from relieving Gloucester, but the new cavalry units were not given any long-term provision for pay or remounts.[106] Over the winter, Parliament had a chance to attempt reform of its finances and administration, but it was not inevitable that this chance would be taken, or that the attempts would succeed. The successes of Essex and Manchester had not decided the war, but they had restored equilibrium.[107]

---

[102] Wanklyn and Jones, *Military History*, 118; Jon Day, *Gloucester and Newbury 1643: The Turning Point of the Civil War* (Barnsley, 2007), pp. 133–5.

[103] Wanklyn and Jones, *Military History*, 120–24.

[104] Malcolm Wanklyn, *Decisive Battles of the English Civil War* (Barnsley, 2006), p. 194.

[105] Holmes, *Eastern Association*, 95–6.

[106] Ibid., 97–8.

[107] Gentles, *English Revolution*, 195.

Conclusion

The new army planned in July 1643 never came into existence. Many of the horses demanded were never supplied, and those that were brought in were used to recruit existing armies. In practice, Parliament could not compel the committees to do as they were told. Hertfordshire and Middlesex had been as forward as Essex in implementing the Propositions in the summer of 1642. It seems that there were new problems in 1643. In Middlesex the deputy lieutenants and constables mostly complied with orders, but were unable or unwilling to compel the many householders who delayed or defaulted. The Kent committee was not in a position to help because it was preoccupied with the rebellion. Even when the full quota was met, as it nearly was in Essex, the system provided no mechanism for a constant supply of remounts, which would always be necessary because of attrition. Like the Propositions, the system had some success at first but was not sustainable. Cavalry officers still had to requisition horses directly from civilians to make up losses. While the targets were not met, the flying army ordinance was not a complete failure. The cavalry of the Eastern Association army was significantly expanded. Manchester's own horse regiment was largely created from troops raised in Essex and Middlesex, including those of John Alford, Nathaniel Rich and William Dingley. Sir John Norwich's Hertfordshire regiment continued to serve under Manchester in 1644.[108] The size of Cromwell's regiment also increased.[109] While Manchester probably got the majority of the horses which were actually brought in, at least some were diverted to his rivals. Essex's army did not necessarily benefit from this very much and continued to seize horses directly from civilians.

The flying army ordinance delegated the raising of forces to the county committees rather than implementing a centralized system controlled from London. Although the ordinance named colonels, the committees seem to have had some freedom to appoint captains in practice. The new troops had distinctive local identities because they were raised at county level. Graham argued that local communities wanted this kind of military representation in 1642, and that Parliament's failure to provide it led to the decline of the Propositions.[110] But the flying army was no more successful despite giving more representation. By trying and often failing to extract the horse quotas, the county

---

[108]   Davies, 'Army of the Eastern Association', 89, 91; TNA: PRO, SP 28/227, unfol.; TNA: PRO, SP 28/153, part 5, Account book of Edward Birkhead, p. 33.

[109]   C.H. Firth, 'Raising the Ironsides', *Transactions of the Royal Historical Society*, 13 (1899): 30–33.

[110]   Aaron Graham, 'Finance, Localism, and Military Representation in the Army of the Earl of Essex (June–December 1642)', *Historical Journal*, 52/04 (2009): 880.

committees demonstrated that their relationship with local communities was more adversarial than representative. County quotas were used again to raise horses for field armies in 1644 and 1645, but never on the same scale.[111]

---

[111] *CJ*, vol. 3, 347; *CSPD 1644*, 114–15; *A & O*, vol. 1, 653–5.

Chapter 5

Purchase

Finance

Parliament's armies tried to get horses by voluntary contributions and various kinds of compulsory requisitioning, but none of these methods was adequate in the long term. Buying horses was a much more reliable source of remounts, but this could not be done without money. The Propositions had provided enough money for the Edgehill campaign, but could not sustain a longer war.

Fifths and Twentieths

The people who had given the resources to create the army did not necessarily have the resources to sustain it for long. On 21 November Richard Shute spoke to the House of Commons on behalf of 'the most active, and the most religious Part of the City' of London, proposing 'that the whole Charge may not lie upon the Good and Godly Party; but that the Malignant Party may be enforced to bear their Share fully according to their Abilities'.[1] Shute framed this proposal in terms of a simple binary opposition: everyone who had not contributed according to their ability was a malignant, and there was nothing in between. As *Meroz Cursed* shows, this polarized view had been advocated by puritan militants for a long time. It became official parliamentary policy in October 1642, when non-contributors began to be secured and disarmed, but it failed to extract sufficient resources. Parliament's next move, on 26 November, was to impose an assessment on non-contributors in the City and suburbs of London.[2] Robert Brenner represented this as a response to Shute's proposal on behalf of City radicals, but it could also be seen as a retreat from the extreme position advocated by the likes of Stephen Marshall.[3]

The assessment ordinance divided people into three groups where the Propositions Ordinance only had two. First there were the 'Papists and other ill-affected Persons' and 'divers Delinquents' who were helping the King to wage

---

[1] Robert Brenner, *Merchants and Revolution: Commercial Change, Political Conflict and London's Overseas Traders 1550–1653* (Cambridge, 1993), p. 430; *CJ*, vol. 2, 857–8.

[2] *A & O*, vol. 1, 38–40.

[3] Brenner, *Merchants and Revolution*, 430–31.

war. The ordinance began with a catalogue of the outrages these people had committed and the threat that they posed to the public, creating an impression of danger as the preamble to the Propositions Ordinance had done. Again, this was a vital part of Parliament's argument from necessity since the ordinance acknowledged that 'by reason of His Majesty's withdrawing Himself from the Advice of the Parliament, there can be no Act of Parliament passed with His Majesty's Assent, albeit there is great Justice that the said Monies should be raised'. The Long Parliament had raised grievances about the King imposing taxes without Parliament's consent, but was now taking the unprecedented step of imposing taxes without the King's consent! The second group consisted of 'divers well-affected Persons, who have freely contributed according to their Abilities' for the support of Essex's army. The established binary was disturbed by a third group: 'divers others … that have not contributed at all towards the Maintenance of the said Army, or, if they have, yet not answerable to their Estates'. These people were clearly distinguished from the ill-affected who were threatening the public, since they were said to 'receive Benefit and Protection by the same Army as well as any others, and therefore it is most just that they should, as well as others, be charged to contribute to the Maintenance thereof'. The identity of non-contributors was mostly left vague. At one point they were referred to as 'able Men', but more often as 'persons' or even vaguer terms such as 'those' or 'any'. Women were not explicitly mentioned, but it seems likely that female property owners were intended to be assessed. The text of the ordinance made ability to pay the key criterion and largely ignored other aspects of identity. These people were to be forced to contribute, but would no longer be treated as enemies. People who refused to pay the assessment were not to be disarmed or classed as delinquents, and they would not forfeit their whole estate. The assessors were given power to distrain goods and receive rents and debts of non-payers only in order to collect the sums assessed. Imprisonment was reserved for cases where the money could not be recovered by any means, although in these cases punishment would be extended to a person's dependants, who were to be expelled from London.

At the same time, membership of the original well-affected group was made more exclusive. Even people who had voluntarily contributed were reassigned to the third group if they had not given a sufficient proportion of their estates. For the first time, Parliament specifically declared a required amount: one twentieth of a person's estate. Before this time, there was apparently no way of knowing whether a contribution was sufficient. A further order on 29 November made it clear that if the assessment was paid in part within 6 days and in full within 12 days a certificate for repayment would be given. In effect, prompt payments of the assessment were to be treated more or less the same as voluntary contributions.

The ordinance compelled neuters to act as if they were well-affected. Parliament still did not tolerate neuters, but the new policy forced them to be friends rather than turning them into enemies, restoring the binary opposition between well-affected and ill-affected. This was still a kind of shibboleth and did not completely ignore internal feelings. The powers of distraint were to be applied to 'those who shall so far discover their disaffection, as not to bring in the several summs of money so assessed upon them'.[4] This still implied that if they covered up their disaffection by paying their assessment there would be no problem.

Like the Propositions, the assessment began with London and later spread further afield, where it was administered by county committees.[5] As with sequestration, this was a slow process because of opposition within Parliament. On 5 December 1642 the Commons debated a proposal to tax non-contributors throughout the kingdom, which Sir Simonds D'Ewes described as 'one of the most fatall and dangerous particulers w[hi]ch wee fell upon this Parliament w[hi]ch was the framing of an Ordinance of Parliament to tax all men through England to pay towards this unnecessary and destructive civill warre', arguing against Parliament's two bodies doctrine that taxing estates

> not by an Acte of Parliam[en]t (by which it can only bee done according to law & according to the ancient propriety of each freeman & the knowen Custome of this Kingdome) but by a meer Ordinance of both howses was a president of soe dangerous a consequence as I did feare it would cause great stirrs & heart burnings ...[6]

It was not until May 1643 that the new assessment, with a maximum rate of a fifth of yearly revenue from land and a twentieth of the value of goods, was introduced.[7] The ordinance named committees to administer the assessment in each county, but ordered them to pay the money to the central treasury at Guildhall. Parliament soon allowed the counties of the Eastern Association to retain the money to pay for their own forces.[8] The treasurer for the southern division of Essex, John Fenning, collected both Propositions money in 1642 and the fifth and twentieth assessment in 1643, each amounting to just over £3,900.[9] The former was all paid to the central treasury at Guildhall, but the latter was kept to support local forces. Fenning paid £100 of assessment money to John

---

[4]   *A & O*, vol. 1, 40.

[5]   James Scott Wheeler, *The Making of a World Power: War and the Military Revolution in Seventeenth Century England* (Stroud, 1999), pp. 102–3.

[6]   *CJ*, vol. 2, 875; BL, Harleian 164, fol. 248r.

[7]   Wheeler, *World Power*, 102–3; A & O, vol. 1, 145–55.

[8]   Clive Holmes, *The Eastern Association in the English Civil War* (Cambridge, 2007), p. 80.

[9]   TNA: PRO, SP 28/153, part 6, Account of John Fenning.

Styles for horses towards the county's quota for Manchester's flying army. Of the 798 individuals named in the account, 345 contributed sufficiently to the Propositions and were not assessed, 66 were assessed because they had given something but not enough and 387 had contributed no money. The lists include 54 women, which is 6.8 per cent of the total. This clearly shows that although female property owners were a minority they were expected to contribute to the war effort. There is no evidence that liability for the assessments depended on having taken the Protestation. Thomas Ballard of Childerditch was assessed for ship money in 1637 and the fifth and twentieth in 1643, but does not appear in the parish Protestation return.[10] Sir Robert Cooke refused the Protestation, but was still assessed for the twentieth part at £2,000 for not contributing to the Propositions. This case also shows that the rules set out in the ordinance were not always followed, since Cooke's whole estate was sequestered in 1643 for non-payment of his assessment.[11] The amounts assessed on individuals were greater than ship money, but fewer people were affected. In Childerditch, 15 residents and seven out dwellers had to pay ship money ranging from 3d to £2, 10s in 1637.[12] Only seven were considered able to contribute to Parliament in 1642 and 1643, but the fifth and twentieth assessments for those who had lent nothing on the Propositions were between £2 and £12.[13]

Like the Propositions, these assessments were one-off payments rather than recurring taxes, but the process of collection dragged on for years. The Committee for Advance of Money was still assessing people for the twentieth part in 1646, when a petition from the City of London complained about its activities.[14] The original ordinance of 26 November 1642 had authorized the mayor and aldermen of London to appoint men in each ward of the City to assess 'any that remaine, or be within the said severall Wards'.[15] When the Committee for Advance of Money took charge, they interpreted these words very literally, imposing assessments on anyone who was present in London even if they did not live there. In 1644 they even demanded money from a Scottish man who had no property in England.[16] In May 1643 the committee had ordered that the

---

[10]   TNA: PRO, SP 16/358, fol. 12r; TNA: PRO, SP 28/153, part 6, Account of John Fenning; 'Childerditch protestation return', *Essex Review*, 26 (1916): 93.

[11]   TNA: PRO, SP 23/173, p. 65.

[12]   TNA: PRO, SP 16/358, fol. 12r.

[13]   TNA: PRO, SP 28/153, part 6, Account of John Fenning.

[14]   Ben Coates, *The Impact of the English Civil War on the Economy of London, 1642–50* (Aldershot, 2004), p. 25.

[15]   *A & O*, vol. 1, 38–40. This 'any' was a false universal because it could only include property owners and erased married women.

[16]   Coates, *Impact*, 25.

value of horses listed on the Propositions after a person had been assessed would not be deducted from the assessment, and then that no horses listed after 29 November 1642 would count towards the assessment.[17] This was justified by the army's urgent need for money, but did not help with its equally urgent need for horses. Removing the incentive to contribute horses did not have a significant effect on the numbers brought in, which were already very small.

Assessments and Excise

After the failure of the Propositions, Parliament took a long time to develop an effective system of regular general taxation which could support its field armies. On 8 December 1642 an ordinance authorized deputy lieutenants to tax their own counties 'from Time to Time, as the Occasion shall require' to support forces raised to help Essex's army.[18] The first recurring tax was the weekly assessment set up in February 1643. This imposed fixed quotas on each county, following the precedent of the ship money and probably influencing the horse quotas which were introduced later that year. County committees then divided the quota between hundreds and parishes, and assessed the inhabitants.[19] While the ordinance insisted that everyone had to pay, it also imposed a double tax on 'every Alien and Stranger born out of the Kings obeysance, as well Denizens as others, inhabiting within this Realm: And also, every Popish Recusant convict or not convict'.[20] This drew a line between English protestants and racial and religious Others, erasing the fact that many of the King's active supporters were also English and protestant. As usual, Parliament used Othering and the impression of imminent danger to emphasize the necessity of its actions, claiming to have taken up arms 'for the necessary defence of themselves and the Parliament from violence and destruction, and of this Kingdome from forraign invasion, and for the bringing of notorious offenders to condigne punishment'.[21] Propositions contributors were liable for the full amount of the assessment. People who had not contributed to the Propositions and not paid their twentieth part were denied the right to appeal against over-rating if the excess was less than or equal to what they should have contributed.[22] This reinforced the boundary drawn by the twentieth part ordinance, counting people who had

---

17 *CCAM*, vol. 1, 19–20.

18 *A & O*, vol. 1, 47.

19 Wheeler, *World Power*, 174–6.

20 *A & O*, vol. 1, 88.

21 *A & O*, vol. 1, 85.

22 John Morrill, *Revolt in the Provinces: The People of England and the Tragedies of War, 1630–1648* (London, 1998), p. 93; *A & O*, vol. 1, 100.

been forced to pay as well-affected and giving no special treatment to people who had contributed to the Propositions before it became compulsory.

A new excise tax on consumption of certain commodities was suggested in Parliament in May 1643, but the plan stalled until after the defeats at Adwalton Moor and Roundway Down.[23] The idea of an excise tax was already actively opposed by the Vintners' and Brewers' Companies before it went through Parliament.[24] The excise ordinance was passed by the Lords on 22 July, the day before the royal army began to besiege Bristol.[25] This ordinance was not implemented until September 1643, when a second ordinance added clarifications to the first one, reduced the rates and ordered the payment of duty on goods bought after 11 September.[26] Like Parliament's other orders for extracting resources, the preamble of the July ordinance gave a justification for its unprecedented actions:

> taking into their serious consideration the great Danger that this Kingdome lyeth under, through the implacable malice and treacherie of Papists, and other Malignant persons, who have, and daily doe wickedly practise, and endeavour the utter ruine and extirpation of the Protestant Religion, the Priviledge of Parliament, and the Liberty of the Subject: Insomuch, that there is no probable way left them for the preservation of this Nation how to prevent the said malitious practises, but by raising of Moneys for the purposes first above-mentioned, untill it shall please Almighty God in his mercy to move the Kings Majesties heart to confide in, and concurre with both his Houses of Parliament, for the establishing of a blessed and happy Peace, which by both Houses is much desired and prayed for.[27]

This was yet another argument from necessity in which Parliament represented itself as protecting the public good, this time specifically from catholics. Like the twentieth part, the excise ordinance drew boundaries between well-affected and malignants. It acknowledged that Parliament had already imposed many taxes, 'which the well-affected partie to the Protestant Religion, have hitherto willingly payd, to their great charge', but that 'the Malignants of this Kingdome have hitherto practised by all cunning wayes and means how to evade and elude the payment of any part thereof', and therefore it was necessary that 'the

---

[23]   Wheeler, *World Power*, 149–50.

[24]   Coates, *Impact*, 34.

[25]   *A & O*, vol. 1, 202–14; Malcolm Wanklyn and Frank Jones, *A Military History of the English Civil War* (Harlow, 2005), p. 190.

[26]   Wheeler, *World Power*, 152; Ben Coates, *Impact*, 30; *A & O*, vol. 1, 287–9.

[27]   *A & O*, vol. 1, 202. Note that although the King's internal feelings were partly to blame, they could be changed by an external factor.

said Malignants and Neutrals may be brought to and compelled to pay their proportionable parts of the aforesaid Charge, and that the Levies hereafter to be made for the purposes aforesaid, may be borne with as much indifferencie to the Subject in generall as may be'. This was very aggressive language, implying that there was little difference between malignants and neutrals, but at the same time it set out a principle of treating everyone equally regardless of allegiance. Parliament effectively acknowledged that allegiance-based taxes were difficult to implement even when allegiance was defined entirely in terms of external actions. Finding out what someone had done and how much their estate was worth could be slow and complicated, and relied on local officials who were in a position to know. The excise avoided this problem by applying equally to everyone who bought the taxable commodities, but taxing consumption at a local level brought new complications and required a very bureaucratic system. The excise applied to all areas under parliamentary influence, but its administration remained highly centralized. Parliament directly appointed the excise commissioners, who then employed sub-commissioners in local offices, giving no responsibility to county committees. This made the revenue available to central treasurers and prevented it from being diverted to local forces. Excise revenues were allocated as security for large loans to finance the field armies and the navy, totalling at least £686,000 during the First Civil War. The excise revenue would have covered the £20,000 per month cost of Essex's army, but Parliament decided to divert some of the money to other forces, including Waller's army and the garrison of Plymouth.[28]

Assessments were simpler to implement than the excise because administration was devolved to county committees, but they had their own problems. The weekly assessment was not collected regularly and the money which was collected was probably diverted to local forces rather than being sent up to London.[29] In March 1644 the weekly assessment on London and Middlesex was replaced by a monthly assessment paid into the central treasury to support Essex's army, which ran until July.[30] The ordinance of Parliament setting up the tax simply asserted 'the necessity of speedy recruiting' of Essex's army without trying to explain why it was necessary.[31] By this time taxation ordinances seem to have become routine, requiring little justification. Another ordinance, passed on 20 January, increased the weekly assessment in the Eastern Association and required county committees to pay the revenue into a new central treasury at Cambridge, which

---

[28] Wheeler, *World Power*, 150–54.
[29] Ibid., 175, 180.
[30] Ibid., 181.
[31] *A & O*, vol. 1, 398.

would fund Manchester's army.[32] This ordinance gave slightly more justification than the one for Essex's army, but much less than ordinances of 1642–43, merely pointing out that the association had incurred great expenses by raising forces 'out of their loyall respect to his Majestie, their pious disposition to the peace and happinesse of this Kingdom, in obedience to the Orders of Parliament'. The same words were repeated when the weekly assessment was renewed on 13 May.[33] The system was improved again in early 1645. Following the precedent set by the ordinance for Essex's army, a monthly assessment was placed on all counties under parliamentary control, which was paid to the treasurers in London to finance the New Model Army.[34] This was kept up for longer than the four-month assessment of 1644, and together with the excise provided a reliable source of funds for long enough for Parliament to win the war.

Although the burden of the excise was to be distributed equally, this was not universally perceived as fair. Distribution of wealth was already unequal, so treating people equally without taking this into account would only perpetuate inequality. The excise ordinance broke an established tradition that the poor should not be taxed by imposing a duty on beer and beef, which were necessities for even the poorest people.[35] The Propositions and subsequent assessments on non-contributors had mostly targeted relatively wealthy people. Arbitrary seizure of horses necessarily hurt middling and elite people who could afford to own horses, and it was usually the most privileged horse owners whose complaints were heard by Parliament (see Chapter 3). The lowest fifth and twentieth assessment in the southern division of Essex was 10s, equivalent to £2, 10s per year in land or £10 in goods. The excise shifted the burden further downwards to people who had not previously been required to provide resources for the war effort and who had less representation in Parliament. Married women were affected because they were responsible for buying food for their household. Attempts to collect the excise sometimes provoked violent protests.[36] Many tradesmen petitioned Parliament to complain about the rates on their commodities and the

---

[32] *A & O*, vol. 1, 368–71; Holmes, *Eastern Association*, 127. Holmes wrote that this was a monthly tax, but the ordinance says weekly. I reproduced this error in Gavin Robinson, 'Horse Supply and the Development of the New Model Army, 1642–1646', *War in History*, 15/2 (2008): 133.

[33] *A & O*, vol. 1, 368, 432.

[34] Wheeler, *World Power*, 181–3.

[35] Ibid., 148; Coates, *Impact*, 35.

[36] Ann Hughes, *Gender and the English Revolution* (Abingdon, 2011), p. 34; Michael Braddick, *God's Fury, England's Fire: A New History of the English Civil Wars* (London, 2008), pp. 422–3.

administrative burden of collecting the tax.[37] Joseph Griffith of Wapping told collectors of the weekly assessment 'That he cared not, if those Parliamentmen were hanged whose Hands were on the Warrant'.[38] The Eastern Association assessments also met some resistance. The excise and assessment ordinances allowed the collectors to use soldiers to enforce collection if necessary, and this power was frequently used.[39] According to the established law, Parliament's taxes were no more legal than the arbitrary requisitioning which they superseded.[40] The Indemnity Committee heard cases in which officials had been prosecuted in court for distraining goods from non-payers. Thomas Marratt and William Smith of Pinchbeck, Lincolnshire, were sued by Richard Baylye for a mare which they had taken in lieu of unpaid excise.[41]

The excise ordinance authorized officers to distrain goods of non-payers at a rate of four times the value of unpaid tax. If sufficient goods could not be distrained then non-payers were to be imprisoned.[42] This was harsher than the twentieth part ordinance, which only allowed distraint up to the value of the unpaid tax, but was basically similar. Non-payers were not to be classed as delinquents or made liable for sequestration. Despite the association of neutrals and malignants in the preamble, this was another attempt to force neutrals to act as if they were well-affected. The weekly and monthly assessments had the same effect, imposing allegiance to Parliament on large numbers of people whether they wanted it or not. Obeying Parliament and financing its armies became a routine, and the excise even forced a choice of sides into normal economic activity. Wherever the excise was being collected, people at all levels of society had to support Parliament or go without basic necessities. This routine applied just as much to people who had actively supported the parliamentary war effort since the summer of 1642. Contributing sufficiently to the Propositions did not secure a permanent 'parliamentarian' identity. Loyalty could only be maintained through repeated performances in response to each new demand. Meanwhile, people who were not enthusiastic about the war were required to perform a public transcript which had material benefits for Parliament no matter how insincere it might have been.

[37] Coates, *Impact*, 33–4.
[38] Dagmar Freist, *Governed by Opinion: Politics, Religion and the Dynamics of Communication in Stuart London, 1637–45* (London, 1997), p. 208.
[39] Holmes, *Eastern Association*, 137, 139; Wheeler, *World Power*, 154.
[40] Morrill, *Revolt in the Provinces*, 93.
[41] TNA: PRO, SP 24/62, part 2, Marratt vs Baylye.
[42] Wheeler, *World Power*, 151–2; *A & O*, vol. 1, 205.

Loans

One of the greatest paradoxes of the parliamentary war effort was that it relied on both puritan zeal and usury at the same time. Puritan sermons often complained about the sin of usury, but helping the Lord against the mighty in the summer of 1642 offered high interest.[43] According to the original Propositions Ordinance, contributions were loans and would be paid back. The ordinance mentioned interest only for money and not for horses, although interest was being offered for horses by December 1642.[44] Cash was to be returned with 8 per cent interest per annum. While this appears to be a very generous return (8 per cent was the maximum allowed by the usury laws, and well above the market rate), it also came with a serious risk since, even if Parliament won the war, there was no mention of where the money for repayments would come from.[45] D'Ewes raised this problem when the ordinance was debated in the Commons: 'I would first desire to know how we shall be able to make this good before we promise it, because I am afraid if there be use for these forces, every man will be disabled to support his own expenses and therefore much less able to satisfy others.'[46] The ordinance passed without this problem being resolved. Therefore Coates was probably right that contributing to the Propositions was not an economic investment.[47] Cromwell's gamble with the bulk of his capital suggests that there was not a clear boundary between religious and economic interests.[48] Contributors could still refuse repayment or interest, but this was quite rare. Katherine Booth, a financially independent spinster and daughter of Sir George Booth baronet, listed a horse on 29 October 1642 which was valued at £6, 'but nothing is expected for hee is given freely'. Similarly, the nag brought in by Robert Warberton of Bawton in Cheshire was 'freely bestowed and nothinge expected'.[49] This implies that the thousands of other people named in the lists did expect repayment for their horses. The accounts of the western division of Surrey kept separate columns for amounts of money that were and were not to be repaid. A total of £1,035, 18s, 2d was lent, but only £77, 5s was

---

[43]   Stephen K. Baskerville, *Not Peace but a Sword: The Political Theology of the English Revolution* (London, 1993), pp. 54, 170.

[44]   *A & O*, vol. 1, 8, 51.

[45]   Coates, *Impact*, 58–9, 80.

[46]   Wilson Coates, Anne Steele Young and Vernon F. Snow (eds.), *Private Journals of the Long Parliament, 2 June to 17 September 1642* (New Haven, 1982), p. 45.

[47]   Coates, *Impact*, 58–9, 87.

[48]   Patrick Little, 'Cromwell and Ireland before 1649', in Patrick Little (ed.), *Oliver Cromwell: New Perspectives* (Basingstoke, 2009), pp. 118–19.

[49]   TNA: PRO, SP 28/131, part 4, fols 7r, 27r.

given.[50] Since interest was offered for cash right from the start, MPs must have been expecting that this incentive would be necessary. Nothing was done about repaying Propositions loans until 1646, when contributors were offered security, but only if they would lend the same amount again.[51] People's motivations for lending money to Parliament are irrelevant to the effects that their actions had. If they contributed out of puritan zeal they were still made into usurers; if they wanted an economic investment they were still taking sides in the civil war.

The Propositions system was an important source of money and horses in 1642, but did not last. Parliament continued to take out secured loans from the City of London throughout the war. The Common Council provided a loan of £100,000 secured against the personal property of MPs in June 1642. Further loans were taken out in the following years to support Essex's army. In February 1643 Parliament borrowed another £60,000 from the Common Council at 8 per cent interest, even though the loan was secured on receipts from the weekly assessment.[52] A loan of £20,000 secured against excise receipts was negotiated in February 1644 to pay for recruiting Essex's army.[53] The creation of the New Model Army in the spring of 1645 was funded partly by an £80,000 loan to be paid off by the monthly assessments.[54] Money was also borrowed at county level to meet the costs of local forces. In June 1643 the Essex committeemen entered into a bond with Ursula Garrett, a London widow, who agreed to lend them £1,000 for a month with £6, 13s, 4d interest (equivalent to 8 per cent per annum) and a penalty of £2,000 for non-payment.[55]

Horse Purchase

The horse trade in mid-seventeenth-century England was dominated by a small group of dealers. The most prominent in the First Civil War were John Styles, Harvey Conway, Richard Clough, Peter Everett, Thomas Crossman and Percival Stanley. These dealers were based in Smithfield market in London, but bought and sold horses in many different parts of England.[56] Most of Parliament's

---

[50]   TNA: PRO, SP 28/334, account book of Richard Wither, p. 6.

[51]   Coates, *Impact*, 65–9.

[52]   Wheeler, *World Power*, 102, 178.

[53]   Ibid., 180; *CJ*, vol. 3, 400.

[54]   Wheeler, *World Power*, 110, 184.

[55]   BL, Egerton 2651, fols 146v–147r.

[56]   Peter Edwards, 'The Supply of Horses to the Parliamentarian and Royalist Armies in the English Civil War', *Historical Research*, 68/159 (1995): 64–5; Peter Edwards, *The Horse Trade of Tudor and Stuart England* (Cambridge, 2004), p. 81.

major armies bought at least some horses from them during the First Civil War. Because the Smithfield dealers were so dominant in their trade, it was hard for parliamentary administrators to avoid doing business with them.[57] They were usually reluctant to sell horses on credit, making it vital for Parliament to secure an adequate supply of money before making contracts.

Essex's Army

The thematic structure of this book risks giving a false impression. The parliamentary war machine did not progress from buying few horses to buying many. From its beginning in the summer of 1642, Essex's army bought large numbers of horses for cash. Initially money was paid out by the Propositions treasurers at Guildhall.[58] In August the Lord General started issuing warrants authorizing payments to army officers from a new treasury under Sir Gilbert Gerard.[59] Cavalry troops were allowed a standard sum of £354 mounting money to buy horses and equipment for the 11 officers, including spare horses for commissioned officers.[60] This money seems to have been paid in many cases.[61] There was also an allowance of £600 to buy 60 troop horses at £10 each, but in most cases this does not appear to have been paid. Ten troops received it from the Propositions treasurers, and one by Essex's warrant.[62] Troopers in most cavalry units were mounted on horses contributed on the Propositions. The gentlemen of Essex's lifeguard each received £15 to buy a horse.[63] Both dragoon regiments, amounting to 1,200 men, bought their horses at £5 each.[64] There were also up to 500 cavalry transferred from the Irish adventure to Essex's army.[65] Each troop of this force had received mounting money for 81 horses.[66] In most cases money was paid directly to officers, who did not record how they spent it,

---

57   Edwards, 'Supply of Horses', 65.

58   TNA: PRO, SP 28/170, Account of Guildhall treasurers.

59   TNA: PRO, SP 28/1A; Tom Crawshaw, 'Military Finance and the Earl of Essex's Infantry in 1642 – a Reinterpretation', *Historical Journal*, 53/04 (2010): 1038.

60   TNA: PRO, SP 28/140, part 17, fol. 401v.

61   TNA: PRO, SP 28/1A; TNA: PRO, SP 28/170, Account of Guildhall treasurers.

62   TNA: PRO, SP 28/170, Account of Guildhall treasurers; TNA: PRO, SP 16/503/62, fol. 59; TNA: PRO, SP 28/2A, part 1, fol. 65.

63   TNA: PRO, SP 28/2B, part 3, fol. 522.

64   TNA: PRO, SP 28/1A, fol. 164; TNA: PRO, SP 16/503/62, fol. 62.

65   *LJ*, vol. 5, 181; *CJ*, vol. 2, 698.

66   TNA: PRO, SP 28/144, part 10, fol. 1.

but the Propositions treasurers paid £530, 4s directly to the horse dealer Thomas Crossman for 51 horses.[67]

Purchase of horses dropped off in 1643. This was partly because there was less money available for Essex's army, and partly because horses had become a very low priority for spending. Holmes argued that Essex's army was still Parliament's highest priority in the first half of 1643 and that it diverted money and attention away from the Eastern Association.[68] More recently, Wheeler argued the opposite: that local forces retained much of the weekly assessment and starved Essex's army of money.[69] Perhaps the best way to reconcile these views is to acknowledge that all of Parliament's forces suffered from insufficient resources at this time, and that it is unfair to make any of them a scapegoat.[70] Even at the best of times there was rarely enough money in the treasury to meet all of an army's needs. The New Model Army was very well financed in 1645, but pay still fell into arrears.[71] Therefore treasurers had to prioritize. Some suppliers would be paid quickly while others had to wait for years. In 1643 Essex was left to find remounts from other sources, leading to immense problems with arbitrary requisitioning (see Chapter 3).

By the spring of 1644 the financial situation had been improved by the excise, monthly assessments and secured loans. At the same time horses became a much higher purchasing priority, perhaps because other methods had proved inadequate. On 23 March 1644 a contract was made with John Styles, Harvey Conway and Richard Clough to supply 1,000 horses for the army at £9 each. These dealers were given an advance payment of £1,000 and further instalments between 2 April and 10 May.[72] The cost of these horses was equivalent to nearly half of the £20,000 excise loan. They were probably all absorbed by existing units, which had been weakened by attrition during the campaigns of 1643 and did not have an adequate supply of remounts. When Essex's army mustered at Tiverton in July 1644 it only had 2,300 cavalry troopers of its own and 400 borrowed from the London militia.[73] This was not many more than Essex had in the previous summer.

---

[67]   TNA: PRO, SP 28/170, Account of Guildhall treasurers.

[68]   Holmes, *Eastern Association*, 82.

[69]   Wheeler, *World Power*, 176.

[70]   Tom Crawshaw's PhD research will settle the debate about the finances of Essex's army.

[71]   Ian Gentles, *The New Model Army in England, Ireland and Scotland, 1645–1653* (Oxford, 1992), p. 49.

[72]   TNA: PRO, SP 28/14, part 2, fol. 243; TNA: PRO, SP 28/14, part 3, fols 292, 327, 362, 387; TNA: PRO, SP 28/15, part 1, fol. 110; TNA: PRO, SP 28/15, part 2, fols 139, 156.

[73]   Richard Symonds, *Diary of the Marches of the Royal Army*, C.E. Long and Ian Roy (eds) (Cambridge, 1997), p. 97.

The Eastern Association

Because the Eastern Association was not very centralized in 1643, the Cambridge committee was unable to buy horses directly. Control of revenue and recruiting was largely retained by the committees of individual counties.[74] The Essex committee was able to buy up to 100 horses from John Styles to fulfil its quota in 1643 as well as compensating individual civilians for horses which had been requisitioned (see Chapter 4). Cavalry units raised in Essex usually joined the association's field army without much trouble, and the county committee rarely insisted that they should be kept for local defence.

The centralization of the association in early 1644 allowed the Cambridge committee to arrange large-scale horse buying, paid for by assessment revenue from the central treasury. Like Essex's army, the Eastern Association seems to have made remounts a high priority for spending at this time. The biggest difference was in who sold the horses. The Cambridge committee rarely did business with the Smithfield dealers who supplied the county committees and Essex's army. Edward Dendy, a captain in Manchester's cavalry regiment, appears to have raised his troop in London in early 1644. His accounts claim £150 for 20 horses which he bought from Richard Clough at Smithfield before joining Manchester's army.[75] This was an exception to the alternative system which operated in the Eastern Association. It was more usual for commissaries to buy remounts directly from civilians without going through middle men. The most prominent of these officers was Lieutenant Russell, who appears in the association's financial records from early 1644 onwards. He often received large sums of money for unspecified numbers of horses which he had bought or was to buy, including a payment of £667, 18s, 2d in February 1644, £1,000 in April and £1,410 in May.[76] In other cases Russell and other commissaries presented detailed lists of horses they had bought, sometimes including the names and addresses of the sellers.[77] At the same time, the treasury issued money directly to cavalry officers to buy mounts for their troopers, as had been common practice in Essex's army in 1642. In April 1644 the Cambridge treasury paid £500 to Colonel Francis Russell for horses to recruit his troop.[78] Cromwell received £1,100 on 22 July to buy 110 horses for his regiment.[79]

---

[74]   Holmes, *Eastern Association*, 88, 99–101.

[75]   TNA: PRO, SP 28/35, part 1, fol. 61.

[76]   TNA: PRO, SP 28/24, part 2, fols 187, 213, 229; TNA: PRO, SP 28/24, part 3, fols 283, 301, 309; TNA: PRO, SP 28/25, part 4, fol. 547.

[77]   TNA: PRO, SP 28/24, part 2, fols 178, 188; TNA: PRO, SP 28/24, part 4, fols 502–3.

[78]   TNA: PRO, SP 28/25, part 3, fol. 430.

[79]   TNA: PRO, SP 28/24, part 4, fol. 518B.

In some cases it was explicitly recorded that horses were bought at fairs. A warrant dated 20 April 1644 authorized £500 to be paid to Lieutenant Russell to buy horses at Northampton fair.[80] Henry Ireton's troop received some horses bought at Cambridge fair in June.[81] The civil wars certainly did not stop markets and fairs from taking place. Captain John Blackwell bought horses for his London militia troop at Hertford fair in April 1644.[82] Even in contested areas the risk of attack did not close down all economic activity. In May 1643 the Earl of Essex's scoutmaster received a report that royal forces under Henry Hastings had tried to raid Nuneaton fair for cattle and horses, but had been driven off by Lord Grey of Groby's men.[83] The Eastern Association commissaries certainly had the opportunity to visit fairs and markets, but there are very few examples of them doing so. Peter Edwards has convincingly argued that the commissaries organized private sales, bypassing traditional venues. According to established law, sales of horses had to be recorded in toll books. The surviving books for the First Civil War period suggest a decline in the numbers and values of horses sold at fairs and markets which is completely at odds with the unprecedented demand from armies of both sides.[84] This was another example of Parliament disregarding law and tradition out of necessity. One of the purposes of toll book records was to create an audit trail which made it easier to trace stolen horses, but officers were not necessarily worried about where their remounts had come from. In fact, many of the state's horses had technically been stolen from civilians, some of whom tried to bring prosecutions, and the disruption of the traditional paper trail did not always prevent owners from finding and recovering their horses (see Chapter 3). The sales organized by the commissaries did have some features in common with fairs and markets. They were held in specific places, with all sales in a town usually recorded on the same day, but the addresses of the sellers, where given, often include several different places. For example, commissaries visited Bedford on 20 April 1644 and bought horses brought in from Bedfordshire and Huntingdon.[85] This strongly suggests that the commissaries' visits were advertised in advance.[86]

The cost of horses for the Eastern Association varied, but was often lower than the prices charged by the Smithfield dealers for other armies. The system

---

[80] TNA: PRO, SP 28/24, part 2, fols 187, 229.

[81] TNA: PRO, SP 28/16, part 2, fol. 220.

[82] TNA: PRO, SP 28/14, part 1, fols 47, 55, 80.

[83] I. G. Philip (ed.), *Journal of Sir Samuel Luke*, Oxfordshire Record Society, vols 29, 31 and 33 (1950), vol. 1, pp. 70–71.

[84] Edwards, 'Supply of Horses', 62–3.

[85] TNA: PRO, SP 28/24, part 2, fols 178, 188.

[86] Edwards, 'Supply of Horses', 62.

of purchase by commissaries worked well as long as money was available. In September 1644 Manchester's army had 40 cavalry troops in five regiments, mustering nearly 4,000 men.[87] This was almost certainly more than any other parliamentary field army had mustered up to that time, and was not surpassed until the formation of the New Model Army in the spring of 1645. In the autumn of 1644 the association suffered a financial crisis as tax receipts failed to meet the cost of the army.[88] Because of this horse purchases dropped off, but the cavalry remained very strong and was able to supply a majority of personnel for the New Model. Cromwell's regiment alone had more than 1,000 men in February 1645.[89]

The Southern Association

Throughout its existence the Southern Association's situation was similar to that of the Eastern Association in 1643. Waller was not given the same central authority as Manchester and the Cambridge committee and had to wait several months for an assessment ordinance.[90] This was finally passed in March 1644, but specified that the revenue raised in each county was only to be used for that county's forces.[91] Waller was left with little scope to buy remounts for his army, but significant purchases were made at county level. The Kent committee employed Charles Bowles as a commissary to buy horses, arms and equipment for local regiments, some of which served in the association's field army. He combined the methods used by Essex's army and the Eastern Association, buying 344 horses in large consignments from the dealers Thomas Crossman and Richard Clough, and another 91 in smaller lots from various other individuals.[92] Lieutenant-Colonel Thorpe of George Thompson's regiment bought at least 23 horses from Harvey Conway and one from Peter Everett, although Everett claimed that Thorpe had also had another of his horses which Sir Richard Grenville took without paying in February 1644.[93] In September 1644 Waller claimed that he only had 700 or 800 cavalry left.[94] This was almost certainly as much a consequence of the association's financial and administrative weakness as of the army's defeat at Cropredy Bridge in June.

---

[87]   Holmes, *Eastern Association*, 236.
[88]   Ibid., 160–61.
[89]   TNA: PRO, SP 28/26, part 1, fols 73–83, 101.
[90]   Holmes, *Eastern Association*, 109–13.
[91]   *A & O*, vol. 1, 416.
[92]   TNA: PRO, SP 28/130, part 3, fols 65–6.
[93]   TNA: PRO, SP 28/265, part 2, fols 143–6.
[94]   *CSPD 1644*, 489.

The New Model Army

The reforms of spring 1645 merged the armies of Essex, Manchester and Waller into the New Model Army under Sir Thomas Fairfax. Robert Scawen moved from the committee for Essex's army to the new Army Committee, bringing his experience of the previous year's reforms.[95] Scawen and his committee went back to the Smithfield dealers who had supplied Essex's army rather than implementing the Eastern Association's successful commissary system. The supply of money from the excise and assessment allowed these purchases to be sustained for an unprecedented length of time. From April 1645 to August 1646 the dealers supplied more than 6,700 horses at a cost of just over £46,000.[96] These horses were paid for by warrants issued by the Army Committee, while deliveries and issues were dealt with by John Smith and Thomas Richardson, the same commissaries who had compiled the Propositions lists in 1642 and 1643. Both the army committee, which had access to large reserves of cash, and the dealers, who dominated the market, negotiated from positions of strength. They agreed a standard price of £7, 10s each for cavalry horses, significantly less than the £9 paid by Essex's army a year earlier, but in return the dealers gained important concessions. As in previous years, they demanded and got advance payment. In March and April 1645 they delivered 1,000 troop horses, all paid for in advance.[97] From July onwards advance payments stopped, but the dealers were usually paid very soon after delivery. On 4 April Parliament made a more unusual concession to the dealers by granting them a month long monopoly on the purchase of troop horses.[98] Bulstrode Whitelocke, who had been an MP at the time, later recorded in his memoirs that the Commons passed the order for buying horses 'whereby the state was cozened'.[99] It is not certain what he meant by this. The state had made an unprecedented concession, but had got a reasonably good deal in return. At this time Whitelocke was aligned with the Presbyterian

---

[95]   John Adamson, 'Of Armies and Architecture: The Employments of Robert Scawen', in Ian Gentles, John Morrill and Blair Worden (eds), *Soldiers, Writers and Statesmen of the English Revolution* (Cambridge, 1998), p. 45; Gentles, *New Model Army*, 31.

[96]   TNA: PRO, SP28/140, part 7. The manuscript gives a total of 6,708, but by adding individual entries together and using warrants to fill in gaps I make it 6,723. Of these, 5,206 were for cavalry, 1,057 for dragoons and 460 draught horses for the artillery train.

[97]   TNA: PRO, 28/140, part 7, fol. 276; TNA: PRO, SP 28/28, part 3, fols 309, 310; TNA: PRO, SP 28/29, part 1, fols 164, 199, 236.

[98]   Edwards, 'Supply of Horses', 63–4.

[99]   Bulstrode Whitelocke, *Memorials of the English affairs from the beginning of the reign of Charles the First to the happy restoration of King Charles the Second* (Oxford, 1853), vol. 1, p. 417.

faction, which was hostile to the New Model Army.[100] Horse dealers generally had a bad reputation, even if they did not always deserve it.[101] These factors could have prejudiced Whitelocke against the deal. Although he probably used contemporary notes, he did not start writing the surviving manuscript versions of his history until the 1660s, by which time would have been expedient to distance himself from Cromwell.[102] Because of all these problems, Whitelocke's testimony is not reliable proof of the dealers being dishonest or the Army Committee being gullible, but it does suggest that the deal was controversial.

A few hundred more horses were bought by the Commissioners of Parliament Residing in the Army, Vincent Potter and Thomas Herbert. Their activities were not quite the same as the Eastern Association commissaries. Rather than visiting different places to buy horses, they usually travelled with the army. Their roles seems to have been buying small numbers of horses locally to make up incidental losses, which was more flexible than waiting for remounts to come up from London whenever they were needed. In October 1645 the Commons ordered that they should receive a regular supply of money, 'to be employed for and towards the Buying and Providing of Horses for the supplying and filling up, from time to time, such Troops as are or shall be defective or broken Troops'.[103] After this they received at least three payments of £200 each.[104] The commissioners' accounts sometimes recorded buying horses from civilians near the army's quarters. For example, Potter bought a bay mare for £4 from Julian Palmer of Buckerell in Devon when Fairfax's headquarters were at Ottery St Mary in November 1645.[105] In many other cases the commissioners paid officers and soldiers for horses which they were already using. The commissioners' payments and Fairfax's warrants authorizing the issuing of the horses were formal abstractions which transferred legal ownership of the horse to the state rather than changing physical possession. For example, their accounts recorded that on 7 November the commissioners bought a horse from George Craven, a trooper in Fleetwood's regiment, and immediately delivered it back to him by authority of a warrant issued by Sir Thomas Fairfax on 11 September.[106]

---

[100]   Ruth Spalding, 'Whitelocke, Bulstrode, appointed Lord Whitelocke under the protectorate (1605–1675)', *ODNB*.

[101]   Edwards, *Horse Trade*, 87, 94, 99–103.

[102]   Blair Worden, 'The "Diary" of Bulstrode Whitelocke', *English Historical Review*, 108/426 (1993): 124.

[103]   *CJ*, vol. 4, 318.

[104]   TNA: PRO, SP 28/33, part 1, fol. 58; TNA: PRO, SP 28/33, part 2, fol. 140; TNA: PRO, SP 28/38, part 4, fol. 388.

[105]   TNA: PRO, SP 28/129, part 10, fol. 13.

[106]   TNA: PRO, SP 28/129, part 10, fol. 10.

Some horses had been bought by cavalry officers before being processed by the commissioners. Captain Packer, commander of a troop in Fairfax's regiment, bought some horses near Bristol in September 1645, but these were not formally bought or issued by Potter and Herbert until 12 November.[107] On 15 November the commissioners paid Captain Grove in Whalley's regiment for 15 horses. Grove had bought some of these horses from countrymen in various places, and others from troopers after the battle of Langport in July 1645.[108] Horses bought from troopers were probably prize goods captured from the enemy. There is no evidence that recruits were required to bring their own horses at this time. Nearly all horses were supplied by the state in one way or another. Only the reformado officers serving as troopers under Captain Knight brought their own horses, for which they were paid an extra 1s per day.[109]

Occasionally the treasurers paid money by warrant directly to army officers, but this was very rare rather than the normal practice which it had been in the old armies. The only known examples are £750 paid to Major Thomas Harrison in April 1645, and £1,200 for Edward Whalley in July.[110] Unlike Essex's officers in 1642, New Model cavalry officers did not normally receive any allowances to buy horses for their own use. Harrison was paid £50 for two horses in July 1645, but this was a reward for bringing news of the victory at Langport.[111] The ability of the commissioners and other officers to buy horses probably removed even more of the need for the spontaneous requisitioning which the old armies had relied on when they lost horses on the march, but supplies from the Smithfield dealers via the London commissaries remained by far the biggest source of remounts. This centralized system largely freed cavalry officers from the burden of finding horses which had preoccupied them in 1643. Cromwell had a much smaller administrative role in the New Model Army than in the Eastern Association, with little or no responsibility for raising money or buying horses. This probably gave him more time to concentrate on tactical and operational leadership, whereas in 1643 he was often distracted by having to write letters to county committees demanding resources. The records created by the centralized administration also make it easier to calculate the equine replacement rate. From 1 June 1645 to 2 June 1646, the cavalry received 3,441 horses from London, 160 bought by Whalley and at least 200 bought by the commissioners in the

---

107 TNA: PRO, SP 28/129, part 10, fol. 11.

108 TNA: PRO, SP 28/129, part 10, fol. 14.

109 *CJ*, vol. 4, 101.

110 TNA: PRO, SP 28/29, part 1, fol. 246; TNA: PRO, SP 28/31, part 5, fol. 548. By this time Whalley had been promoted to colonel of a horse regiment.

111 TNA: PRO, SP 28/31, part 5, fol. 547; Whitelocke, *Memorials*, vol. 1, 476–7.

army.[112] This comes to 63 per cent of the army's establishment of 6,000 cavalry (excluding Rossiter's regiment, which does not appear in the central records of horse purchase). Okey's dragoon regiment replaced 78 per cent of its horses in the same period.[113]

Winning and Losing

1644: The Indecisive Year

In absolute terms, Parliament was in a stronger military position in early 1644 than ever before. There were more field armies with a greater flow of resources extracted from more people than in previous years. But this did not give a great advantage over the King, who had also tapped more resources and built new armies. Both sides seem to have been fairly evenly balanced despite their increased resources. The resource situation made it impossible for either side to win the war in a single battle because there were too many armies in existence. Destroying one or two was not enough to tip the balance. It would take a run of several victories to cripple the enemy, and this was inherently unlikely because battles were so unpredictable. Even in 1643, when Parliament's forces were at their weakest, the King and his generals had failed to complete the sequence by destroying Essex's army, and Parliament recovered from defeats at Adwalton and Roundway.

Parliament's financial and administrative reforms of early 1644 made the main field armies stronger and more sustainable. Manchester had already received the largest share of the cavalry quotas in 1643. With the new central treasury receiving the weekly assessment, the Eastern Association was able to send out the English Parliament's biggest field army.[114] The excise and monthly assessment gave Essex's army a more sustainable source of revenue than the Propositions. Waller was in a weaker position, but managed to field a respectable army which played a significant part in the year's campaigns. Lord Fairfax had rebuilt his army in the East Riding, despite having less help from London than Essex or Manchester got.[115] As a result of negotiations following the defeat at

---

[112]   TNA: PRO, SP 28/140, part 7, fols 276v–287Av; TNA: PRO, SP 28/129, part 10; TNA: PRO, SP 28/31, part 5, fol. 548.

[113]   TNA: PRO, SP 28/140, part 7, fols 276v–287Av; TNA: PRO, SP 28/129, part 10; TNA: PRO, SP 28/36, part 6, fols 646, 659, 707.

[114]   Holmes, *Eastern Association*, 1.

[115]   Andrew J. Hopper, *'Black Tom': Sir Thomas Fairfax and the English Revolution* (Manchester, 2007), p. 46.

Adwalton Moor, a very large Scots army under the Earl of Leven advanced into England in January.[116] To coordinate these forces, Parliament set up the Committee of Both Kingdoms. Some of the committee's decisions have been criticized by historians, but there was probably no alternative to having a central authority in a fixed location to manage the operational strategy and logistics of the diverse parliamentary forces. Without it, Parliament's armies might have been even more disjointed than they were.

The King benefited from gains of territory in the previous year. Although administrators could not automatically get civilian property, access to a greater area and population probably increased the flow of resources even if the full potential was not realized. Gaining Bristol and Weymouth made importing arms and ammunition from France easier.[117] In early 1644 Prince Rupert was put in charge of north Wales and the marches, where he reformed the administration and built a new army. This allowed him to capture Liverpool and gain control of a large part of Lancashire.[118] Parliament's alliance with the Scots Covenanters was partly balanced by the ceasefire negotiated between Ormond and the Irish rebels, which allowed the King to bring reinforcements from Ireland. The numbers and ethnic identities of these soldiers are controversial, but they must have increased the available forces.[119]

With such huge quantities of resources mobilized on both sides, the campaigns of 1644 would necessarily be an attritional grind. The campaigning season began well for Parliament when Waller, reinforced by a strong detachment of Essex's cavalry under Sir William Balfour, defeated Hopton's army at Cheriton in Hampshire on 29 March.[120] This was not a battle which could have had a major impact on the outcome of the war by itself. If the result had been reversed, Essex, Manchester and the London militia could probably have limited the strategic damage. Hopton would have needed the good luck to win the battle and further good luck to outmanoeuvre the remaining parliamentary forces and link up with potential rebels in Kent and Sussex. The Second Civil War shows that coordinating spontaneous rebellions was impractical. For Parliament, the victory at Cheriton at least gave a temporary advantage. With Hopton weakened, Essex and Waller were free to combine forces against the

[116] Ian Gentles, *The English Revolution and the Wars in the Three Kingdoms, 1638–1652* (London, 2007), pp. 205–7; Wanklyn and Jones, *Military History*, 171.

[117] Peter Edwards, *Dealing in Death: The Arms Trade and the British Civil Wars* (Stroud, 2000), p. 205.

[118] Ronald Hutton, *The Royalist War Effort, 1642–1646* (London, 1984), pp. 129–42.

[119] Ibid., 122, 140; Wanklyn and Jones, *Military History*, 15; Mark Stoyle, *Soldiers and Strangers: An Ethnic History of the English Civil War* (New Haven, 2005), pp. 53–4.

[120] Wanklyn and Jones, *Military History*, 144–6.

Oxford army. Despite the animosity between the two generals, they did manage to cooperate as their armies advanced on Oxford up both banks of the Thames in May, but Charles and his army still escaped. This created a strategic dilemma because even with the increased resources of 1644 there were not enough armies available to chase the King, besiege Oxford and relieve Lyme in Dorset, which was under threat from Prince Maurice's army. After some disputes between the generals and the Committee of Both Kingdoms, Essex marched into the west while Waller continued to shadow the King. This strategy was initially successful as Essex relieved Lyme and captured Weymouth and Taunton, but on 29 June Waller was unexpectedly defeated by the Oxford army at Cropredy Bridge in Oxfordshire.[121] The Southern Association army was not wiped out by this setback, but Waller was unable to stop the King, who went west in pursuit of Essex's army. After he was informed of the Oxford army's approach, the Lord General marched his army into Cornwall. At Lostwithiel he was surrounded by the combined forces of the King, Prince Maurice and Sir Richard Grenville. Although this position was on the coast, the parliamentary navy was not much help because the wind was blowing in the wrong direction – the weather was another factor which could influence operations. Sir William Balfour led the cavalry through the royal lines and brought them safely home, although losses of horses and men were probably quite heavy. Essex himself escaped by boat, leaving Major-General Philip Skippon to negotiate the surrender of the rest of the army on 2 September. The infantry were disarmed and allowed to go on condition that they did not fight again until they reached Southampton, but the entire artillery train was left behind.[122] This defeat was embarrassing for Essex, but had surprisingly little effect on the parliamentary war effort.[123] The army was rebuilt when it reached Hampshire and was back in action by late October. In the interim the King had little chance to win the war and was not even able to recapture Taunton.

At the time of Cropredy Bridge, Manchester, Fairfax and Leven were besieging Newcastle's northern army at York, and Prince Rupert was on the way to relieve the city. Before Rupert arrived, the balance of forces in the north strongly favoured Parliament. In addition to his old enemies the Fairfaxes, Newcastle had to deal with new threats from the Scots to the north and the Eastern Association to the south. The 'popish army' took refuge in York as the three armies closed in. Rupert brought his new army across from Lancashire to break the siege and decided to give battle. Whether this decision was based on

[121]   Ibid., 161–9.

[122]   Ibid., 193–7.

[123]   Clive Holmes, *Why Was Charles I Executed?* (London, 2006), p. 73.

the Prince's assessment of the situation or on a misinterpretation of the King's orders, the gamble did not pay off. After a long stand-off the two royal armies were attacked by the combined Scots and parliamentary forces at Marston Moor on 2 July and badly beaten. Although many of Rupert's soldiers and the northern horse escaped, Newcastle's infantry had been wiped out.[124] The garrison which Rupert left at York surrendered after two weeks.[125] This battle could not decide the war in itself, but defeating Rupert and Newcastle was one of the necessary steps towards parliamentary victory. Holmes cited the different effects of Marston Moor and Lostwithiel as evidence of Parliament's resource superiority, but this is not comparing like with like.[126] At Lostwithiel only one parliamentary army was defeated and the infantry were allowed to march away, but there were two royal armies at Marston Moor and one lost most of its infantry. Marston Moor increased the probability of parliamentary victory, but this is not the same as making it inevitable. The combined effect of Cheriton and Marston Moor meant that parliamentary forces *could* now win the war by the end of the year *if* they took out the Oxford army.

The chance to destroy the King's army came at the second battle of Newbury on 27 October.[127] The political controversies which followed this battle continue to influence the historiography, making it more difficult to discuss what happened and why.[128] It seems likely that many politicians had an unrealistic expectation of decisive victory, fuelled partly by the example of Marston Moor and perhaps just as much by the militant puritan millenarianism which had led from confidence to disappointment and recriminations in the first campaign of the war. But this alone does not explain the bitterness which the Newbury campaign provoked. Factional politics were a crucial part of the dispute. During the summer of 1644 the various factions in Parliament and its armies coalesced into two large groups, conventionally called Presbyterians and Independents. The Marston Moor campaign was a crucial part of this realignment. There was increasing animosity between the Presbyterian Scots and the sects which were tolerated in Manchester's army when they came into contact with each other at the siege of York.[129] Both factions worked together to win the battle of Marston Moor, but

---

[124]   Wanklyn and Jones, *Military History*, 171–89; Braddick, *God's Fury*, 328–9.
[125]   Wanklyn and Jones, *Military History*, 190; Gentles, *English Revolution*, 222.
[126]   Holmes, *Why*, 73.
[127]   Wanklyn and Jones, *Military History*, 205.
[128]   Malcolm Wanklyn, *Decisive Battles of the English Civil War* (Barnsley, 2006), p. 142; Malcolm Wanklyn, 'A General Much Maligned: The Earl of Manchester as Army Commander in the Second Newbury Campaign (July to November 1644)', *War in History*, 14/2 (2007): 135–7, 146–9.
[129]   Holmes, *Eastern Association*, 203–4.

this only drove them further apart as they disputed who should get the credit for the victory.[130] The Scots commissioners in London went on to ally with English presbyterians, conservatives and former members of the peace group against the radicals, sectaries and extreme militants of the Independent faction.

Historians have traditionally seen the Presbyterians as being more inclined to a negotiated peace than winning the war, but Wanklyn has recently suggested that Cromwell and his cavalry were reluctant to fight at second Newbury because decisive victory was not in the interests of the Independents at that time.[131] Peacey has shown that writers outside Parliament sometimes represented both factions as being similar to each other and motivated by self-interest rather than differences of principle.[132] Given the dispute over Marston Moor and their opposing views of what the political and religious consequences of victory should be, each faction had a vested interest in taking sole credit for victories and blaming the other for failures. Essex tried unconvincingly to blame Waller for his defeat in Cornwall, but if the operation had been a success, his rivals would have been denied a share of the glory. The chances of wiping out the King's army would be increased by concentrating as many parliamentary forces against it as possible, but joint responsibility might disadvantage one faction or the other, as it had with Marston Moor. A further complication was that the Eastern Association field army was divided.[133] Combining forces was necessary because the parliamentary field armies were in a relatively poor condition despite having greater access to resources than in 1643. Armies always expended resources and lost strength while campaigning, but each had specific problems of its own in addition to normal attrition. Waller was in a very weak position because the Southern Association could not provide the resources to maintain a field army; Essex had used up extra resources to compensate for losses sustained in Cornwall, and the monthly assessment had expired in July; Manchester was better off, but the Eastern Association's cash flow was becoming inadequate.[134] These problems made it unlikely that the autumn campaign would go smoothly.

In October 1644 the armies of Essex, Waller and Manchester linked up in the Thames valley to oppose the Oxford army. The senior generals of the three armies and two civilian commissioners formed a committee to make joint

---

[130]   Joyce Macadam, 'Soldiers, Statesmen and Scribblers: London Newsbook Reporting of the Marston Moor Campaign, 1644', *Historical Research*, 82/215 (2009): 105–6.

[131]   Malcolm Wanklyn, 'Oliver Cromwell and the Performance of Parliament's Armies in the Newbury Campaign, 20 October–21 November 1644', *History*, 96/321 (2011) : . 21–3.

[132]   Jason Peacey, 'Perceptions of Parliament: Factions and the "Public"', in John Adamson (ed.), *The English Civil War: Conflict and Contexts, 1640–1649* (Basingstoke, 2009), pp. 88–9.

[133]   Holmes, *Eastern Association*, 199–204.

[134]   Ibid., 178–9; Wheeler, *World Power*, 181.

decisions, which seems to have functioned perfectly well until after second Newbury.[135] Essex himself was absent through ill health and so could not personally take any credit or blame for anything which happened, although any failures attributed to Manchester, Crawford, Balfour or Stapleton would damage the whole Presbyterian faction. The royal army was outnumbered by the parliamentary forces, but stayed in a reasonably strong defensive position near Newbury. To overcome this disadvantage the council of war agreed on a very ambitious plan involving a fixing and flanking manoeuvre. Manchester and his infantry were to keep the royal forces occupied with a diversionary attack while Waller led the rest of the infantry and most of the cavalry around to attack from the rear. This plan came close to succeeding, but there was not enough daylight to complete it.During the night the King and his army escaped. The armies faced each other again at the relief of Donnington Castle, but the council of war decided not to risk Parliament's combined armies by fighting another battle.[136] In purely military terms this failure was disappointing but hardly fatal to the parliamentary cause, and not as bad as it could have been. By assaulting a defensive position, the parliamentary forces risked suffering much heavier casualties for no gain. It was tensions between the factions which blew it up into a major political crisis, as Manchester and Cromwell accused each other of incompetence and betrayal.[137] The unbroken run of victories needed to win the war by the end of the year was always improbable, and the plan implemented at second Newbury depended on luck as much as ability. A decisive victory could never be relied upon, even if there were no mistakes or deliberate sabotage. The greater resources available in 1644 reduced the effects of individual battles. Even Marston Moor and Lostwithiel could not end the equilibrium on their own. Breaking out of this situation by the end of the year would have required an implausible run of good luck for either side.

1645: Decision

Neither side started 1645 with a clean slate. The campaigns of the previous year left the King in a weaker position than he had been a year earlier, having lost armies and territory without being able to replace them. These losses were contingent on the defeats of 1644 rather than an inevitable consequence

[135] Wanklyn, 'Oliver Cromwell', 9.
[136] Wanklyn and Jones, *Military History*, 204–8; Wanklyn, 'General Much Maligned', 145–8. Wanklyn, 'Oliver Cromwell', 6, 11, argued that the west of the King's position was not as formidable as it seemed and that his army was ineffectively deployed, but taking advantage of this still required a long flank march on a short day.
[137] Wanklyn, 'General Much Maligned', 150.

of any natural disadvantages. Parliamentary victory was still not inevitable. Parliament's field armies had also been weakened by attrition and resource shortages. The factional infighting which produced the Self-Denying Ordinance and the remodelling of the army could just as easily have led to paralysis and defeat. Without the reforms of early 1645, the parliamentary armies might not have been capable of fighting effectively. As it was, the improvements in finance and administration made the New Model Army the most efficient force to take part in the war. Even the new system of gathering resources could not necessarily sustain the war effort indefinitely. Both sides were running short of infantry. The King had to empty garrisons to strengthen his field army, and lost some important strongholds even before Naseby.[138] Meanwhile, Parliament found that turning unwilling civilians into soldiers was much harder than turning them into taxpayers. The New Model Army did not inherit enough infantry from the old armies and could not find enough volunteers to make up the deficit. Impressing men and transporting them to the army was difficult and expensive, and many of the new conscripts deserted.[139]

The infantry shortage and the concentration of resources into two large armies made a decisive battle much more likely than in 1644. While Parliament probably had enough spare forces and resource flow to recover if the New Model Army was destroyed, the controversies over second Newbury made it likely that a military failure would have disproportionate political consequences. The remodelled army was dominated by Independent officers who had to gamble with the fortunes of their faction whenever they fought a battle. There were still Presbyterian colonels, such as Richard Greaves and Sir Robert Pye, who were not removed until 1647, but the faction's leading grandees (Essex, Manchester, Stapleton) and high-ranking Scots officers (Balfour, Crawford, Middleton) could expect to be insulated from defeat as much as denied a share in victory.[140] The King still had some forces in the west, but winning the war would be extremely difficult without the Oxford army. Ultimately Charles and Fairfax staked everything at Naseby, and it was the King who happened to lose. Rather than occupying a strong defensive position as at Newbury, the royal army attacked in the open early on a summer day, which probably accounts for much of the difference between the two battles.[141] The superior numbers of the New Model, augmented with local forces sent by direction of the Committee of Both Kingdoms, might have been expected to increase Fairfax's chances of victory, but some parliamentary units performed very badly, and the battle

---

138   Hutton, *Royalist War Effort*, 178–9.
139   Gentles, *New Model Army*, 32–3.
140   Ibid., 168.
141   Wanklyn and Jones, *Military History*, 204–5, 244, 246–8.

was very close.[142] As at Marston Moor, the royal cavalry escaped. The infantry, who would be much harder to replace, were mostly killed or captured. Hutton suggested that the royal cause 'committed suicide' at Naseby by attacking under unfavourable circumstances without waiting for reinforcements.[143] The risk may still have been worth taking, and if the gamble had paid off historians might well have said that it was Fairfax who committed suicide, but it was never safe to rely on winning a battle.

Naseby was the most decisive battle of the First Civil War, but it would not have been possible without the cumulative attrition of 1644 or Parliament's financial and administrative reforms in early 1645. The amalgamation of the three field armies made sense by late 1644 because the King had one major army, and only a combined force would have a chance of beating it. Earlier in the year this was not an option because there were several royal armies to be dealt with in different places. The strategic problems facing Essex, Waller and the Committee of Both Kingdoms in the summer of 1644 arguably demanded a greater number of armies rather than more centralization. This was a resource problem which could only be solved by more money, not by reform of the command structure. Even in 1645, the need to relieve Taunton, besiege Oxford and destroy the King's army caused problems.[144] After Naseby, Fairfax had much more freedom to operate than his predecessors because the balance of forces was strongly in his favour. It was this as much as his aggressive leadership which allowed a quick march into the west to deal with Goring as soon as Leicester was recaptured. At Langport on 10 July the western army collapsed surprisingly quickly after being engaged by a relatively small part of the New Model's advance guard.[145] From this point, parliamentary operations consisted mostly of mopping up garrisons. This was tedious and expensive work which dragged on for more than a year, but the King no longer had the military force to make winning the war possible. His only hope was to exploit divisions between English and Scots, and between Presbyterians and Independents.

Conclusion

The First Civil War started with two rival governments competing for obedience. By the middle of 1646, one had collapsed and the other was dominant. After the last garrisons surrendered, the only way to avoid submitting was to go into exile.

---

[142] Wanklyn, *Decisive Battles*, 173, 176–7.
[143] Hutton, *Royalist War Effort*, 178.
[144] Gentles, *New Model Army*, 53–4; Wanklyn and Jones, *Military History*, 231–2.
[145] Gentles, *New Model Army*, 67–9.

The few who chose this were likely to be the King's most sincere supporters, although fear of punishment and sensitivity about honour could also be factors. The Marquess of Newcastle was apparently running away from the court as much as from Parliament when he fled to the continent after Marston Moor.[146] For the majority who stayed in England, 'true' allegiance became more obscure and blurred as they compromised with their enemies. In just a few years Parliament had taken executive power, enforced ordinances without royal assent, raised armies, introduced new taxes and new state oaths, drastically changed property rights and punished people for obeying the King's person. The result was not only victory in the civil war but also the creation of a new state.

---

[146]   Lynn Hulse, 'Cavendish, William, first duke of Newcastle upon Tyne (bap. 1593, d. 1676), writer, patron, and royalist army officer', *ODNB*.

Conclusion

Deciding the War

This book has focused on the parliamentary war effort, partly because of an arbitrary decision based on personal taste, but also because of the survival of records. There is a huge collection of parliamentary documents in the National Archives, and their potential is nowhere near exhausted. Because there was no need to keep records of the losing side, and because many commanders destroyed their papers as incriminating evidence, it is impossible to know as much about the administration and finance of royal armies. When the surviving fragments are compared with parliamentary systems, they often appear similar, with large voluntary contributions of horses at first, followed by county quotas and direct requisitioning by soldiers. The biggest difference is that there is no direct evidence of royal armies buying horses on the same scale as Parliament, but this could easily be a result of record loss rather than a real difference in practice. There are examples of small-scale purchases among the surviving records.[1] Ultimately, the royal armies must have got their horses somewhere since they were never short of cavalry. Infantry were a much bigger problem for both sides, especially in the later years of the war.

Because of the imbalance in surviving administrative records, it is impossible to make any definitive claims about whether one side or the other had a resource advantage at any particular time. The quantity of available parliamentary records risks giving a false impression, but examining them in detail reveals serious problems, particularly in 1643. The solving of Parliament's resource problems does not fit into a narrative of progress. Essex's army was very well funded and supplied in the summer and autumn of 1642, but declined in 1643. This was partly caused, and partly balanced, by the creation of local and regional forces, but by August 1643 every field army other than Essex's had been defeated and Parliament was losing territory. The available resources were increased by the excise and the flying army quotas, but these were not enough to win the war on their own. Reforms of Essex's and Manchester's armies in the spring of 1644 improved the situation further, but they were still not adequately financed in the long term.

---

[1] Peter Edwards, *Dealing in Death: The Arms Trade and the British Civil Wars* (Stroud, 2000), pp. 159–62.

The Eastern Association was unable to support Parliament's biggest field army to date, even though the assessments were efficiently collected. Meanwhile, Essex's army was weakened because its assessment was not renewed, probably as a result of factionalism. Although the experiments of 1644 were not entirely successful, they provided valuable experience which fed into the creation of the New Model Army's efficient administration and adequate funding in 1645.

The King probably did not implement anything like the new modelling, but still had a field army capable of fighting in 1645. In early 1644, his forces appear to have been similar in strength to Parliament's; in the summer of 1643, royal field armies almost certainly gained a numerical advantage by wiping out the armies of Waller and the Fairfaxes. Parliament probably had a resource advantage by 1645, but it is a big step from having an advantage to being guaranteed to win. The same is true of holding London. The development of the arms industry meant that by 1644 parliamentary armies had easy access to adequate supplies and got more for their money because increased supply pushed prices down.[2] This was certainly an advantage, but it is hard to make it into a determinant of inevitable victory. The navy was able to supply garrisons such as Hull and Plymouth by sea, making them much harder to capture, but it could not stop arms imports from reaching the King's armies or rescue Essex's army from Cornwall. To the extent that the navy was an advantage, it was a very expensive one which swallowed up most of the customs revenue and so partly negated the advantage of controlling the largest port.[3]

If the traditional determinist model is inadequate, so is an approach which privileges battles and largely ignores resources. According to Wanklyn, 'in the last resort it is how military force was used in the decisive engagements that ultimately decided which side won the war'.[4] At best this is only partly true. Battles *could* be decisive, but this depended on circumstances outside the battlefield, particularly the distribution of resources. Edgehill had the potential to decide the war because both sides concentrated most of their available forces there and did not have the resources to replace them quickly. Parliament could have lost the war at first Newbury because it staked its last field army on the relief of Gloucester. Similarly, the King's last major army was at risk of being destroyed at second Newbury. But sometimes the balance of forces and resources prevented a single battle from deciding the war, no matter how well the armies and generals fought. Marston Moor could not possibly have made victory or defeat inevitable for either side

    [2]   Ibid., 72; Ben Coates, *The Impact of the English Civil War on the Economy of London, 1642–50* (Aldershot, 2004), p. 211.

    [3]   James Scott Wheeler, *The Making of a World Power: War and the Military Revolution in Seventeenth Century England* (Stroud, 1999), pp. 132–5, 173.

    [4]   Malcolm Wanklyn, *Decisive Battles of the English Civil War* (Barnsley, 2006), p. 1.

because there were too many other armies in existence. This does not mean that it was irrelevant to the outcome of the war. The result made parliamentary victory more probable, which is not the same as inevitable.

In an article published in 1985, Ann Hughes offered a different explanation of Parliament's victory which acknowledged that getting resources from civilians was difficult rather than automatic, and that early-modern politics necessarily depended on compromise. According to this argument, Parliament was better at negotiating with localism because MPs were part of central government and local communities at the same time, whereas personal loyalty to the King was harder to reconcile with local interests. While Charles's supporters went to court to serve in person, the creation of county committees was 'part of the common-sense and institutional routine of Parliamentarianism'.[5] Parliament had a long tradition of negotiating consensus through deliberation. While Hughes admitted that Parliament and its committees and armies were divided by factional conflict, she interpreted this as a strength rather than a weakness. Because there was no single ultimate authority, there was always hope that a decision could be reversed, and in order to take advantage of this, supporters had to stay within the parliamentary war effort, unlike the many disillusioned commanders who deserted the King. Hughes made a crucial link between allegiance and the material world by pointing out that maintaining even the appearance of support necessarily involved providing or gathering resources for Parliament. In this way, disaffected factions could still serve a useful purpose.[6] While the parliamentary war effort was open, inclusive and flexible, Charles alienated supporters by making arbitrary and capricious decisions in private, and by concentrating too much power in the hands of individuals such as Prince Rupert.[7] Disputes between the King's supporters all too easily became matters of personal honour. These weaknesses of the royal war effort 'were in no sense the product of chance but implicit in the very structure and character of personal monarchical rule in the context of previous political processes in England. Parliament's strengths, again illustrated through the nature of local and central connections, were equally integral.'[8] While this argument was much more sophisticated than those based on London and the navy, it still made the result of the war inevitable.

Hughes made some valuable insights which have been expanded in this book, but ultimately her argument depended on selecting the best examples

---

[5]   Ann Hughes, 'The King, the Parliament and the Localities during the English Civil War', *Journal of British Studies*, 24/2 (1985): 241–5.

[6]   Ibid., 247–9.

[7]   Ibid., 250, 254, 257.

[8]   Ibid., 262.

from one side and the worst examples from the other. Sometimes the King's commanders cooperated more effectively than Parliament's. Waller was defeated at Roundway Down partly because the Oxford army responded immediately to Hopton's call for help. Diverse royal forces united at Lostwithiel, where Essex had isolated himself partly because of his feud with Waller. The rivalry between them seems to have had a personal as well as a political dimension. Essex threatened to resign as Lord General in June 1643 if he did not get his own way.[9] Colonel Long made his dispute with the Essex gentry into a matter of honour and reputation. According to Hughes, 'Fairfax, Cromwell, or Brereton as much as Essex, Manchester, or Waller surely did not see themselves simply as military leaders, in opposition to civilian interests.'[10] But my examples of horse requisitioning have shown that at times Essex and Waller acted exactly as if they were purely military figures who were opposed to civilian interests. Hughes cited Viscount Conway's defection in 1644 as an example of how the King's supporters were alienated, neglecting to mention that he had deserted Parliament in the previous year.[11] It may be that their personal connections with both the court and the House of Lords made it easier for peers such as Conway and the Earl of Carlisle to change sides repeatedly.

Parliament's decisions could be just as arbitrary and capricious as the King's. It empowered Bard and Browne to requisition horses regardless of allegiance and property rights, then threatened them with criminal prosecution, then denied having done so and granted them indemnity. While this proves Hughes's point that unfavourable decisions could always potentially be reversed, the opposite must also be true. Bard and Browne could never be certain that their indemnity would not be withdrawn, and it was always possible that they might be hanged before their allies in Parliament could intervene. The fluidity and deliberative traditions of Parliament contributed to such rapid and arbitrary changes, but at other times made the process of gathering resources painfully slow. The ordinances for sequestration and the national fifth and twentieth assessment each took a very long time to pass through both houses. Even the Propositions system, which in its original voluntary form was less controversial than taxation and sequestration, took three months from the original ordinance to a general order to implement it in all counties. Before the 1640s, Parliament did not exercise executive power, and in practice its role was often to stop the King from doing things. When it took on new responsibilities in 1642, it was prone to indecision and mistakes. Slow deliberation and sudden arbitrary decisions

    [9]   Vernon F. Snow, *Essex the Rebel: the Life of Robert Devereux, the Third Earl of Essex 1591–1646* (Lincoln, NE, 1970), p. 370.
    [10]   Hughes, 'King, Parliament and Localities', 253 note 50.
    [11]   Ibid., 252.

combined to create a paradox on 14 October 1642, when the order for disarming and imprisoning non-contributors was passed quickly, but the sequestration ordinance was not, wrecking a coherent plan and (probably inadvertently) erasing the boundary between neutrals and enemies. The delay between the initial twentieth part ordinance in November 1642 and similar assessments in the counties created a double standard whereby non-contributors were treated as friendly taxpayers in London and as dangerous enemies elsewhere. The mixed response to the flying army ordinance in 1643 suggests that MPs and peers had not yet found a way to reconcile the conflicting demands of field armies and county committees. Parliament did eventually develop effective and sustainable systems for extracting resources, but this was contingent, not inevitable. It depended on ordinances passing both houses and being implemented at lower levels. If attendance at Westminster had been different on certain days, then some ordinances might have passed sooner or later or not at all. It was not inevitable that county committees would put ordinances into effect, or that civilians would comply.

Hughes was right to point out that local versus central is a false dichotomy because MPs synthesized local and central roles. I would go further and suggest that it is also a false dichotomy because the categories 'local' and 'central' are false universals. Who were the 'locals'? There were many different interests outside Parliament (whether opposed or indifferent to it) which cannot easily be lumped together. MPs and county committees did not represent the whole of any community. The centre is no easier to define. The particular argument that Hughes put forward in 1985 depended on a monolithic 'Parliamentarianism' which is no longer widely accepted (if it ever was). Even the simplistic paradigm which divides Parliament into 'peace' and 'war' groups in 1643, and continues them as the Presbyterian and Independent factions from 1644 onwards, necessarily has 'parliamentarians' fundamentally divided over what parliamentary victory would mean, how it could be achieved and whether it was desirable. While factions certainly did have to bring in resources to maintain their influence, they often disagreed over how these resources should be used. At the time, there was no consensus on what Parliament's war aims should be or how they could best be achieved. Furthermore, Sir Simonds D'Ewes remained in Parliament, but consistently spoke and voted against all resource gathering ordinances on the grounds that it was fundamentally wrong to fight a civil war and override traditional property rights. Meanwhile, Henry Marten's horse seizures provoked or exacerbated conflicts which were probably not balanced by the number of cavalry he raised. He was expelled from the Commons and imprisoned for advocating a position which was too 'parliamentarian' for most MPs.

In order to take advantage of the structure of Parliament or limit the damage of unfavourable decisions, MPs and peers needed to be present at Westminster in the same way that royal commanders needed to spend time at court. This necessarily distracted them from their military commands and local administrative responsibilities, a problem which was not solved until late in the war by the Self-Denying Ordinance. The simultaneous demands of local and central government could also help to explain Parliament's strength in the south-east. Because of the short distance from Westminster to Buckinghamshire, Hertfordshire and Essex, MPs could more easily divide their time between the Commons and their constituencies (although this did not guarantee a good response: the Propositions and the flying army levies were not very successful in Kent or Surrey). Members for more remote northern and western areas could not switch so easily. The complexity of the parliamentary administration and the political divisions among its personnel were sources of weakness and not the advantage that Hughes claimed. The war effort came very close to failure in 1643, partly because resource gathering was disrupted by factional divisions and disputes over property rights. Parliament tended to get more things done when one faction was dominant. The infighting after second Newbury resulted in better finance and administration, and less pluralism, but it could just as easily have led to paralysis and prevented any factions from achieving their war aims.

Making Sides

Determinism and essentialism intersect at the concept of 'puritan zeal': the puritans just were more zealous, and this made their victory inevitable.[12] This book has shown that while puritan sermons do appear to have influenced the conduct of parliamentary leaders, this could be counterproductive for resource gathering. Acting as if 'he that is not with me, is against me' did not stop the decline of Propositions contributions in the autumn of 1642. Pym and his allies arguably put too much effort into devising shibboleths which mostly failed to find out what people 'really' thought or draw a definite line between in-group and out-group. The puritan ideal of a Godly minority shunning the reprobate masses could not solve the practical problems of fighting a long attritional war. The determinist model made zeal into a mysterious metaphysical essence or supernatural force, erasing the difficulty of becoming Godly. Puritan texts emphasized that people constantly had to struggle against their own weakness and corruption. Puritans experienced depression and inactivity as much as confidence

---

[12]   Clive Holmes, *Why Was Charles I Executed?* (London, 2006), pp. 78–81.

and violent action.[13] Determinist and essentialist historiography effectively set puritans apart, exempting them from motivations and weaknesses that would be considered normal for other people. This made them both more and less than human. The construction of humanity must be crucial to any study of identities. The essential categories 'royalist' and 'parliamentarian' are anthropocentric, not just because they have always been applied exclusively to people, but also because they depend on certain views of human nature. Most twentieth-century studies of allegiance, whether they were for or against quantification and determinist explanations, assumed that there was a 'real' allegiance somewhere inside, even though they disagreed on how easily it could be discovered and whether it could change. The intentionalism of Morrill and Sadler privileged this 'true' inner allegiance very strongly. While they rejected a clear boundary between 'royalist' and 'parliamentarian', they effectively reinforced a binary opposition between animal and human because allegiance was supposed to be founded on reason or emotion, and these things were consistently and unquestioningly attributed only to people. Being a rational autonomous human subject with an authentic inner self was presented as a necessary precondition to having allegiance. Therefore the essence of allegiance was also the essence of humanity.

Thinking about horses offers a way of challenging essentialism. The outcome of the war must have depended on them whichever causal explanation we prefer. If resource superiority was the deciding factor, horses laboured to gather and transport resources, and were treated as resources. If tactical and operational contingency were more important, horses helped armies to move and to gather intelligence, and they fought in the decisive battles. Why should these actions be any less significant than what people did? If we fail to ask then we necessarily reinforce essentialist and anthropocentric assumptions that the actions of horses do not count because they were not expressing a 'true' allegiance. But Morrill had to stress that many human actions were not necessarily sincere or enthusiastic. If this is the case, then in terms of allegiance, what set non-militant people apart from animals? The only logical answer is nothing. Men and horses were conscripted into armies without being given any choice and they tried to escape, with varying degrees of success. Civilians and horses worked to pay taxes to fund the parliamentary war effort even if they did not want to or did not fully understand the consequences. Every action had effects which were independent of motives and intentions. Horses were agents just as much (or as little) as many people. My extreme anti-essentialist argument might be hard to accept,

---

[13] Paul S. Seaver, *Wallington's World: A Puritan Artisan in Seventeenth-Century London* (London, 1985), pp. 16, 21–4; Ian Gentles, *Oliver Cromwell: God's Warrior and the English Revolution* (Basingstoke, 2011), p. 6; William Hunt, *The Puritan Moment: The Coming of Revolution in an English County* (Cambridge, MA, 1983), pp. 119–21, 221–2, 224.

but at the very least it is no more absurd that McElligott and Smith's extreme intentionalist argument that the Scottish army which fought for Charles I in 1648 was 'not a royalist army' because what the Scots *wanted* was not in the King's best interests.[14]

Gender and feminism are as important as animals for my understanding of allegiance. As Hughes recently stressed, gender is 'fundamental to identity', and we cannot understand the civil wars and revolution without paying attention to it.[15] Throughout this book I have tried to show how gender intersected with the political and military history of the First Civil War. The rights and duties of women, what made a man a man, and who counted as a person were all contested at the time. Gender can be found everywhere, even in ordinances of Parliament and routine financial documents, if we are prepared to stop ignoring it. It is certainly not anachronistic to draw attention to gender issues or to gain new insights from feminist perspectives. According to Glenn Burgess, anachronism is 'the use of present-day standards and concepts to organize our study of the past, or to judge the past'.[16] By this definition, essential allegiance is anachronistic, and we can add to Butler's reworking of Nietzsche: the doer is not just a fiction but a historically specific fiction. The fixed allegiance required by Blackwood and Underdown does not fit with what seventeenth-century people actually did, or with what they wrote about identities. Morrill and Sadler have provided more subtle and sophisticated models of allegiance, but these still depend on an ideal of the authentic self and are too dismissive of actions and their effects. Familiarity with women's and gender history makes these problems very clear. Early-modern gender was an external performance which depended on clothes and behaviour, and was not rooted in a metaphysical essence or in the physical reality of the body. Rather than providing a definite origin for gender, the humoral body was dangerously unstable. Like gender, allegiance became a real thing that existed outside people's minds despite not having any physical or metaphysical foundations. There was no way of securing a permanent allegiance. It had to be performed repeatedly in response to new demands. Even for the militants who were not obviously coerced, making the war happen was a process of becoming something new, not of expressing what was already there.

The identities made possible by the outbreak of civil war in the 1640s do not fit into a simple binary opposition. Parliament was primarily for privileged

---

[14]   Jason McElligott and David L. Smith, 'Introduction: Rethinking Royalists and Royalism', in Jason McElligott and David L. Smith (eds), *Royalists and Royalism During the English Civil Wars* (Cambridge, 2007), p. 13.

[15]   Ann Hughes, *Gender and the English Revolution* (Abingdon, 2011), p. 149.

[16]   Glenn Burgess, 'On Revisionism: An Analysis of Early Stuart Historiography in the 1970s and 1980s', *Historical Journal*, 33/3 (1990): 615.

English protestant men, but many of its supporters did not live up to this ideal. Meanwhile, identifying the enemy caused many problems and contradictions. Othering was necessary to secure support, and catholics were the most convenient scapegoats. The 'papist' was a common and unusually essentialized stereotype which could be blamed for almost anything. The problem for the Long Parliament was that not all English catholics acted as enemies, and not all active enemies were catholic by any definition. In 1642 Parliament had no adequate vocabulary to describe militant supporters of the King. The identity of 'delinquent' emerged slowly and was often redefined, at times becoming so broad that it could easily describe people who had never willingly done anything for either side. Morrill was almost certainly right that these people were a majority. They posed a serious problem for the parliamentary war effort. Puritan preachers such as Stephen Marshall tried to exhort neuters into action, or at least used them as an Other to exhort puritans. Official parliamentary policy rarely acknowledged the existence of neutrals as a distinct group, instead fluctuating between conflating them with enemies and forcing them to act as friends. Ordinances of Parliament and fast sermons both attempted to draw lines between the well-affected and the ill-affected, but there was no stable consensus about exactly where the line should be. Shibboleths failed to clarify the situation: the Protestation was too broad while the Vow and Covenant and the Solemn League and Covenant were too narrow. Discovering protestant enemies was far more difficult than discovering catholics because both sides were very diverse and claimed to be fighting for more or less the same things. Puritan militants tried to make the First Civil War into a war of religion, not least because this was the only culturally available way to describe and explain civil strife, but it would not quite fit the existing template.

By trying to fight a war of religion, puritan militants became divided rather than united. Like a puritan soul, Parliament was at war with itself as much as with the King. It is well known that when Sir Jacob Astley surrendered at Stow-on-the-Wold on 21 March 1646, he said, 'You have now done your work and may go play, unless you will fall out among yourselves.'[17] This was not very prescient as they had been falling out among themselves since 1642, and things only got worse as the war went on. People who were 'parliamentarians' according to twentieth-century taxonomies found that other 'parliamentarians' threatened, denounced, insulted and arrested them, broke into their houses and stables, and took or destroyed their property. 'Parliamentarian' politicians and generals repeatedly tried to get other 'parliamentarian' politicians and generals sacked

[17]   Michael Braddick, *God's Fury, England's Fire: A New History of the English Civil Wars* (London, 2008), p. 467.

or demoted. Armies and political factions which were ostensibly on the same side competed for the same resources and cut off each other's supplies. Factional strife became even worse for the King's supporters as they came closer to losing the war. The 'royalist' versus 'parliamentarian' binary was reduced to absurdity in January 1646, when Goring's cavalry tried to retreat across the Tamar but were fought off by Sir Richard Grenville's Cornish infantry.[18] Who was 'royalist' now? Did their opponents therefore become 'parliamentarians'? And if so, were they 'trimmers' or had they 'really' been 'parliamentarians' all along? The people labelled as 'royalists' and 'parliamentarians' by modern historians really existed (as did the horses that have never been labelled in that way), but the labels do not accurately represent the identities which they fashioned for themselves or had imposed on them. These identities were created by doing things, and there is no empirical proof of any essential being behind the deeds. Nobody actually *was* 'a royalist' or 'a parliamentarian'.

---

[18]   Mark Stoyle, *Soldiers and Strangers: An Ethnic History of the English Civil War* (New Haven, 2005), p. 188.

Bibliography

Manuscript Sources

British Library, London

Add. 18777–80 Diary of Walter Yonge
Add. 22619 Papers relating to Norwich
Add. 31116 Diary of Lawrence Whitaker
Egerton 2643–51 Barrington papers
Harleian 162–6 Diary and papers of Sir Simonds D'Ewes
Stowe 189 Letters and papers of the Civil Wars and Commonwealth

Bodleian Library, Oxford

Tanner 59–64 Clerk of Parliament's papers

Essex Record Office, Chelmsford

D/Y 2 Morant manuscripts

Parliamentary Archives, Westminster

HL/PO/JO/10/1 House of Lords Main Papers 1509–1700

The National Archives of the UK: Public Records Office, Kew, Surrey

SP 16 State Papers Domestic, Charles I
SP 23 Compounding Committee papers
SP 24 Indemnity Committee papers
SP 28 Commonwealth Exchequer Papers

Published Sources

Abbott, W.C., *Writings and Speeches of Oliver Cromwell*, 2 vols (Cambridge, MA: Harvard University Press, 1937).

Adamson, John, 'Of Armies and Architecture: The Employments of Robert Scawen', in Ian Gentles, John Morrill and Blair Worden (eds), *Soldiers, Writers and Statesmen of the English Revolution* (Cambridge: Cambridge University Press, 1998), pp. 36–67.

——, *The Noble Revolt: The Overthrow of Charles I* (London: Weidenfeld & Nicolson, 2007).

——(ed.), *The English Civil War, Conflict and Contexts, 1640–49* (Basingstoke: Palgrave Macmillan, 2008).

Adolph, Anthony R.J.S., 'Papists' Horses and the Privy Council 1689–1720', *Recusant History*, 24 (1998): 55–75.

Anderson, Virginia DeJohn, *Creatures of Empire: How Domestic Animals Transformed Early America* (Oxford: Oxford University Press, 2004).

Atkyns, Richard, 'The Praying Captain: A Cavalier's Memoirs', Peter Young (ed.), *Journal of the Society for Army Historical Research*, 35/141 (1957): 3–15, 53–70.

Aylmer, Gerald, *Rebellion or Revolution? England 1640–1660* (Oxford: Oxford University Press, 1987).

Baker, Thomas, *Some speciall passages from London, Westminster, Yorke Hull, Ireland and other partes Collected for the satisfaction of those that desire true informarion.*, Early English Books Online (London: Thomas Baker, 1642) TT E.108[33].

Barber, Sarah, *A Revolutionary Rogue: Henry Marten and the English Republic* (Stroud: Sutton, 2000).

Barry, Jonathan and Brooks, Christopher (eds), *The Middling Sort of People: Culture, Society and Politics in England, 1550–1800* (Basingstoke: Macmillan, 1994).

Baskerville, Stephen K., *Not Peace but a Sword: The Political Theology of the English Revolution* (London: Routledge, 1993).

Beaver, Daniel C., *Hunting and the Politics of Violence before the English Civil War* (Cambridge: Cambridge University Press, 2008).

Bennett, Judith M., *History Matters: Patriarchy and the Challenge of Feminism* (Manchester: Manchester University Press, 2006).

Bennett, Martyn, 'Contribution and Assessment: Financial Exactions in the English Civil War, 1642–6', *War and Society*, 4/1 (1986): 1–11.

——, 'Between Scylla and Charybdis: The Creation of Rival Administrations at the Beginning of the Civil War', *Local Historian*, 22/4 (1992): 191–202.

Blackwood, B.G., 'Parties and Issues in the Civil War in Lancashire and East Anglia', in R.C. Richardson (ed.), *The English Civil War: Local Aspects* (Stroud: Sutton, 1997), pp. 261–85.

Boehrer, Bruce, *Shakespeare Among the Animals: Nature and Society in the Drama of Early Modern England* (New York: Palgrave, 2002).

——, 'Shakespeare and the social devaluation of the horse', in Karen L. Raber and Treva J. Tucker (eds), *The Culture of the Horse* (Basingstoke: Palgrave Macmillan, 2005), pp. 91–111.

Boroditsky, Lera, 'Sex, Syntax, and Semantics', in D. Gentner and S. Goldin-Meadow (eds), *Language in Mind: Advances in the Study of Language and Cognition* (Cambridge, MA: MIT Press, 2003), pp. 61–79.

Boulton, Jeremy, 'Wage Labour in Seventeenth-Century London', *Economic History Review*, 49/2, New Series (1996): 268–90.

Braddick, Michael, *God's Fury, England's Fire: A New History of the English Civil Wars* (London: Allen Lane, 2008).

——, *The Nerves of State: Taxation and the Financing of the English State 1558–1714* (Manchester: Manchester University Press, 1996).

Braddick, Michael and Walter, John (eds), *Negotiating Power in Early Modern Society: Order, Hierarchy and Subordination in Britain and Ireland* (Cambridge: Cambridge University Press, 2001).

Brenner, Robert, *Merchants and Revolution: Commercial Change, Political Conflict and London's Overseas Traders 1550–1653* (Cambridge: Cambridge University Press, 1993).

Brooks, Christopher, 'Professions, Ideology and the Middling Sort in the Late Sixteenth and Early Seventeenth Centuries', in Jonathan Barry and Christopher Brooks (eds), *The Middling Sort of People: Culture, Society and Politics in England, 1550–1800* (Basingstoke: Macmillan, 1994), pp. 113–40.

Bulstrode, Richard, *Memoirs and reflections on the reign and government of King Charles Ist and king Charles IId* (London: 1721).

Burgess, Glenn, 'On Revisionism: An Analysis of Early Stuart Historiography in the 1970s and 1980s', *Historical Journal*, 33/3 (1990): 609–27.

——, *Absolute Monarchy and the Stuart Constitution* (New Haven: Yale University Press, 1996).

——, 'Was the Civil War a War of Religion? The Evidence of Political Propaganda', *Huntington Library Quarterly*, 61/2 (2000): 173–201.

Butler, Judith, *Gender Trouble* (Abingdon: Routledge, 2006).

Campbell, Mildred, *The English Yeoman Under Elizabeth and the Early Stuarts* (London: Merlin, 1960).

'Childerditch protestation return', *Essex Review*, 26 (1916): 93.

Clarendon, Edward Hyde, Earl of, *The history of the Rebellion and civil wars in England begun in the year 1641*, William Dunn Macray (ed.) (Oxford: Clarendon Press, 1888).

Coates, Ben, *The Impact of the English Civil War on the Economy of London, 1642–50* (Aldershot: Ashgate, 2004).

Coates, Wilson, Young, Anne Steele and Snow, Vernon F. (eds), *Private Journals of the Long Parliament, 2 June to 17 September 1642* (New Haven: Yale University Press, 1982).

Coffey, John and Lim, Paul C.H. (eds), *The Cambridge Companion to Puritanism* (Cambridge: Cambridge University Press, 2008).

Cranmer, Thomas, *Certaine sermons or homilies appoynted to be read in churches. In the time of the late Queene Elizabeth of famous memory. And now thought fit to be reprinted by authority from the Kings most excellent Maiesty* (London: 1635).

Crawshaw, Tom, 'Military Finance and the Earl of Essex's Infantry in 1642 – a Reinterpretation', *Historical Journal*, 53/04 (2010): 1037–48.

Cressy, David, *Agnes Bowker's Cat: Travesties and Transgressions in Tudor and Stuart England* (Oxford: Oxford University Press, 2001).

——, 'The Protestation Protested, 1641 and 1642', *Historical Journal*, 45/2 (2002): 251–79.

——, *England on Edge: Crisis and Revolution 1640–1642* (Oxford: Oxford University Press, 2007).

Cuneo, Pia, 'Just a Bit of Control: The Historical Significance of Sixteenth- and Seventeenth-Century German Bit-Books', in Karen L. Raber and Treva J. Tucker (eds), *The Culture of the Horse* (Basingstoke: Palgrave Macmillan, 2005), pp. 141–74.

Curth, Louise Hill, 'English Almanacs and Animal Health Care in the Seventeenth Century', *Society and Animals*, 8/1 (2000): 71–86.

——, '"The Most Excellent of Animal Creatures": Health Care for Horses in Early Modern England', in Peter Edwards, Karl Enenkel and Elspeth Graham (eds), *The Horse as Cultural Icon: The Real and the Symbolic Horse in the Early Modern World* (Leiden: Brill, 2011), pp. 217–40.

Cust, Richard, 'The "public man" in late Tudor and early Stuart England', in Peter Lake and Steven Pincus (eds), *The Politics of the Public Sphere* (Manchester: Manchester University Press, 2007), pp. 116–43.

Dale, Thomas Cyril (ed.), *The Members of the City Companies in 1641 as Set Forth in the Return for the Poll Tax* (London: Society of Genealogists, 1934).

Davies, Godfrey, 'The Army of the Eastern Association', *English Historical Review*, 46/181 (1931): 88–96.

——, 'The Parliamentary Army Under the Earl of Essex', *English Historical Review*, 49/193 (1934): 32–54.

Day, Jon, *Gloucester and Newbury 1643: The Turning Point of the Civil War* (Barnsley: Pen & Sword, 2007).

Dolan, Frances E., *Whores of Babylon Catholicism, Gender, and Seventeenth-Century Print Culture* (Notre Dame: University of Notre Dame Press, 2005).

Donagan, Barbara, 'Family and Misfortune in the English Civil War: The Sad Case of Edward Pitt', *Huntington Library Quarterly*, 61/2 (2000): 223–40.

——, *War in England 1642–1649* (Oxford: Oxford University Press, 2008).

Dunn, Diana (ed.), *War and Society in Medieval and Early Modern Britain* (Liverpool: Liverpool University Press, 2000).

Earle, Peter, 'The Middling Sort in London', in Jonathan Barry and Christopher Brooks (eds), *The Middling Sort of People: Culture, Society and Politics in England, 1550–1800* (Basingstoke: Macmillan, 1994), pp. 141–58.

Edwards, Peter, 'The Supply of Horses to the Parliamentarian and Royalist Armies in the English Civil War', *Historical Research*, 68/159 (1995): 49–66.

——, *Dealing in Death: The Arms Trade and the British Civil Wars* (Stroud: Sutton, 2000).

——, *The Horse Trade of Tudor and Stuart England* (Cambridge: Cambridge University Press, 2004, first published 1988).

——, *Horse and Man in Early Modern England* (London: Hambledon Continuum, 2007).

Edwards, Peter, Enenkel, Karl and Graham, Elspeth (eds), *The Horse as Cultural Icon: The Real and the Symbolic Horse in the Early Modern World* (Leiden: Brill, 2011).

Erickson, Amy Louise, *Women and Property in Early Modern England* (London: Routledge, 1995).

——, 'Possession—and the Other One-Tenth of the Law: Assessing Women's Ownership and Economic Roles in Early Modern England', *Women's History Review*, 16/3 (2007): 369–85.

Firth, C.H., 'Raising the Ironsides', *Transactions of the Royal Historical Society*, 13 (1899): 17–73.

Fissel, Mark Charles, *English Warfare, 1511–1642* (London: Routledge, 2001).

Fletcher, Anthony, *The Outbreak of the English Civil War* (London: Edward Arnold, 1981).

——, *Gender, Sex and Subordination in England 1500–1800* (New Haven: Yale University Press, 1995).

Fletcher, Anthony and Stevenson, John (eds), *Order and Disorder in Early Modern England* (Cambridge: Cambridge University Press, 1985).

Foard, Glenn, *Naseby: The Decisive Campaign* (Barnsley: Pen & Sword, 2004).

Foxley, Rachel, 'Royalists and the New Model Army in 1647: Circumstance, Principle and Compromise', in Jason McElligott and David L. Smith (eds), *Royalists and Royalism During the English Civil Wars* (Cambridge: Cambridge University Press, 2007), pp. 155–74.

Freist, Dagmar, *Governed by Opinion: Politics, Religion and the Dynamics of Communication in Stuart London, 1637–45* (London: Tauris, 1997).

French, H.R., 'Social Status, Localism and the "Middle Sort of People" in England 1620–1750', *Past and Present*, 166/1 (2000): 66–99.

Fudge, Erica, *Perceiving Animals: Humans and Beasts in Early Modern English Culture* (Urbana: University of Illinois Press, 2002).

Gardiner, Samuel Rawson, *The Constitutional Documents of the Puritan Revolution 1625–1660* (Oxford: Clarendon Press, 1899).

Gentles, Ian, *The New Model Army in England, Ireland and Scotland, 1645–1653* (Oxford: Blackwell, 1992).

——, '"This Confused, Divided and Wretched City": The Struggle for London in 1642–43', *Canadian Journal of History*, 38/3 (2003): 467–79.

——, *The English Revolution and the Wars in the Three Kingdoms, 1638–1652* (London: Longman, 2007).

——, *Oliver Cromwell: God's Warrior and the English Revolution* (Basingstoke: Palgrave Macmillan, 2011).

Gentles, Ian, Morrill, John and Worden, Blair (eds), *Soldiers, Writers and Statesmen of the English Revolution* (Cambridge: Cambridge University Press, 1998).

Gibson, J.S.W. and Dell, Alan, *Protestation Returns, 1641–42 and Other Contemporary Listings* (Bury: Federation of Family History Societies, 2004).

Gilbert, C.D., 'The Catholics in Worcestershire, 1642–1651', *Recusant History*, 20/3 (1991): 336–57.

Glete, Jan, 'Warfare, Entrepreneurship, and the Fiscal-Military State', in Frank Tallett and D.J.B. Trim (eds), *European Warfare 1350–1750* (Cambridge: Cambridge University Press, 2010), pp. 300–21.

Graham, Aaron, 'Finance, Localism, and Military Representation in the Army of the Earl of Essex (June–December 1642)', *Historical Journal*, 52/04 (2009): 879–98.

——, 'The Earl of Essex and Parliament's Army at the Battle of Edgehill: A Reassessment', *War in History*, 17/3 (2010): 276–93.

Green, Mary Anne Everett (ed.), *Calendar of the Proceedings of the Committee for Advance of Money, 1642–56* (London: HMSO, 1888).

——, *Calendar of the Proceedings of the Committee for Compounding 1643–60* (London: HMSO, 1889).

Greenblatt, Stephen J., *Renaissance Self-fashioning: From More to Shakespeare* (Chicago: University of Chicago Press, 2005).

Griffiths, Paul, Fox, Adam and Hindle, Steve (eds), *The Experience of Authority in Early Modern England* (Basingstoke: Macmillan, 1996).

Gwynne, John, *Military Memoirs of the Great Civil War* (Edinburgh: Constable, 1822).

Harding, Vanessa, 'The Population of London, 1550–1700: A Review of the Published Evidence', *London Journal*, 15/2 (1990): 111–28.

Henrich, Joseph, Heine, Steven J. and Norenzayan, Ara, 'The Weirdest People in the World', *Behavioural and Brain Sciences*, 33/2–3 (2009): 61–83.

Herrup, Cynthia B., 'The King's Two Genders', *Journal of British Studies*, 45/3 (2006): 493–510.

Hexter, J.H., *The Reign of King Pym* (Cambridge, MA: Harvard University Press, 1941).

Hirst, Derek, *The Representative of the People? Voters and Voting in England Under the Early Stuarts* (Cambridge: Cambridge University Press, 1975).

Holmes, Clive, 'The Affair of Colonel Long: Relations Between Parliament, the Lord General and the County of Essex in 1643', *Transactions of the Essex Archaeological Society*, 3rd series, 2 (1970): 210–16.

——, 'Colonel King and Lincolnshire Politics, 1642–1646', *Historical Journal*, 16/3 (1973): 451–84.

——, 'The County Community in Stuart Historiography', *Journal of British Studies*, 19/2 (1980): 54–73.

——, *Why Was Charles I Executed?* (London: Hambledon Continuum, 2006).

——, *The Eastern Association in the English Civil War* (Cambridge: Cambridge University Press, 2007, first published 1974).

——, 'Centre and Locality in Civil-War England', in John Adamson (ed.), *The English Civil War: Conflict and Contexts, 1640–1649* (Basingstoke: Palgrave Macmillan, 2009), pp. 153–74.

Hopper, Andrew J., '"The Popish Army of the North": Anti-Catholicism and Parliamentarian Allegiance in Civil War Yorkshire, 1642–46', *Recusant History*, 25/1 (2000): 12–28.

——, 'Fitted for Desperation: Honour and Treachery in Parliament's Yorkshire Command, 1642–1643', *History*, 86/282 (2001): 138–54.

——, *'Black Tom': Sir Thomas Fairfax and the English Revolution* (Manchester: Manchester University Press, 2007).

——, 'The Wortley Park Poachers and the Outbreak of the English Civil War', *Northern History*, 44/2 (2007): 94–114.

——, 'The Self-Fashioning of Gentry Turncoats During the English Civil Wars', *Journal of British Studies*, 49/2 (2010): 236–57.

Hribal, Jason, '"Animals Are Part of the Working Class": A Challenge to Labor History', *Labor History*, 44/4 (2003): 435–53.

Hughes, Ann, 'The King, the Parliament and the Localities During the English Civil War', *Journal of British Studies*, 24/2 (1985): 236–63.

——, 'Parliamentary Tyranny? Indemnity Proceedings and the Impact of the Civil War: A Case Study from Warwickshire', *Midland History*, 11 (1986): 49–78.

——, 'Men, the "Public" and the "Private" in the English Revolution', in Peter Lake and Steven Pincus (eds), *The Politics of the Public Sphere* (Manchester: Manchester University Press, 2007), pp. 191–212.

——, *Gender and the English Revolution* (Abingdon: Routledge, 2011).

Hunt, William, *The Puritan Moment: The Coming of Revolution in an English County* (Cambridge, MA: Harvard University Press, 1983).

Hutton, Ronald, *The Royalist War Effort, 1642–1646* (London: Longman, 1984).

Jenkins, Keith, *Re-Thinking History* (Abingdon: Routledge, 2003).

Jones, David Martin, *Conscience and Allegiance in Seventeenth Century England: The Political Significance of Oaths and Engagements* (Rochester, NY: University of Rochester Press, 1999).

Josselin, Ralph, *The Diary of Ralph Josselin 1616–1683*, Alan MacFarlane (ed.) (London: Oxford University Press for the British Academy, 1976).

Keeler, Mary Frear, *The Long Parliament 1640–1641, a Biographical Study of its Members* (Philadelphia: American Philosophical Society, 1954).

Knights, Mark, 'How Rational Was the Later Stuart Public Sphere?', in Peter Lake and Steven Pincus (eds), *The Politics of the Public Sphere* (Manchester: Manchester University Press, 2007), pp. 252–67.

Kyle, Chris R. and Peacey, Jason (eds), *Parliament at Work: Parliamentary Committees, Political Power, and Public Access in Early Modern England* (Woodbridge: Boydell, 2002).

Lake, Peter, 'Anti-Popery: The Structure of a Prejudice', in Richard Cust and Ann Hughes (eds), *The English Civil War* (London: Arnold, 1997), pp. 181–210.

Lake, Peter and Pincus, Steven (eds), *The Politics of the Public Sphere in Early Modern England* (Manchester: Manchester University Press, 2007).

Laqueur, Thomas, *Making Sex: Body and Gender from the Greeks to Freud* (Cambridge, MA: Harvard University Press, 1992).

Leys, Mary, *Catholics in England, 1559–1829: A Social History* (London: Longman, 1961).

Lindley, Keith, *Popular Politics and Religion in Civil War London* (Brookfield, VT: Scolar Press, 1997).

Little, Ann M., *Abraham in Arms: War and Gender in Colonial New England* (Philadelphia: University of Pennsylvania Press, 2007).

Little, Patrick (ed.), *Oliver Cromwell: New Perspectives* (Basingstoke: Palgrave Macmillan, 2008).

——, 'Cromwell and Ireland before 1649', in Patrick Little (ed.), *Oliver Cromwell: New Perspectives* (Basingstoke: Palgrave Macmillan, 2009), pp. 116–41.

Locke, John, *Two Treatises on Government* (London, 1821).

Lovejoy, Arthur O., *The Great Chain of Being* (Cambridge, MA: Harvard University Press, 1972).

Macadam, Joyce, 'Soldiers, Statesmen and Scribblers: London Newsbook Reporting of the Marston Moor Campaign, 1644', *Historical Research*, 82/215 (2009): 93–113.

MacCannell, Daniel, '"Dark Corners of the Land"? A New Approach to Regional Factors in the Civil Wars of England and Wales', *Cultural and Social History*, 7/2 (2010): 171–89.

MacInnes, Ian F., 'Altering a Race of Jades: Horse Breeding and Geohumoralism in Shakespeare', in Peter Edwards, Karl Enenkel and Elspeth Graham (eds), *The Horse as Cultural Icon: The Real and the Symbolic Horse in the Early Modern World* (Leiden: Brill, 2011), pp. 175–89.

Malcolm, Joyce Lee, *Caesar's Due: Loyalty and King Charles 1642–6* (London: Royal Historical Society, 1983).

Manning, Brian, *The English People and the English Revolution, 1640–1649* (London: Heinemann, 1976).

——, *The Far Left in the English Revolution 1640 to 1660* (London: Bookmarks, 1999).

Marshall, Stephen, *Meroz cursed, or, A sermon preached to the honourable House of Commons, at their late solemn fast, Febr. 23, 1641 by Stephen Marshall ...* (London: 1642) TT E.133[19].

McElligott, Jason and Smith, David L. (eds), *Royalists and Royalism During the English Civil Wars* (Cambridge: Cambridge University Press, 2007).

McShane, Angela, 'Subjects and Objects: Material Expressions of Love and Loyalty in Seventeenth-Century England', *Journal of British Studies*, 48/4 (2009): 871–86.

Monti, Martin M. et al., 'Willful Modulation of Brain Activity in Disorders of Consciousness', *New England Journal of Medicine*, 362/7 (2010): 579–89.

Morrill, John, *The Nature of the English Revolution* (London: Longman, 1993).

——, *Revolt in the Provinces: The People of England and the Tragedies of War, 1630–1648* (London: Longman, 1998).

Nenner, Howard, 'Loyalty and the Law: The Meaning of Trust and the Right of Resistance in Seventeenth-Century England', *Journal of British Studies*, 48/4 (2009): 859–70.

Newman, Peter, 'Catholic Royalists in Northern England, 1642–1645', *Northern History*, 15 (1979): 88–95.

——, 'Roman Catholics in Pre-Civil War England: The Problem of Definition', *Recusant History*, 15 (1979): 148–52.

——, 'Roman Catholic Royalists: Papist Commanders Under Charles I and Charles II, 1642–1660', *Recusant History*, 15 (1981): 396–405.

Nishimoto, Shinji et al., 'Reconstructing Visual Experiences from Brain Activity Evoked by Natural Movies', *Current Biology*, 21/19 (2011): 1641–6.

Nusbacher, Aryeh J.S., 'Civil Supply in the Civil War: Supply of Victuals to the New Model Army on the Naseby Campaign 1–14 June 1645', *English Historical Review*, 115/460 (2000): 145–60.

Peacey, Jason, 'Politics, Accounts and Propaganda in the Long Parliament', in Chris R. Kyle and Jason Peacey (eds), *Parliament at Work: Parliamentary Committees, Political Power, and Public Access in Early Modern England* (Woodbridge: Boydell, 2002), pp. 59–78.

——, *Politicians and Pamphleteers: Propaganda During the English Civil Wars and Interregnum* (Aldershot: Ashgate, 2004).

——, 'The Print Culture of Parliament, 1600–1800', *Parliamentary History*, 26/1 (2007): 1–16.

——, 'Perceptions of Parliament: Factions and the "Public"', in John Adamson (ed.), *The English Civil War: Conflict and Contexts, 1640–1649* (Basingstoke: Palgrave Macmillan, 2009), pp. 82–105.

Pennington, Donald H., 'The Accounts of the Kingdom 1642–1649', in F.J. Fisher (ed.), *Essays in the Economic and Social History of Tudor and Stuart England* (Cambridge: Cambridge University Press, 1961), pp. 182–203.

Pennington, Donald H. and Roots, Ivan (eds), *The Committee at Stafford 1643–1645: The Order Book of the Staffordshire Committee*, Staffordshire Record Society, 4th Series, vol. 1 (1957).

Philip, I.G. (ed.), *Journal of Sir Samuel Luke*, Oxfordshire Record Society, vols 29, 31 and 33 (1950).

Poyntz, Nick, 'The Attack on Lord Chandos: Popular Politics in Cirencester in 1642', *Midland History*, 35/1 (2010): 71–88.

Purkiss, Diane, *The English Civil War: A People's History* (London: HarperCollins, 2006).

Raber, Karen L. and Tucker, Treva J. (eds), *The Culture of the Horse: Status, Discipline, and Identity in the Early Modern World* (New York: Palgrave Macmillan, 2005).

Richardson, R.C. (ed.), *The English Civil Wars: Local Aspects* (Stroud: Sutton, 1997).

Robinson, Gavin, 'Horse Supply and the Development of the New Model Army, 1642–1646', *War in History*, 15/2 (2008): 121–40.

——, 'The Military Value of Horses and the Social Value of the Horse in Early Modern England', in Peter Edwards, Karl Enenkel and Elspeth Graham (eds), *The Horse as Cultural Icon: The Real and the Symbolic Horse in the Early Modern World* (Leiden: Brill, 2011), pp. 351–76.

——, 'Equine Battering Rams? A Reassessment of Cavalry Charges in the English Civil War', *Journal of Military History*, 75/3 (2011): 719–31.

Rogers, Clifford J., 'Tactics and the Face of Battle', in Frank Tallett and D.J.B. Trim (eds), *European Warfare 1350–1750* (Cambridge: Cambridge University Press, 2010), pp. 203–35.

Rowlands, M.B., ' "Rome's Snaky Brood": Catholic Yeomen, Craftsmen and Townsman in the West Midlands, 1600–1641', *Recusant History*, 24 (1998): 147–65.

Roy, Ian, 'Royalist Reputations: The Cavalier Ideal and the Reality', in Jason McElligott and David L. Smith (eds), *Royalists and Royalism During the English Civil Wars* (Cambridge: Cambridge University Press, 2007), pp. 89–111.

Russell, Conrad, *The Fall of the British Monarchies 1637–1642* (Oxford: Clarendon Press, 1991).

——, 'The Scottish Party in English Parliaments, 1640–1642', *Historical Research*, 66 (1993): 35–52.

Sadler, S.L., ' "Lord of the Fens": Oliver Cromwell's Reputation and the First Civil War', in Patrick Little (ed.), *Oliver Cromwell: New Perspectives* (Basingstoke: Palgrave Macmillan, 2009), pp. 64–89.

Scott, Christopher L., Turton, Alan and Arni, Eric Gruber von, *Edgehill: The Battle Reinterpreted* (Barnsley: Pen & Sword, 2004).

Seaver, Paul S., *Wallington's World: A Puritan Artisan in Seventeenth-Century London* (London: Methuen, 1985).

Shagan, Ethan, 'Constructing Discord: Ideology, Propaganda, and English Responses to the Irish Rebellion of 1641', *Journal of British Studies*, 36/1 (1997): 4–34.

Shedd, John A., 'Legalism over Revolution: The Parliamentary Committee for Indemnity and Property Confiscation Disputes, 1647–1655', *Historical Journal*, 43/4 (2000): 1093–1107.

——, 'Thwarted Victors: Civil and Criminal Prosecution Against Parliament's Officials During the English Civil War and Commonwealth', *Journal of British Studies*, 41/2 (2002): 139–69.

——, 'The State Versus the Trades Guilds : Parliament's Soldier-Apprentices in the English Civil War Period, 1642–1655', *International Labor and Working-Class History*, 65 (2004): 105–16.

Shepard, Alexandra, *Meanings of Manhood in Early Modern England* (Oxford: Clarendon Press, 2006).

Smith, Hilda L., *All Men and Both Sexes: Gender, Politics, and the False Universal in England, 1640–1832* (University Park, PA: Pennsylvania State University Press, 2002).

Smith, Steven R., 'The London Apprentices as Seventeenth-Century Adolescents', *Past and Present*, 61 (1973): 149–61.

——, 'Almost Revolutionaries: The London Apprentices During the Civil Wars', *Huntington Library Quarterly*, 42/4 (1979): 313–28.

Snow, Vernon F., *Essex the Rebel: The Life of Robert Devereux, the Third Earl of Essex 1591–1646* (Lincoln, NE: University of Nebraska Press, 1970).

Sommerville, Johann P., *Royalists and Patriots: Politics and Ideology in England, 1603–1640* (London: Longman, 1999).

Spicksley, Judith M., 'Usury Legislation, Cash, and Credit: The Development of the Female Investor in the Late Tudor and Stuart Periods', *Economic History Review*, 61/2 (2008): 277–301.

Steel, Karl, 'How To Make A Human', *Exemplaria*, 20/1 (2008): 3–27.

Stoyle, Mark, *Loyalty and Locality: Popular Allegiance in Devon During the English Civil War* (Exeter: University of Exeter Press, 1994).

——, 'Caricaturing Cymru: Images of the Welsh in the London Press 1642–46', in Diana Dunn (ed.), *War and Society in Medieval and Early Modern Britain* (Liverpool: Liverpool University Press, 2000), pp. 162–79.

——, 'English "Nationalism", Celtic Particularism, and the English Civil War', *Historical Journal*, 43/04 (2000): 1113–28.

——, *Soldiers and Strangers: An Ethnic History of the English Civil War* (New Haven: Yale University Press, 2005).

Symonds, Richard, *Diary of the Marches of the Royal Army*, C.E. Long and Ian Roy (eds) (Cambridge: Cambridge University Press, 1997).

Tallett, Frank and Trim, D.J.B. (eds), *European Warfare, 1350–1750* (Cambridge: Cambridge University Press, 2010).

Thomas, Keith, *Man and the Natural World: Changing Attitudes in England 1500–1800* (London: Allen Lane, 1983).

Thomson, Alan (ed.), *The Impact of the First Civil War on Hertfordshire 1642–1647*, Hertfordshire Record Society, vol. 23 (2007).

Tincey, John, 'Armed Complete', *English Civil War Times* 55 (1998): 17–22.

To the honorable the House of Commons, now assembled in Parliament. The humble petition of the inhabitants of Watford, in the county of Hertford. (London: John Bellamy and Ralph Smith, 1642) TT 669.f.5[52].

Turton, Alan, *Chief Strength of the Army: Cavalry in the Earl of Essex's Army* (Leigh-On-Sea: Partizan Press, c. 1992).

Tutino, Stefania, 'The Catholic Church and the English Civil War: The Case of Thomas White', *Journal of Ecclesiastical History*, 58/2 (2007): 232–55.

Underdown, David, *Revel, Riot, and Rebellion: Popular Politics and Culture in England 1603–1660* (Oxford: Clarendon Press, 1985).

Vallance, Edward, 'The Kingdom's Case: The Use of Casuistry as a Political Language 1640–1692', *Albion: A Quarterly Journal Concerned with British Studies*, 34/4 (2002): 557–83.

——, 'Loyal or Rebellious? Protestant Associations in England 1584–1696', *Seventeenth Century*, 17/1 (2002): 1–23.

——, 'Preaching to the Converted: Religious Justifications for the English Civil War', *Huntington Library Quarterly*, 65/3 (2002): 395–419.

——, *Revolutionary England and the National Covenant: State Oaths, Protestantism and the Political Nation, 1553–1682* (Woodbridge: Boydell, 2005).

Walter, John, *Understanding Popular Violence in the English Revolution: The Colchester Plunderers* (Cambridge: Cambridge University Press, 1999).

Wanklyn, Malcolm, *Decisive Battles of the English Civil War* (Barnsley: Pen & Sword, 2006).

——, 'A General Much Maligned: The Earl of Manchester as Army Commander in the Second Newbury Campaign (July to November 1644)', *War in History*, 14/2 (2007): 133–56.

——, 'Oliver Cromwell and the Performance of Parliament's Armies in the Newbury Campaign, 20 October–21 November 1644', *History*, 96/321 (2011): 3–25.

Wanklyn, Malcolm and Jones, Frank, *A Military History of the English Civil War* (Harlow: Pearson, 2005).

Waters, Ivor, *Henry Marten and the Long Parliament* (Chepstow: Chepstow Society, 1976).

Webb, John, 'The Siege of Portsmouth in the Civil War', in R.C. Richardson (ed.), *The English Civil War: Local Aspects* (Stroud: Sutton, 1997), pp. 63–90.

Weil, Rachel, 'Thinking About Allegiance in the English Civil War', *History Workshop Journal*, 61/1 (2006): 183–91.

——, 'Matthew Smith Versus the "Great Men": Plot-Talk, the Public Sphere and the Problem of Credibility in the 1690s', in Peter Lake and Steven Pincus (eds), *The Politics of the Public Sphere* (Manchester: Manchester University Press, 2007), pp. 232–51.

Wharton, Nehemiah, *Letters of a Subaltern in the Earl of Essex's Army*, Henry Ellis (ed.) (London: J.B. Nichols and Sons, 1854).

Wheeler, James Scott, *The Making of a World Power: War and the Military Revolution in Seventeenth Century England* (Stroud: Sutton, 1999).

Whitelocke, Bulstrode, *Memorials of the English affairs from the beginning of the reign of Charles the First to the happy restoration of King Charles the Second* (Oxford: Oxford University Press, 1853).

——, *The Diary of Bulstrode Whitelocke 1605–1675*, Ruth Spalding (ed.) (Oxford: Oxford University Press, 1990).

Wilson, Robert Anton, 'Towards Understanding E-Prime', in D. David Bourland Jr and Paul Dennithorne Johnston (eds), *To Be or Not: An E-Prime Anthology* (International Society for General Semantics, 1991): 23–6. Available at http://nobeliefs.com/eprime.htm

Winawer, Jonathan et al., 'Russian Blues Reveal Effects of Language on Color Discrimination', *Proceedings of the National Academy of Sciences*, 104/19 (2007): 7780–85.

Wood, Andy, 'Beyond Post-Revisionism? The Civil War Allegiances of the Miners of the Derbyshire "Peak Country"', *Historical Journal*, 40/1 (1997): 23–40.

——, 'Fear, Hatred and the Hidden Injuries of Class in Early Modern England', *Journal of Social History*, 39/3 (2006): 803–26.

Wootton, David, 'From Rebellion to Revolution: The Crisis of the Winter of 1642/3 and the Origins of Civil War Radicalism', *English Historical Review*, 105/416 (1990): 654–69.

Worden, Blair, 'The "Diary" of Bulstrode Whitelocke', *English Historical Review*, 108/426 (1993): 122–34.

Wrightson, Keith, '"Sorts of People" in Tudor and Stuart England', in Jonathan Barry and Christopher Brooks (eds), *The Middling Sort of People: Culture, Society and Politics in England, 1550–1800* (Basingstoke: Macmillan, 1994), pp. 28–51.

Young, Peter, *Edgehill 1642: The Campaign and the Battle* (Kineton: Roundwood Press, 1967).

Unpublished Theses

All of these theses can be downloaded free of charge from http://ethos.bl.uk

Jordan, Sally Anne, 'Catholic Identity, Ideology and Culture: The Thames Valley Catholic Gentry from the Restoration to the Relief Acts' (PhD, Reading University, 2002).

Nagel, Lawson Chase, 'The Militia of London 1641–1649' (PhD, University of London, 1982).

Robinson, Gavin, 'Horse Supply in the English Civil War, 1642–1646' (PhD, Reading University, 2001).

Sadler, S.L., 'Cambridgeshire Society During the First and Second Civil Wars c.1638–c.1649: Some Aspects of Patterns of Allegiance' (PhD, Anglia Polytechnic University, 1998).

Index

For Product Safety Concerns and Information please contact our
EU representative GPSR@taylorandfrancis.com Taylor & Francis
Verlag GmbH, Kaufingerstraße 24, 80331 München, Germany